Praise for *Multi Asset Class Investment Strategy*:

".. . pension fund trustees right around the globe should read the book . . . it is certain to stir up some much needed debate . . . has received rave reviews from within the UK pension industry" (*Global Pensions*)

".. . time and money well spent . . . the tectonic plates are shifting under the UK investment establishment" (*Daily Telegraph*)

".. . an indispensable roadmap for anyone looking to create a successful investment programme . . ." (*The Securities Investment Review*)

"It's some time since I read anything as clear and punchy . . . if you are involved in setting investment strategy for a pension fund, this book cannot help but clarify your thinking." (*Benefits & Compensation International*)

"This book stakes Fraser-Sampson's claim to be recognised as one of the great thinkers on portfolio theory, ranking alongside Markowitz and Swensen." (*Rebecca Meijlink, AlphaBet Capital*)

"I somehow expected another version of Swensen's "Pioneering Portfolio Management". However, this is in my eyes a huge improvement and a surprisingly entertaining and satisfying read." (*Thomas Meyer, EIF, author: Beyond the J-Curve*)

Private Equity
as an Asset Class

Private Equity
as an Asset Class

Guy Fraser-Sampson

John Wiley & Sons, Ltd

Other Wiley Editorial Offices

John Wiley & Sons Inc., 111 River Street, Hoboken, NJ 07030, USA

Jossey-Bass, 989 Market Street, San Francisco, CA 94103-1741, USA

Wiley-VCH Verlag GmbH, Boschstr. 12, D-69469 Weinheim, Germany

John Wiley & Sons Australia Ltd, 42 McDougall Street, Milton, Queensland 4064, Australia

John Wiley & Sons (Asia) Pte Ltd, 2 Clementi Loop #02-01, Jin Xing Distripark, Singapore 129809

John Wiley & Sons Canada Ltd, 6045 Freemont Blvd, Mississauga, ONT, L5R 4J3, Canada

Wiley also publishes its books in a variety of electronic formats. Some content that appears in print may not be available in electronic books.

British Library Cataloguing in Publication Data

A catalogue record for this book is available from the British Library

ISBN 978-0-470-06645-4 (HB)

Typeset in 11/13pt Times by SNP Best-set Typesetter Ltd., Hong Kong
Printed and bound in Great Britain by TJ International Ltd, Padstow, Cornwall, UK
This book is printed on acid-free paper.

Contents

Introduction

There are a number of books already in print on the subject of private equity, and (I believe) a couple more in the course of preparation, so it may be felt that a book such as this requires some justification. If so, it can very simply be provided. I have always felt the lack of a single comprehensive guide to private equity; something that does not seek to examine the relationship between GPs and LPs, or to indulge in esoteric analysis of private equity returns, but which sets out simply to answer the key questions, such as "what is private equity?" and "how does it work?".

Surprisingly for an asset class whose roots go back to before the second world war, there is no such book available and it is precisely this gap that this work is designed to fill. There is, for example, no one standard text book which can be used for the private equity elective in business schools, and I have designed the overall structure of the book in consultation with academics who teach such courses in an attempt to achieve as close a fit as possible with the course outline (not as easy as it sounds since there seems to be no one universally accepted list of course content!). Nor is there one that can be recommended to entry level professionals in private equity firms, nor for institutional investors who may be looking to enter the asset class for the first time, nor for pension consultants and their trustee clients.

However, please do not assume that just because you might have many years of private equity experience you will come across nothing new in this book. Concepts such as Total Return investing, and treasury and portfolio secondaries, have been in my thinking for several years but have been articulated for the first time in this book. These are novel ideas and may seem controversial to some, but I trust you will at least find them thought-provoking. Similarly, my analysis of historic private equity returns, both buyout and venture, has been performed specifically for this book, using the most up-to-date figures available at the time of writing (Autumn 2006), and my conclusions and suggestions in this regard are original and newly formed.

My previous book *Multi Asset Class Investment Strategy*, also published by John Wiley & Sons, answered the questions "why should I invest in private equity?", "how much should I allocate to it?", "how should private equity returns be compared and analysed against those of other asset classes?" and "how does private equity fit within an overall portfolio?". These two books are designed to be read in conjunction and therefore I do not propose to repeat any of that content here. In any event, it would seem to fit much more naturally within a book on overall asset allocation than within a specialist work of this nature. I would, therefore, strongly recommend that you read the other book first if you have not already done so.

Before we get into the main body of the book, there are a number of points which I would like to make by way of general introduction in the hope that it will enhance your understanding of what is to follow. I must also confess that this hope is somewhat self-serving, since there were a number of general issues running as a thread through every chapter but which were difficult to classify sufficiently to identify exactly where they might properly be discussed in detail.

NUMBERS, THEIR USES AND LIMITATIONS

The first is that while numbers are all we have to work with, we should constantly remind ourselves that they do not paint a perfect picture. This is true of all investment, but probably more so with private equity than with any other asset class. Private equity is different in so many ways, but most importantly it is the only asset class where (1) annual returns are meaningless, invalid and irrelevant and (2) true returns can only be measured many years in arrears. Thus, while we should make full use of the available data we should always be ready to temper the results with perceived trends and personal experience, particularly where we may be in the midst of structural change.

Similarly, we should always think about what lies behind the figures. As an industry we seem prone to looking at figures, particularly performance figures, and drawing quick and seemingly obvious conclusions from them. Yet in many cases, if we stopped and asked ourselves some intelligent questions as to how the figures have been prepared and presented, or as to what they actually represent, or as to what factors might have influenced them, we would almost certainly arrive at a totally different, and certainly a more insightful, result. We will see that the figures purporting to represent European venture performance are a particularly clear example of this, but there is hardly a single aspect of private equity data where the same point does not hold true to some lesser degree. Understanding what lies behind the figures is infinitely more valuable than a simple presentation of their surface values. Indeed, one of my main objectives in agreeing to write this book was the hope that this one important truth could be conveyed and understood.

THE NEED FOR TRANSPARENCY AND FULL DISCLOSURE

This leads us on to the second point, which is a plea for full transparency within the industry. Time and again in the book we find ourselves wishing to analyse a particular point only to find that the data we need is not available, and thus having to make some hopefully intelligent deductions and assumptions instead. The private equity industry is now large, mature and well developed. Surely we have reached a stage where full details of every individual transaction can happily and safely be released, classified according to a commonly agreed analytical model, and the data made publicly available, if necessary for a fee? It is quite ridiculous that an industry which raises hundreds of billions of dollars every year should be unable to tell, for example, whether leverage ratios have risen or fallen in European buyout within a particular period, or to what extent certain investors are being diluted or otherwise by the terms of US venture funding rounds.

I would argue that transparency and full disclosure would actually help rather than harm the industry. We are subjected to an enormous amount of ill-informed criticism, ranging from blogs in the United States that may have got hold of a small part of the portfolio data of a public pension plan, or even an individual fund, and publish it without understanding that something like the J-curve could completely alter its apparent meaning, to (regrettably) articles in the European national press which fail to understand even fundamental concepts such as the difference between venture and buyout funds, or between allocated, committed and invested capital. Were the information publicly available to rebut these stories then surely life would be made easier, not more difficult? Just what is it that GPs are afraid of, that they feel the need to shelter behind such massive ramparts of confidentiality?

ALLOCATED, COMMITTED AND INVESTED CAPITAL

As signalled in the previous section, the third point I wish to make is that time and again over the years I have been struck by how few people really understand the difference between allocated, committed and invested capital (very few LPs, for example, actually over-commit as they should). As you will see, I argue that once the distinction is fully appreciated, then it calls for a radical new approach, which I have chosen to call Total Return investing, to how we should look at a private equity fund programme as a whole, and that this in turn has serious implications as to, for example, how we look at the secondaries space.

It is difficult to exaggerate the importance of this key distinction, which does not just impact the question of programme management but in fact runs through discussion of every aspect of private equity. Is it better, for example, to earn a 60% IRR for 6 months or a 25% IRR for 6 years? The answer is, of course, that it all depends. It depends on whether you are going to be able to reinvest that money straight away at a private equity rate of return. In only about one case out of a million is the answer to this question going to be "yes", so the answer to the original query would clearly be the latter rather than the former. Yet in that case why do we use IRR as a measure of fund performance (rather than, say, money multiples), which might incentivise the GP in the above case to give you the former course of action rather than the latter? And why do we base the GP's management fee on committed rather than invested capital, but the carried interest (in many cases) on invested rather than committed capital? Illogical, captain.

CAN THE INDUSTRY ABSORB MORE CAPITAL?

There is also the question of the amount of capital being raised by the industry, and the resulting rise in average fund sizes. This is a topic of particular relevance since my earlier book argues that most investors worldwide should be making an allocation of 25% to the asset class. Were anything like this to occur it would of course result in massive influx of new capital and fears have been raised of the capacity of the industry to handle this much money.

The first point to make is that this new capital would not of course be coming into the industry all at once but rather over about an 8-year period in the case of each new investor, and some of these may take some years even to make the decision in the first place, which means that we could be looking at anything between 10 and 15 years. Thus, we would be looking at a steady and fairly slow (though admittedly sizeable) expansion rather than a sudden explosion.

The second point is that the capacity of, say, the buyout industry to absorb new money appears to be almost infinite. I have written many articles in recent years about this phenomenon so I think my views are well known, but let me say again that there seems to me no logical reason why the size of mega buyout funds could not rise very considerably beyond their present levels. Clearly if any one fund has the ability by itself to absorb, say, an extra $10 billion of new capital in any one vintage year then this should considerably lower people's anxiety levels.

This clearly has implications for patterns of equity ownership, and we can expect many more companies to be transferred, at least temporarily, from the quoted markets into the hands of private equity players. It also suggests that even very large companies may no longer be beyond their grasp, particularly if the current trend for hunting in packs and laying off equity to potential competitors continues. It has implications, too, for returns. You will have to read the relevant chapters to see what I have to say about this, but one general point bears making at the outset. There is a clear common sense relationship, which is in general borne out by the available data, between the amount of money poured into any particular class of private equity investment and the return which that class is likely to produce. Perhaps fortunately for those few of us who *do* understand this, it is a truth which the vast majority of LPs and their advisers have apparently failed to grasp.

ACCESS, AND WHAT THIS MEANS FOR INVESTMENT MODELS

Another point which is not at all understood by most LPs is access, and this problem is of course particularly acute in the case of US venture and what little is left of the European mid-market. How many LPs realise, for example, that US venture returns are driven by a small number of no more than about 20 firms, and that there is effectively no chance of committing new capital to any fund which they manage, since this is likely to be over-subscribed at least one hundred and possibly one thousand times? Clearly virtually none, but this is perhaps both understandable and excusable. Without wishing to ascribe any cynical motive to them, the situation is hardly helped by investment managers and advisers who claim to be able to deploy large amounts of capital here when clearly on any view they cannot.

The truth is stark: if you seek to commit anything other than a miniscule amount of money to US venture then the best possible outcome is that you will end up in the upper quartile but outside that all-important top decile. A more likely outcome (given the amount of money seeking a home and the number of available funds) is that you will find yourself with second, third or even bottom quartile performance. I am not by any means suggesting that investors should not attempt to do so, since I am a big supporter of US venture, but they should go into it with their eyes open and realistic expectations, and this will not happen so long as some people within the fund of funds and advisory communities continue to make self-serving extravagant claims that cannot be reconciled with the facts.

THE GP/LP RELATIONSHIP

This is a topic which I do not propose to discuss within the body of the book. This may cause some surprise, since it is a subject to which whole chapters have been devoted in books both actual and planned by other writers, and I therefore owe the reader an explanation of why this is.

Rather like access, this is an area where whole battle fleets of theory and discussion founder upon one massive rock of reality. Except perhaps for the case of LPs who invest on a truly massive scale (some of the US public pension plans, for example), and even then only where they are investing with GPs who are determined to raise as much money as possible in order to maximise their management fee income, this is simply no longer an issue. The GP has almost supreme bargaining power, and any individual LP effectively has no bargaining power at all. Consider the situation: the LP's only sanction when faced with what may be deemed an unacceptable situation is not to invest, but to invest elsewhere. The fund, if it is a quality fund, will be potentially over-subscribed almost immediately. It therefore matters not one jot to the

GP whether the LP invests or not; if that particular LP does not proceed, there are others who will. Conversely, if the LP goes elsewhere and finds that her views are now listened to, this should raise questions about the level of investor interest in this new fund generally, and thus of its quality (there are obvious exceptions here, where an asset class falls out of favour for reasons which may have little to do with investment logic, such as European venture, but for the most part it will be true).

Let me qualify this statement of general truth, however. There are obviously some things which even with such supreme power a GP simply could not get away with, but I am not sure that we have really tested the limits yet of what that might be, particularly in the case of golden circle US venture firms. There was initially resistance to the idea of a 30% carry, for example, but this went on to become almost commonplace (I know of one LP, a US endowment, who as a matter of principle stopped investing with a golden circle firm on this issue, and has presumably lived to rue the lost investment returns ever since). Similarly, there was resistance to the dramatic fund size increases which occurred just before the collapse of the bubble, but these still went ahead. Indeed, one or two firms successfully resisted all investor attempts to reduce them again, even when the need for this had become starkly obvious, and many of their peers had already done so. This general principle must logically hold true: as long as there are new investors waiting to crowd into a fund if existing ones fail to take up their offered entitlement, then GPs will be able to call the shots.

Please understand that I am not condoning the position. Personally, I find it extremely regrettable that the economic interests of GPs and LPs are for the most part so badly misaligned, and that friendly and constructive professional discussion of fund terms now seems to belong to a vanished golden age. I am simply recording and recognising reality. This book is designed to be a practical guide to private equity, and I have therefore decided that there is no place in it for sterile academic discussion of what should ideally be the case if only things were different. It is rather like a lot of finance theory, which is fine in theory when you learn it at business school but collapses as soon as you try to put it into practice in the real world. For those who may disagree, let me say this: not only is the situation not going to improve, but if anything it is going to get even worse given the large amounts of extra capital which will be seeking a home in the asset class in future. So, as an American might say (but I, being a courteous and well-brought-up European, couldn't possibly): "get real!". For the foreseeable future, fund terms will be more or less whatever GPs want them to be.

An obvious question, one which I am often asked but to which I do not have an answer, is why LPs do not band together to combine their bargaining power, perhaps even drawing up standard approved sets of legal terms, such as has happened in other industries, for example shipping, international sale of goods, etc. I do know that some attempts have been made to do this, particularly in the USA, and you do occasionally find it happening on an ad hoc basis within the investor base of a particular fund, e.g. on the fund size reduction issue, but I have certainly never come across any really effective large and long-term grouping. Perhaps there is a pointer here for the future. Many LPs come across each other on a regular basis anyway, and there really is no logical reason why they should not formalise these encounters into some sort of industry standards board. Perhaps one day we will come across funds being raised "on International LP committee standard terms (2100)", but somehow I doubt it.

One final point before I leave this rather controversial subject. There are many LPs who say that they view terms and fund economics as the most important single factor in deciding whether to commit to a fund or not. With great respect, I find this view completely illogical. A glance at some of the figures presented later in this book will show that the potential for out-performance by the very best funds in almost any private equity discipline, and most obviously in venture capital, is huge. Even in the case of buyout, it is huge compared with some other asset classes, such as quoted equities. I have not run the calculations, but it seems inconceivable that the impact of any fund term (for example, the difference between a 20% carry and a 30% carry) could make such a difference to the overall performance that it would invalidate the investment decision. That fund is still going to be a dramatically out-performing fund. Do you really care that it will only return 9× to you rather than 10×? And can you really be so sure of your own judgement that if you turn it down you will choose another one that will achieve 10× (the odds against which are immense) rather than, say, 2×? If you are the sort of person who is going to turn down a chance to invest with the likes of Kleiner Perkins or Sequoia on the basis of any disagreeable fund term (unless it is something which makes it legally impossible for you to invest because of your own regulatory or constitutional situation) then I would respectfully suggest that you have not grasped the way private equity returns work, and would be better employed in a different area of investment.

It is for much the same reasons that, after much reflection, I have decided not to comment specifically on fund terms. First, this discussion more properly belongs in a book aimed at an audience of lawyers, and would involve a lot of detailed issues which a non-legally-qualified reader may find very challenging. Second, it would be very difficult to do within the confines of a single chapter, and, if done properly, would probably require a whole book to itself. Third, there are specialist lawyers who will guide you through the process should you encounter it in practice, so this is knowledge which you as an investor do not really necessarily need. Fourth, it would unbalance the book, since I wanted to discuss direct investment (i.e., in companies) as well as indirect investment (i.e., in funds). Finally, and most importantly, even if you *do* understand everything there is to know about fund terms, this knowledge will for the most part be largely irrelevant since the terms will be more or less what the GPs decide they will be, and the scope for any meaningful negotiation will be strictly limited.[1]

So, just to recapitulate, this book is intended as a practical guide to how to go about the business of making private equity investments, whether at the company or (probably more usually) at the fund level. It attempts to describe reality as I, as a practitioner, have experienced it over the years, and to stick to the highways of the possible, not to explore the back lanes of intellectual perfection. Private equity investing is quite difficult enough already without getting distracted by largely irrelevant issues.

---

[1] Since about 1998 I can only remember one instance where a major change was made to the fund terms during the legal documentation review, and this was where something was inconsistent with an assurance which had been given verbally during the fundraising process. In all other cases, the changes that occurred were simply to correct drafting errors which were clearly nonsensical, though in the case of one well-known buyout firm, the lawyers once said to me "to be honest, we don't understand what it means either, but we're not going to change it".

Acknowledgements

Once again Thomson Financial have kindly made available their VentureXpert database to me, and so once again I must express my sincere gratitude and appreciation, particularly to Bob Keiser who again patiently and uncomplainingly dealt with all the minutiae of copyright releases and so forth. Without access to their figures this book could not have been written.

The team at Wiley have again done a superb job. I would like to express thanks tinged with sadness to Rachael Wilkie and Jenny McCall, both of whose efforts have been rewarded with well deserved promotion to other areas of responsibility within Wiley. I will miss working with them both, particularly Rachael who was my original editor and takes the credit (blame?) for first enticing me into print in book form. The continuing members of the team are Chris Swain, Julia Bezzant, Caroline Baines and Samantha Hartley and I would like to express my thanks to all of them, plus Caitlin Cornish, who proved an able substitute for Rachael on a temporary basis. To them in particular must go the credit for publishing the book outside their normal production schedule in order to have it available for launch at SuperReturn.

A number of people kindly read the book, or individual chapters, in draft and provided their comments, which I have striven to incorporate wherever possible. I would like to single out in particular David de Weese of Paul Capital Partners and Joanna Jordan of Greenpark Capital, who both took time out of their busy schedules to provide very helpful information on the secondaries market. My friend and former colleague Joe Schorge, now with PA Consulting Group, again rendered valuable assistance with the graphics as well as early morning brainstorming sessions at the Belsize Café.

1
What is Private Equity?

It used to be quite easy to define what was and was not a private equity investment: "any equity investment in a company which is not quoted on a stock exchange". In truth, however, this rather simplistic description has been in trouble for a long time. What about investments that are structured as convertible debt? What about companies which are publicly listed but are taken private? Or where the company remains listed but the particular instrument into which the new investment occurs is not?

What about a situation where an interest in a company is acquired not for itself but with the intention of gaining ownership of underlying assets, particularly property (real estate) related assets? Even a few years ago many would have drawn back from classifying this as a pukkah private equity transaction, yet today funds are being raised specifically to target such opportunities.

There again, there is the whole secondaries scene, where existing interests in private equity are traded between investors. Just to complicate matters still further, secondary players are today equally happy to buy directly the underlying investments of the fund, and frequently to make primary investments in new funds as well.

Clearly the question "what is private equity?" is no longer capable of a quick and simple answer, even if it ever was. Without wishing to confuse you still further, there is an increasing convergence between the activities of private equity funds, hedge funds and property funds, and by the time this book is published we may well have seen the first recorded example of all three co-operating together on the same transaction; it can only be a matter of time. However, there was a well-known law case in England many years ago when a judge famously said that although you cannot define an elephant you still recognise one when you see it (though some believe he may have pinched this idea from Doctor Johnson without acknowledgement). I think all of us will have an instinct for what a private equity transaction is or is not, but it is growing increasingly difficult to be certain about this as the parameters of the asset class are being stretched all the time.

In this chapter I am going to set out some basic concepts of how private equity functions as an asset class, many of which will then be developed in more detail in the following chapters. This opening chapter will thus be of most use to those with no prior experience of private equity, but I would urge the rest of you to stay with us rather than turning straight to the next chapter, as I will be referring later in the book to these concepts intending them to have precisely the meaning and context to which I am just about to ascribe them.

FUND INVESTING VERSUS DIRECT INVESTING

The first and most fundamental distinction in the private equity world is between those who invest in funds and those who then manage the capital invested in those funds by making investments into companies. This distinction is sometimes defined by the terms "fund investing" and "direct investing", and confusingly some investors do both.

We also have to deal with what Oscar Wilde described as "a single people divided by a common language", although to be fair US private equity terminology has become increasingly common in Europe and I shall usually be adopting it as industry standard, except where it is absolutely essential to draw some particular distinction of meaning.

In America, those who invest in funds are called "LPs", since the most common form of private equity fund is a limited partnership, the passive investors in which are called Limited Partners. In Europe, such folk have historically been called simply "investors". There are various different types of LP and it is worth spending some time examining these here since they will all have different investment criteria and, most importantly of all, different levels of knowledge of the asset class (typically referred to rather arrogantly as "sophistication").

At the top end of the scale are the Fund of Funds managers. These will typically do nothing except invest in private equity, and the best of them will have staff with perhaps 20 years' specialist experience. Some (Horsley Bridge would be a good example) might specialise in one particular area (traditionally early stage US venture in their case) whereas others (Harborvest, to give an example of similar vintage) are generalist both as to the type of investments which they make and the geographical areas which they cover. As we will see, however, the bulk of private equity activity occurs in the USA and in Europe, and it is these two areas into which the private equity world has traditionally been subdivided.

Perhaps perversely, many of the Fund of Funds also make direct investments alongside their fund investments (this is known as "co-investment" because it usually takes the form of persuading the manager of a fund into which you have put money to allow you to invest alongside the fund in one or more of its portfolio companies). I say "perversely" because there is an argument that by indulging in co-investment one actually harms exactly that diversification which is one of the advantages usually cited by Fund of Funds managers of investing in their pro-grammes. They would argue, on the contrary, that the amounts involved are relatively small, that the overall impact of management fees is lessened, albeit very slightly, and that it enables investors to put more money to work in the asset class than would otherwise be the case. Notwithstanding these cogent arguments, there is nonetheless a vociferous minority who regard this approach as stark staring sophisticated.

For most investors seeking to enter the asset class, the fund of funds approach will be preferred. Few will have the relevant levels of specialist expertise available in-house to be able consistently to select the best partnerships and, even if one could, many of the best are "invitation only" so that gaining access to them may well prove impossible anyway; this is a particular issue with US venture funds. Outside the USA there is a further issue which is that allocations to private equity are usually unrealistically low (so low, in fact, that most investors would do better not to be making any allocation at all), so that not only can the cost of acquiring such expertise never be contemplated, but there is no way in which even unskilled time can be made available to study and analyse the couple of hundred fund offerings which are likely to be received in any one year.

The Fund of Funds approach provides skilled fund selection expertise. It also ensures that capital will be committed on a scientific basis every year (very important to obtain diversification by time, as we will see), and that all reporting and accounting at the partnership level will be taken care of. In fact, the Fund of Funds route into the asset class can be thought of as the "fire and forget" option. Provided one commits to each successive Fund of Funds vehicle from that manager (typically every 3 years) then one can simply sit back and manage the cash inflows and outflows.

The next step up might be to use some aspects of the Fund of Funds approach but perhaps supplemented by one's own efforts. For example, a European investor who has taken the trouble to set a proper allocation level and to acquire relevant internal expertise, may feel confident enough to start making, say, European buyout selections themselves but wish to use specialist Fund of Funds products aimed at, for example, US buyout and venture. Alternatively, such specialist funds can be used simply to add a "tilt" to a private equity programme by going underweight or overweight in a particular area.

Direct investment is the final layer in the private equity environment, where money actually gets channelled into investee companies, and this is the role of the private equity manager ("GP"). The investment process may therefore be seen as consisting broadly of two levels, the fund level and the company level, and it is this distinction which I label as the difference between "fund investment" and "direct investment".

Each requires its own particular modelling and analysis, and we will be looking at this in more detail in later chapters. Importantly, each also requires its own skills. This is often overlooked by investors who, not content with fund investing, decide they would also like to share in some of the "fun" of direct investing. As we have already noted, where this takes the form of co-investment it will usually have an adverse impact on diversification. Where it takes place directly, without even the comforting umbrella of a fund co-investor, then it is frequently a recipe for disaster since few investors have the skills of a specialist GP. This was a particular problem during the dot.com bubble as various family offices, banks and large corporates scrambled to take stakes in technology and internet companies without the relevant company building skills to ensure their success and also without the discipline and mental toughness to ride out the bad times when they inevitably arrived. Many of these companies would have been doomed in any event, with hopelessly ill-conceived business plans and poor management, but not all. Who knows how many struggling but worthwhile companies might have survived the maelstrom if the business of direct investing had been left to the professionals?

TERMINOLOGY

I have referred to the Oscar Wilde factor above and while I propose to deal with this largely by ignoring it, there are some important points to make right at the outset, since there are some differences in terminology which go to the very heart of understanding the asset class, and which are a constant source of confusion for the uninitiated.

In Europe, the asset class as a whole is called "private equity", and it is broadly subdivided into "buyout" and "venture capital" (or just "venture"), as we will see below. While this broad classification also holds good in the USA, different terms are frequently used. There, the asset class as a whole is usually called "venture capital" and buyouts (particularly large ones) are often referred to as "private equity". I think you will see at once the huge scope for confusion which this creates. I am frequently consulted by journalists working for national newspapers who are about to write an article on the sector, and find myself having to make this point again and again; it seems that I have been only partially successful, since I have lost count of the number of times I have seen large European buyout firms referred to as "venture capitalists".

In fairness to the journalists involved, none of whom pretend to be experts on the sector, this confusion is to a certain extent perpetuated and encouraged within Europe for the rather cynical purposes of those concerned. In the right hands, venture capital is a powerful tool for economic growth. Research suggests that even by the end of 2000, venture capital had directly created about 8 million new jobs in the USA (roughly equivalent to one job for every $36000 of investment), and that if one added into the mix the jobs created indirectly in supporting and related businesses then the total rose to a staggering 27 million.[1] No comparable studies have been made in Europe; the deliberate confusion between venture and buyout makes any reference to "venture-backed" companies meaningless in this context. However, it is logically impossible that venture has had no effect whatever. It must therefore be accepted that venture capital is socially and economically desirable since it has a clear tendency to boost both GDP and employment. Venture capital typically represents less than 1% of total capital investment in any one year in the USA, yet venture-backed companies are said to create about 13% of GDP.[2]

Buyout, by contrast, can be seen by those European governments who practise what might be termed a "social economic" model (most of the continental countries, and increasingly the UK) as undesirable. As we discuss how buyout operates it will become clear that buyout transactions generally have the effect of reducing employment through restructuring and rationalisation, and certainly of decreasing tax yield since financial structuring will use loan interest to reduce taxable earnings. Small wonder, then, that industry bodies in Europe have sought

---

[1] *Public Sector Review*: Finance, Summer 2004, pp. 62 and 63.
[2] *Public Sector Review*, as before.

to wrap themselves in the flag of venture capital. The British Venture Capital Association, for example, speaks (despite its name), not, as one might expect, for the venture community in the UK but overwhelmingly by member fund size for the buyout community transacting deals across Europe.

This is unfortunate for all sorts of reasons, not least that the venture community in Europe is left without any body to lobby on its behalf. Fortunately for the BVCA and the European buyout community, European politicians are sufficiently "unsophisticated" that this deception goes unmasked. Unfortunately for the European venture community they are forced unjustly to endure the brickbats which are regularly aimed at "venture capitalists" (meaning buyout firms) by left-wing politicians.

It will be apparent from the title of this book that I have chosen to adopt "private equity" as the name of the asset class as a whole, and "buyout" and "venture" as its two main constituents. I believe that this is the least confusing approach available and it reflects the way in which I have always viewed the asset class. I will generally be adopting the US expressions "LP" (Limited Partner) and "GP" (General Partner) for "investor" and "firm" or "manager", respectively, but there will be occasions when the context suggests that the European terms should be preferred. Incidentally, it may come as a surprise for American readers to learn that the terms "LP" and "GP" were largely unknown in Europe until a very few years ago.

PRIMARY VERSUS SECONDARY FUND INVESTING

When I wrote my book *Multi Asset Class Investment Strategy* I was able to devote only one chapter to private equity and these constraints meant that I was able to give only a passing reference to secondary transactions. This was unfortunate, as secondary investing has become a very significant part of the private equity landscape, and also has an important part to play in the planning of private equity fund programmes, particularly in the early stages. We will examine both these areas in more detail later, but for the moment I am happy to be able to devote some time to explaining what secondary transactions are and how they work.

It is widely assumed by investors that private equity funds are illiquid investments. While this is strictly true as a matter of law (in the sense that they are not quoted on an exchange) it is not true as a matter of practice, because of the very active secondary market which exists.

Briefly, if you hold an interest in a private equity fund and wish for whatever reason to sell it (thus also bringing to an end your obligation to continue to fund capital calls) then there are a significant number of specialist secondary purchasers who will be happy to quote you a price for it. Various investors and Funds of Funds also play in this space, though it does not form the main thrust of their activities.

The specialist secondary players have grown rapidly in recent years, both in number and in size, to the extent that there is now usually an excess of demand over supply for secondary product, reflected in very firm pricing, at least for buyout funds (venture funds are still affected by the uncertainty created by the technology bubble, particularly those that are not well known and/or may be seen as having kept some companies alive unnecessarily).

Thus the myth that private equity as an asset class is illiquid is just that – a myth. It should be perfectly possible to dispose of an entire private equity fund programme in the space of 3 months or so should one for some reason wish to do so. I have personally conducted a secondary transaction in less than a month from start to finish. Of course one will not usually realise the full potential value of the interest, but then that is the nature of selling any future cashflow for a present value. It should also be borne in mind that having to sell a large holding of quoted equities on a fire sale basis is unlikely to bring in their full book value.

Secondary transactions also take place at the company level, typically taking the form of a GP seeking to sell the remaining portfolio of a fund in order to be able to wind it up in a timely fashion. Very rarely one may see a GP who has been unable to raise a new fund selling the active portfolio of their existing fund or funds at the urging of their LPs; these situations are much more likely to involve one of the corporate or banking investors to whom we referred earlier panicking and compounding their original error by seeking to sell their investments at the worst possible time.

The skills of a secondary investor are different again to those of a GP or a conventional LP, but are probably the closest of all to standard finance theory and thus the easiest to learn. Certainly they are at the most objective and quantitative ends of the relevant continuum.

A BROAD DELINEATION: BUYOUT AND VENTURE

Buyout can be distinguished from venture capital in a number of ways. Chief among these are the fact that it generally focuses on established companies rather than young businesses, and the fact that it uses debt as well as equity financing (and frequently hybrids of the two). It is also generally true that it tends to concern itself with "traditional" business activities rather than technology, although this distinction is becoming somewhat blurred as former "dot.com" and technology businesses mature. We have already seen a number of buyouts in the telecoms space (some of them very large) and there is no logical reason why a company which has originally been venture backed should not in the full course of time be the subject of a buyout transaction.

Size is also often advanced as a differentiating factor and now that the excessive valuations of the dot.com bubble have subsided this can also probably be adopted with some confidence as a general truth. However, this too should be treated with some caution. While it is certainly true that the average size of buyout funds is getting larger and larger, enabling them in turn to transact larger and larger deals, there are still a few buyout firms who are happy to operate at the smaller end of the market.

Another apparent distinction is that between "control" and "non-control" investing, the former being where the private equity manager either owns a majority of the shares in the company or at least has control over the majority of the voting rights. Tread carefully, here, though. While it is extremely unusual to find a venture capitalist having control over a company, except where this may have occurred through the failure of the company to achieve its targets and the triggering of default and/or preference rights, this is by no means the same thing as saying that control will always be present in a buyout transaction.

Indeed, non-control investing used to be extremely prevalent, and even at the time triggered arguments about whether it could properly be called "buyout" investing. There is now general agreement that such transactions probably constitute a separate class altogether, called either "expansion capital" or "development capital". The importance of such deals should not be underestimated, since while they have largely faded from view in the UK and the USA there are still some firms who specialise in them even in these countries and many managers in such countries as France, Italy and Spain undertake development capital deals alongside buyouts in the same fund. Note too that the historic buyout return figures will contain large elements of development capital, particularly the European figures for the early and mid-1990s.

These factors are advanced as suggested guidelines and while they will prove helpful, and perhaps even definitive in most cases, I think it

Table 1.1 Guidelines for classifying private equity transactions

Venture	Buyout
Small enterprise value (particularly in Europe)	Large enterprise value, sometimes very large (multi-billion)
Bank debt almost never used	Bank debt almost always used
Young companies, even start-up	Generally mature, established companies
Investee companies rarely profit-making	Profit levels of investee companies crucial (although turnaround situations are considered)
Investee company will always be developing or applying new technology	Technology considerations largely irrelevant
A minority stake will always be taken. Control will usually only arise through default and/or refinancing	Control always present in true buyouts, though some firms practice development capital
Valuation largely a matter of instinct and experience	Firm rules of financial theory available with which to calculate valuation (e.g., earnings multiple)
Venture managers will often have been successful start-up entrepreneurs and/or will have specialist technology expertise	Buyout managers typically come from an accountancy, investment banking or management consultancy background

will be obvious even from the brief outline above that there will always be some that defy precise definition. How would you classify, for example, a firm that took majority stakes in fairly mature technology companies using only equity, or a firm that used debt financing to take a majority stake in a troubled early stage company? Happily, common sense will usually prevail but Table 1.1 may prove helpful.

CAPITAL: ALLOCATED, COMMITTED, DRAWN DOWN AND INVESTED

We will be examining in some detail how private equity funds and transactions work, but this may be greatly facilitated by an explanation right at the outset of the different categories of capital which one encounters. This point is absolutely key as, for example, a failure to understand the difference between committed and invested capital lies at the heart of the very fundamental mistakes which one sees being made habitually by investors who have either recently entered the asset class for the first time, or who see it as a tiresome distraction from the main business of investing in bonds and quoted equities and thus never bother to acquire the required level of knowledge. Without wishing to be unduly paranoid or cynical, could it be that it is perhaps in the interests of such people, who may never have really believed in the asset class anyway, to see its returns artificially depressed in their hands? At the very least, they are unlikely to be unhappy should such an eventuality occur.

It may be helpful first to see a basic graphic (Figure 1.1) showing the way in which private equity funds work. Allocated capital is that amount of their capital which an investor notionally sets aside in their mind to be devoted to private equity. For example, if a €500M pension fund decides to make a 15% allocation to private equity, then its allocated capital will be €75M. Allocated capital can be thought of as roughly representing the total amount of capital which an investor would ideally like to have actually invested in private equity investments (i.e., companies) at any one time.

Committed capital is that amount of capital which an investor has actually legally promised to provide to private equity funds by signing Limited Partnership Agreements. Two points need to be made here. First, in the early years of a private equity fund programme this figure will necessarily be quite small. Second, because of the way in which private equity funds work, which we will be examining in detail below, it is necessary to over-commit. In other words, your target committed capital should not be the same as your private equity allocation, but considerably more (usually at least 160% of allocated capital). This is the one single point which is most frequently misunderstood about private equity and leads to dramatic under-investment.

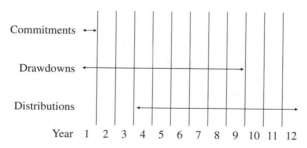

Figure 1.1   How a private equity fund works

Drawndown capital is that amount of your committed capital which has actually been drawn down (i.e., requested by a private equity fund and paid to them). This will include both capital to be invested in companies and also money required for fees and expenses.

Invested capital, as the name suggests, is that part of drawn-down capital which has actually been invested in companies. I think it will be apparent already that there can be a dramatic difference between allocated capital and invested capital. A common misconception amongst those who have been used to investing in quoted shares and bonds is that one can somehow pick up the phone and order a certain amount of private equity, thus fully investing your allocation all at once, rather than realising that it needs at least 8 years of careful planning and execution (including significant over-committing) to get anywhere near your objective.

HOW DO PRIVATE EQUITY FUNDS WORK?

Structure

We have already seen that private equity funds are invariably structured as limited partnerships, thus leading to the steady adoption of the American terminology "LP" (for Limited Partner) for an investor in such funds and "GP" (for General Partner) for a manager. Yet here again we find ourselves having to qualify this definition almost immediately.

It is probably more correct to say that institutional private equity funds are customarily structured as limited partnerships. Many funds which are intended for retail use are structured as quoted vehicles, and these are often also used by investors looking to "park" uninvested allocated capital.[3] As we will see in a later chapter, these vehicles are frequently cash rich and rarely approach the level of returns achieved by institutional partnerships, at least measured in IRR terms.

There are other funds aimed predominantly at retail investors and driven by tax breaks: examples would be a VCT (Venture Capital Trust) in the UK or an FCPR[4] (Fonds Commun de Placement à Risques) in

---

[3] This is not a good practice as there are much better ways of doing this. See my earlier book "*Multi Asset Class Investment Strategy*", John Wiley & Sons, London, 2006, particularly pages 177 to 180.

[4] This does not even need to invest exclusively in private equity. An FCPR will enjoy special fiscal advantages if even 50% of its capital is invested in European unlisted securities.

France. In these cases, again, high quality institutional returns are unlikely to be achieved, but investors will hope that the benefit of the associated tax breaks will make up for this.

In certain countries, notably continental Europe, legal and regulatory reform has been slow to catch up with reality with the result that even today other legal forms are sometimes forced upon an institutional fund, but there will usually always be a limited partnership available as a parallel structure for those whose own jurisdiction permits them to invest in one.

Some jurisdictions go further and almost force a limited partnership structure on an investor. In America, for example, pension funds are subject to ERISA[5] regulations. While these do not impose any strict requirement to restrict private equity investment to limited partnerships (reference is to Venture Capital Operating Companies (VCOCs) and there is a particular issue with regard to the making of capital contributions before the date of the fund's first investment[6]), in practice US lawyers have become adept at drafting LPAs (Limited Partnership Agreements) in such a way as to accommodate these and so as a matter of practice few American pension funds will contemplate any other structure.

A limited partnership is known as a closed-end fund since it has a finite lifetime (typically either 10 or 12 years, depending on whether it is a buyout or venture fund, respectively, but in each case with the option of two annual extensions). This has always been the model in the USA and the UK (at least for institutional funds), where the limited partnership has long been accepted as a way of doing business, but less so in other regions. In continental Europe, for example, much private equity investing took place through open-ended structures. These "evergreen" vehicles were the subject of much criticism from Anglo-Saxon observers, who claimed that they provided little incentive to managers to force exits from their investments, and that their returns could not validly be compared with limited partnerships because typically there was no mechanism for them to return capital to investors.

---

[5] Employee Retirement Income Security Act.
[6] Broadly, to qualify as a VCOC, at least 50% of capital must be invested in venture capital investments and the entity must exercise actual management rights in respect of at least one of the underlying companies.

Cashflow

Private equity funds are unlike any other form of investment in that they represent a stream of unpredictable cashflows over the life of the fund, both inward and outward. These cashflows are unpredictable not only as to their amount, but also as to their timing. For example, while funds will typically select their investments over a 3-year period, the period during which they are legally able to do so (the "investment period") is usually set at 5 years to provide flexibility and even then some funds (particularly venture funds) will make follow-on investments into their portfolio companies for some years thereafter. We will be considering later what this means for the way in which we should model private equity funds, and analyse returns, but let us for the moment examine how this all happens in practice.

When a fund needs cash, either for the payment of fees or the making of investments, the GP will issue a Drawdown Notice (sometimes called a Capital Call, though strictly speaking the Capital Call is the process to which the Drawdown Notice gives effect). This will ask for a certain amount of money to be paid into a specified bank account by a certain date and will give brief details of what the money is required for.

The LP will check that the purposes for which the money is required are valid according to the terms of the LPA (is the investment within the stated scope of the fund?, is there a restriction on the amount of money that may be called in any one year, or for any one investment?, etc.) and that the amount has been correctly calculated. It will then take steps to honour the Drawdown Notice by making the required bank transfer. An important point to note here is that funds are generally not allowed to draw down money to hold on account, although they are allowed to do so in anticipation of a specific transaction which they hope to close shortly, and frequently to return it and draw it down again if the transaction does not complete, although this can give certain types of investors, particularly Funds of Funds, procedural headaches of their own.

Distributions are the other side of the cashflow coin. Whenever a fund exits an investment by sale or flotation (American: IPO) then they will have cash available to return to investors. This is usually effected by a distribution notice, which is just the opposite of a Drawdown Notice, and will notify each individual investor of how much money they may expect to have transferred into their bank account, and when.

Since the timing of exits is unpredictable then so necessarily is the timing of distributions. To inject yet further uncertainty into the situation, a fund may actually sell its holding in a particular company in tranches over time, particularly where the exit is by flotation.

One important point which is often overlooked is the tendency of some private equity funds, particularly US venture funds, to make distributions in specie. All this means is that instead of selling shares in an underlying company and then distributing cash, they distribute the shares themselves, leaving the individual investors to decide when and how to sell them. Indeed, with US venture funds, distributions in specie are probably more numerous than cash distributions. A further complication is that such shares are frequently restricted stock, i.e., they cannot be traded (sold) for a certain length of time (usually 6 months). This imposes a requirement for a specialist "end game" team within any investor in such funds, firstly because that investor may not already have a mechanism in place for trading quoted stocks (it may, for example, be a specialist private equity Fund of Funds), secondly because the management of restricted stocks requires complex compliance and regulatory systems, and finally because even if the investor does already deal in quoted stocks they are unlikely to have an analyst covering the company in question. This means that most investors simply sell their shares on the first available day, which can obviously lead to them having to accept a disappointing price as many shares are thrown into the market together.

There were some European funds who used this practice in the mid-1990s, but the problems described above led to such adverse investor reaction that almost without exception European funds decided to eschew such measures, and it will now be found only in the very unusual and highly theoretical circumstance of a fund being wound up while still holding active investments. However, in the USA it is commonplace and those who rush into investing directly in US funds, particularly of the venture capital variety, without putting in place mechanisms for dealing with it (there are various third-party quoted distribution management services that are prepared to provide the service for a fee) may be in for an unpleasant surprise. In fairness, the widespread adoption of electronic registration and dealing services in recent years have made this less onerous than once it was, but it still imposes a prodigious regulatory burden, and in any event only a specialist professional investor is likely to have access to these expensive facilities.

Investment

The most important thing to understand about the way in which a private equity fund invests is that investment power is confined to the manager (GP). The LPs have no voice at all in the investment process and, indeed, should not want to have since there is a significant risk of them losing their limited liability if they can be shown to have played an active part in the management of the partnership.

The combination of passive investing and long fund lifetimes has made private equity an unpalatable dish for some, and emphasises the need for extreme care and specialist skills in the selection of managers in the first place. Any private equity fund is likely to last longer than the average marriage and while an active secondary market does exist, a private equity fund commitment should be thought of as essentially long term.

There are some investors who chafe at the bit and find ways of influencing the investment process, either from behind the scenes, or through sitting on the investment committee or even quite blatantly with a power of veto. This will be dramatically unpopular with most investors, however, even to the extent of putting them off committing to the fund at all. A golden rule of private equity fund selection is that those responsible for the investment process should be members of the full-time executive team, but nobody else.

Historically there was an interesting juxtaposition here between practice and attitudes in continental Europe and elsewhere. On the continent, it was commonplace for private equity funds to be affiliated to, or even owned by, entities such as banks and insurance companies. Even where this was not openly the case, GPs would seek to position themselves within the semi-formal networks that permeated all local business dealings by bringing senior people from such organisations into the investment decision process. The juxtaposition arose because this was found to be very attractive to local investors (who liked both the idea of enhanced dealflow and some check or balance on the investment team) but deeply unpopular with Anglo-Saxon investors, who deplored the lack of independence and possible interference with the investment process for reasons which might not be purely financial. There was a period in France, for example, when banks were inclined simply to park troublesome debtors in their captive private equity portfolio.

To be fair, there were instances of this in the UK and the USA as well, but these were mostly resolved some years ago by the executive team buying themselves out from their parent organisation (CVC splitting away from Citibank would be an obvious example). This took much longer on the continent, where many GPs were curiously reluctant to go it on their own, and indeed there are still many captive and semi-captive firms in operation. Interestingly, however, the teams are at least at great pains nowadays to stress their independence.

This is a delicate matter and I do not wish to provoke contro-versy. However, it does seem to me that even where there may be no out-siders involved on the investment committee it is probably illusory to talk about independence within any large group. Deutsche Bank, for example, simply closed down their supposedly independent private equity operation in London one day, regardless of the interests of the outside investors which the team had managed to attract into their fund, and there have recently been persistent rumours of a similar nature surrounding another bank. All in all, I would agree whole-heartedly with an aphorism which is credited to Phil Horsley, a very senior and respected private equity fund investor (and a former partner of mine) to the effect that you should never invest with a private equity team if you have to go to somebody else's office to meet them.

Fundraising

In a sense we should have discussed fundraising first, since it is chrono-logically at the beginning of the fund cycle and forms an obvious pre-requisite to any form of investment activity. You cannot invest money unless you have it in the first place. Let us explore briefly how the fundraising process plays itself out in practice.

Most funds (including Funds of Funds) tend to work to a 3-year fund cycle which means that in the third year of Fund I they will be out fundraising for Fund II, and so on. This is an important factor which is often overlooked by those seeking to enter the sector for the first time. For example, European pension funds will frequently put a desired private equity allocation out to tender, ignoring the fact that (1) some of the best private equity managers do not participate in such processes, (2) on average only a third of them will be fundraising at any one time, and (3) the tendering process does not apply to investment funds anyway! There are many other objections to the tendering process which probably lie beyond the scope of this book,[7] but let us simply

---

[7] "Got time to kill?", Guy Fraser-Sampson, *Pensions World*, January 2006.

note that this is a deeply sub-optimal way of choosing private equity managers; indeed, as you will see when we come to look at manager selection, this is really just a complete abrogation of responsibility when compared with best practice.

The first step in the fundraising process should be for the team to sit down and plan their investment model for their next fund. This should consist of mapping out where the most lucrative returns are likely to be made, assessing how many of these investments they can secure (this is likely to be a strictly limited number in most circumstances), and thus how many are likely to be made in a 3-year period and how much money is required for them. They will then resolve to raise exactly that amount of money (plus a small contingency) and no more, since to do so would pull them away from the sweet spot which they have identified.

You will notice that I say "should". Sadly, what I have just described is best practice but is increasingly now honoured in the breach rather than the observance. Particularly in the case of the large buyout funds, there is an increasing feeling that they will simply adjust their target fund size to meet investor demand. This is not necessarily damaging, or even reprehensible (see my comments on fund size in the buyout chapter), but it is certainly not best practice, and does raise worrying issues about what exactly motivates buyout managers. In fairness, I should point out that if one glosses over the unfortunate excesses of the dot.com bubble then this best practice is still largely observed in other quarters, most notably by the best US venture firms.

The next stage in the process is to prepare an Offering Memorandum (sometimes called a Private Placement Memorandum) which is the legal document on the basis of which investment will take place, although the actual contractual document is of course the Limited Partnership Agreement, which will be signed separately by each investor, or made the subject of a subscription agreement, which will be signed separately by each investor. While the precise status of an OM in relation to a private equity fund has never been definitively established (and would in any event differ from one jurisdiction to another), it does seem that its representations will be incorporated into the resulting contract,[8] whether expressly or impliedly, and that knowingly

---

[8] It is probably more correct to say that the contract will be deemed to have been entered into by the parties on the basis of the representations made in the OM.

making a false or misleading statement within an OM could well leave one open to criminal charges.

In practice, marketing often takes place without an OM, at least in final form, and I have known the OM to be produced right at the end, and delivered to investors with all the other contractual documentation, i.e., after they have actually taken their decision to invest, which would doubtless raise a number of nice legal points. For marketing purposes, the most important documentation is the presentation, which is exactly what it sounds like: a set of Powerpoint slides which are used as the focus for a face-to-face fundraising meeting. There are some investors who ask to see the presentation in advance. Personally, I would discourage this practice. A well-crafted presentation will act merely as a counterpoint or backdrop to what the team want to say and should not be considered as a stand-alone document. If the investor wants to know specific information to help decide whether or not to take the meeting, then why not simply ask for it? GPs could be better prepared here. It should be possible, for example, to have ready to hand a standard form fund performance slide (preferably on a single sheet of paper) which can be updated quarterly. Once the meeting has taken place, the presentation will act as a useful aide memoire in conjunction with the meeting note which will be prepared by a member of the investor's team.

Practice is divided amongst LPs as to what happens next. This is a complex area and most investment decision processes pass through several stages. However, in broad terms the decision process will be either preceded or followed by a period of due diligence, during which the LP's team will endeavour to carry out as much analysis and as many background checks as possible on the GPs. In practice, it is probably more accurate to say that in most cases the decision process will be accompanied by the due diligence process, since some analysis may well be done at a very early stage (on the historic financial performance, for example) while the final decision may well be expressly subject to due diligence which has yet to be carried out.

My views on due diligence may be slightly eccentric, but I must say that in my opinion much of the due diligence which is performed by LPs is excessive, and in many cases ineffective or even irrelevant. Due diligence should be an intelligent exercise during which the LP team members discuss what are the issues that they see with the offering, and set out specific steps to answer these particular questions. Unfortunately in practice one is more likely to meet the scattergun approach, which I once heard described as "asking for my grandmother's birth certificate", and which is aptly known as "papering the file" in the USA.

The really ironic thing is that the intelligent approach is much more likely to disclose useful information than the scattergun approach. Approaching the referees proposed by the GPs, for example, particularly with a standard form set of questions, is unlikely to yield any surprises; the GP would hardly have suggested them in the first place unless they knew in advance roughly what they were going to say. One or two of these calls should be made as a matter of form, but far more interesting will be approaching people "off the list" as it were. Particular attention should be paid to tracking down anyone who has recently left the firm, the CEO of any portfolio company which has got into difficulties, and any other private equity professionals with whom the GP habitually co-invests. Investment bankers and head-hunters can also prove productive sources of intelligence.

Once an investor is ready to indicate that they are minded to invest a certain amount, they become a "soft circle" and once they have actually taken a firm decision to invest subject only to due diligence and agreement on the legal terms they become a "hard circle". This is what GPs and their placing agents are referring to when they talk of having a certain amount "hard circled" or "soft circled". With successful, established groups it is not unusual to find that existing investors from prior funds are already hard circles before the offering goes out to potential new investors; indeed, it would be surprising if it were otherwise, since the existing LPs will want to make sure of their allocations.

The final stage in the process sees the lawyers being unleashed as the terms of the LPA are debated and negotiated. In truth, such is the bargaining strength of the GPs in desirable funds that little of any substance is usually conceded to LPs, and their choice is effectively between signing the LPA or walking away. Perhaps surprisingly, there is little attempt made by LPs to get together and negotiate terms collectively, nor to agree "industry standard" terms amongst themselves and then say that they will invest only on this basis, though common sense would appear to commend both these courses of action. A cynic would doubtless venture that, human nature being what it is, LPs might never be able to trust each other sufficiently not to break ranks, thus leaving the remainder horribly exposed.

SUMMARY

- Private equity investing can be divided generally into two streams, fund investing and company investing. Fund investing is essentially one level removed from company investing, as the fund will in turn invest in underlying portfolio companies. For this reason, company investing is often called "direct" investing.
- Fund investments are in turn divided into primary and secondary. A primary investment is a commitment to invest in a new fund which is as yet unformed. A secondary investment is the purchase and transfer of an interest in an existing fund from another investor.
- Direct private equity investing, i.e., at the company rather than the fund level, can be described as typically being an investment of an equity nature in a company which is not listed on any public equity market. While there are a number of possible exceptions, this definition remains broadly true.
- All private equity investing, whether at the fund or company level, can be subdivided into buyout and venture. Buyout transactions typically include debt and involve established and usually profitable companies. Venture transactions typically do not include debt and involve young, even start-up companies and some element of technological innovation.
- Fundamental to a proper appreciation of how private equity funds work is an understanding of the difference between allocated, committed, drawdown and invested capital. Allocated capital represents that part of the overall asset mix which has been set aside for investment in private equity. Committed capital is that amount of allocated capital which has been committed (i.e., become the subject of a legally binding agreement to be paid on demand) to a private equity fund. Drawdown capital is that part of committed capital which has been paid on demand. Invested capital is that part of drawdown capital which has actually been invested in portfolio companies (the other main use of drawdown capital being the payment of fees and expenses).
- The bulk of private equity funds are these days typically structured as institutional limited partnerships, though other legal forms exist, including some which are quoted and/or aimed at least in part at retail investors.

- A private equity fund may be thought of as a stream of cashflows (both into and out of the fund) which are essentially unpredictable both as to their timing and amount.
- Sole investment powers rest with the GP (manager) of the fund. Thus all private equity fund investors are wholly passive in the strict legal sense.
- Fundraising typically takes place at 3-year intervals, although some funds, such as secondary funds, have in recent years been investing more rapidly, and thus fundraising at shorter intervals. This phenomenon also occurred with venture funds during the bubble period.

Private Equity Returns –
The Basics

We are going to dive straight into an explanation of private equity returns at this point, firstly because I think it follows on logically from what we were discussing in the last chapter, and secondly because learning private equity without first understanding how the returns work is rather like learning to play bridge without understanding how to score. In private equity, there are interconnections which mean that the nature and circumstances of a deal, and of the firm which transacts it, will tend to operate in a certain way on its likely return, both as to amount and as to timing. Ideally one could discuss both of these aspects at once, but of course that is impossible in practice and so I think it is best if we first familiarise ourselves with the general characteristics of private equity returns. How are these measured, and why? How will they tend to react in different circumstances? How may we compare them with the returns of other asset classes? What industry benchmarks are available to assist us, and how should we seek to use these?

UNDERSTANDING THE J-CURVE
AND COMPOUND RETURNS

If people with no prior experience of private equity have ever heard one thing about it in passing it tends to be the J-curve. Sadly, since this lies at the heart of comprehending how private equity returns work, it is widely misunderstood, sometimes even after several attempts at explanation. This is not because it is an unduly difficult or complex concept, or that the people struggling with it are unintelligent. It is because the background to it is (to those brought up in a conventional investment environment) somewhat revolutionary and unless and until one can grasp and accept this background, then the concept of the J-curve makes little sense or, even worse, can be seen as some sort of attempted confidence trick on behalf of the private equity industry.

This will probably be the first of many times in this book that I say that private equity is different from just about any other asset class. For our present purposes, one of the main differences is that annual returns cannot be used as a guide to private equity performance, whereas for most people this is the only return that matters for every other asset class. The reason that annual returns are not a valid measure of private equity performance rests on one of the other differences with other asset classes.

Unlike other asset classes, an investment in a private equity fund represents an investment in a stream of cashflows. Of course there are other assets which would appear to satisfy this definition, most notably bonds, but in fact there is a huge difference between the two. When you buy a bond you typically have just one cash outflow (on day one, when you buy the bond) and then a series of cash inflows (the coupon payments and then the face value of the bond at the end of its life), the dates and amounts of which can be precisely predicted. That is why, for example, you can calculate the redemption yield of a bond at any time.

With a private equity fund, you will have a whole series of cash outflows as money is drawn down by the GP, but both the timing and the amount of these outflows is totally uncertain (the only thing you do know is that their total value cannot exceed the amount of your committed capital). Similarly there will be a number of cash inflows as the GP distributes the proceeds of investments as they are realised, but again it is completely impossible to predict in advance how much each one of these will amount to, or when it will occur. You might like to look back at Figure 1.1 to refresh yourself on this.

So, yes, the way of calculating the total return of both a bond and a private equity fund can be by calculating a compound return over time, but there the similarity ends. The calculation in respect of a bond can be done on the day of purchase; indeed, it is this very certainty which is a major selling point for things such as so-called Liability Driven Investment. The calculation in respect of a private equity fund can only be made once the very last cashflow has occurred; in other words, the true return will only be known retrospectively. I hope it will be obvious though, that the later in the lifetime of the private equity fund you find yourself then the more accurate your guesstimate of the final result is likely to be, since the outcome will become steadily less uncertain with every passing year and every recorded cashflow.

Of course there is some element of this in the case of the bond also, but it is really nothing more than the normal operation of the time value of money. As you approach the redemption date then the redemption amount will play a bigger and bigger part in the total return calculation, but this is only because it is becoming closer in time terms. Thus looking only at the annual return in terms of the coupon received could actually give a very misleading result, especially in the case of a short bond that has only a few years left to run. However, the bond markets are as near perfect as makes no difference, and this difference would of course be reflected in the market price of the bond, which is after all only a simple arithmetic calculation. Thus, provided that you take into account both the coupon (the running yield) and the redemption effect, then a perfectly valid annual return can be calculated for any bond.

Not so with a private equity fund. The cashflows are unpredictable, as we have seen, and to complicate matters still further the best is kept until last from an investor's point of view, as the biggest inflows tend to occur towards the end of the fund's life rather than towards the beginning (this is particularly the case with venture funds, whose average investment holding period will be longer than that of a buyout fund). Thus any attempt to calculate an annual return will be hostage to fortune; the fortune of how many cashflows might be received that year. Increase in capital values does not work here, either, as most private equity firms are very conservative on valuation, particularly in Europe where stringent valuation guidelines are enforced. A company may be sold for much more than its latest valuation in the fund's accounts.

It is clear, then, that we need to look at the compound return over time (the IRR) of a private equity fund in order validly to assess its performance. What happens, though, if we attempt to do so at an early stage of its life? It is here that we meet the J-curve phenomenon.

I hope that if you have understood what I have been saying about the nature of private equity returns then this part will now seem very obvious. Briefly, the J-curve is produced by looking at the cumulative return of a fund to each year of its life. In other words, the first entry will represent the IRR of the fund for the first year of its life. The second entry will represent the IRR of the fund for the first two years of its life, the third the IRR for the first three years, and so on.

Any private equity fund will exhibit strongly negative returns in the early years as money is drawn down, if only through the effect of management fees. However, as distributions start to flow back to the investor then the downward march of the IRR will be reversed and there will come a day when the amount of inflows precisely matches the amount of outflows, thus creating a cumulative IRR of zero. This is the point where the J-curve crosses back over the horizontal axis and subsequent IRRs start to become positive (see Figure 2.1).

A particular problem which arises with this diagram is that people are so used to looking at annual returns that, try as they will, they find it very difficult to grasp what the chart is depicting. It is *not* saying that the fund returned minus 25% in year 3. It *is* saying that if you map all the cashflows from the beginning of the fund to the end of year 3 you may calculate an IRR of minus 25%. Similarly, if you look at year 6 it is *not* saying that the fund's performance for that year was flat. It *is* saying that from the beginning of the fund to the end of year 6 the positive cashflows exactly match the negative cashflows, so that the IRR of the first 6 years is zero.

It is this difficulty in being able to abandon the blinkers of annual returns and view the world afresh from the perspective of compound returns that gets in the way of people understanding private equity returns. Once this has been grasped, then everything else falls very easily into place. Private equity returns are calculated and stated not as the annual returns of any particular year, but as compound returns *from* a certain year (the year of formation of the fund) *to* a specified year. When looking at benchmark figures for the industry as a whole, or indeed any part of it, then all the funds which form part of the sample that were formed in the same year are grouped together and their returns become the vintage year return.

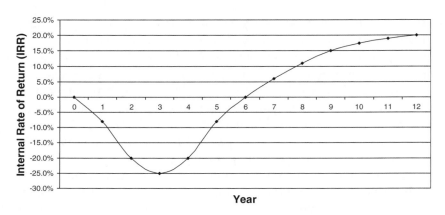

Figure 2.1   J-curve illustration

Again, this concept seems to cause even intelligent, well-educated people a lot of problems, so let me expand on it a little to make quite sure that the concept is fully understood. This is important since from now on we will be making frequent references to vintage year returns.

Take the following example, which shows a simple sequence of returns. I have chosen a few years of upper quartile European buyout returns and presented them as a table (Table 2.1). The 1996 figure shows not the annual return for all constituent funds during 1996, but the compound return (the IRR) for all constituent funds which were formed during 1996, from 1996 to the end of 2005. Similarly, the 1997 figure shows not the annual return for all constituent funds during 1997, but the compound return for all constituent funds formed during 1997, from 1997 to date.

Rule: the vintage year return will always show (in respect of any one vintage year) the compound return of all constituent funds formed during the vintage year, from the vintage year to the date specified.

(In practice, because of the way in which the figures are compiled and released, the specified date will usually be the end of the last complete year for which the figures are available, with the switch typically taking place in about May of each year.) For those who are familiar with such terms, it may help to think of them as "from inception" returns.

Now if you look at the J-curve you will realise something else. At any one time, the vintage year returns for the last few years (i.e., most recent) should be very low – even negative. That is because they represent the equivalent of the first few years of the J-curve, a time when even the best private equity fund in the world will show negative returns. Sadly, I cannot demonstrate this to you with actual figures at this time because the last year and a half has been a bumper exit market and clearly some funds have had an opportunity to "turn" some investments very quickly, thus resulting in some very high IRRs which have

Table 2.1 Upper quartile European buyout; vintage year returns to December 2005, cumulative IRR to date (%)

1996	1997	1998	1999	2000	2001	2002	2003
26.5	25.1	11.4	10.6	10.5	19.7	4.3	48.8*

Source: Thomson Financial.
*See text.

badly skewed the figures. There is one 2003 vintage European buyout firm, for example, which as at December 2005 boasted an IRR of over 1200%! This is clearly both unrealistic and unsustainable.

This does however illustrate another important principle when it comes to looking at vintage year returns, namely that figures which are very "young" are inherently unreliable. Indeed, in normal circumstances as a guideline to what the final performance of the fund is likely to be, they are all but meaningless. You can be certain only of one thing: they will most certainly not be the same as the final result. The effect of the time value of money, however, means that the more years a rolling compound return gets under its belt, the closer it will be to the final result. By the end of a fund's life it becomes increasingly difficult to influence the outcome of the final figure – if a fund has achieved 15% IRR for the first 11 years of its life then even a 50% 1-year return in year 12 will only lift it to about 16.6% overall. It is for this reason that I have in the past discussed weighting vintage year returns in order to recognise that a young return gained over just a couple of years is largely meaningless, while an old return gained over 10 or more years is very robust; but this idea has yet to gain the acceptance of the industry benchmark providers.[1]

Rule: the greater the number of years over which a vintage year compound return is calculated, the more robust it becomes, i.e., the less deviation there is likely to be between it and the final fund return.

Given the current anomalies in the figures, I must stress that the J-curve here does not represent the J-curve of any particular fund in real life, but it is a broad generalisation of what you can expect to find in every case. The only difference will be the shape of the curve; a buyout fund, for example, will tend to pay back its capital more quickly than a venture fund. Yet even this generalisation is enough to show us that it is meaningless to look at the performance of a private equity fund in its early years. Opinion may vary as to what that period might be (and it will certainly be longer in the case of a venture fund than in the case of a buyout fund), but there is no dispute that it exists. I tend typically to ignore the last 5 years' or so vintage year returns when looking at industry figures and I would urge you to do the same.

Having now explained how private equity returns are measured and presented, we are able to understand a basic set of vintage year return

---

[1] For some worked examples, see my earlier book *Multi Asset Class Investment Strategy*, already referenced.

figures and also how the J-curve operates. We now need to look at the basics of how these figures are "sliced and diced", and the first concept we need to grasp is that of the upper quartile.

UPPER QUARTILE FIGURES

The upper quartile is that data point in a sample population that stands exactly one quarter down from the top in order of ranking. This may seem a rather simplistic point, but I make no apology for it, since it is widely and surprisingly misunderstood when it comes to private equity. There are two aspects in particular which I wish to stress because they seem to cause the most confusion.

The first is that the upper quartile is one quarter below the top in terms of rankings, not amount. Let us take a random list of values:

31	
26	
19	
18	Upper quartile
17	
13	
12	
12	Median*
11	Median*
10	
9	
5	
3	Lower quartile
2	
0	
−3	

*Strictly speaking, the median is the middle observation and is found by the formula $\frac{1}{2}(n + 1)$ where n is the number of observations in the sample populations. However, as a matter of practice, where a sample contains an equal number of observations then the two middle observations are added and divided by two (in other words averaged). Thus in this case the median would be calculated as 11.5.

In the above list of values, 18 will be the upper quartile, since it is the fourth of the observations by ranking. It has no reference at all to the values of the other observations save in this sense. I am labouring this point because there are those who seem to believe that it is a number which lies halfway between the average (about 11.56) and the value of the top observation (31), i.e., 19.44. This is not the case.

Neither is it the return of all the funds within the upper quartile grouped together. It is quite simply the return of the individual fund which sits at the bottom of the upper quartile, i.e., one quarter of the way down the ranked list of observations.

This leads us on to the second important point. The upper quartile can be a very useful statistical device but, as all statisticians know but many investors overlook, it takes no account of the spread of the observations. In particular, it takes no account of the spread of the individual values within the upper quartile. It marks the bottom of the upper quartile, but gives no clue as to where the top might lie. Perhaps surprisingly, since the "upper quartile" figures are bandied around so readily, the return of the top fund in any vintage year is not.

The significance of this will be apparent from Table 2.2, which sets out the upper quartile and top fund vintage year performance for US venture funds from 1991 to 2000. While the years are chosen more or less at random, the picture they paint is roughly typical of all vintage years. I hope it will be obvious that this is a point of crucial importance and is, sadly, yet another example of people looking at private equity returns without really understanding what they are looking at, or at least being willing to engage their brain and think about what lies behind them. We will see later that this is a particular problem with European venture returns.

Table 2.2   US venture fund cumulative IRRs (%), vintage years 1991 to 2000

	1991	1992	1993	1994	1995	1996	1997	1998	1999	2000
U/Q	25.7	38.1	39.5	41.5	65.1	114.5	61.2	11.8	−1.5	−1.7
Top	61.4	102.3	116.4	112.9	247.8	415.9	296.0	721.0	140.6	48.1

Source: Thomson Financial.
Figures prepared to 31.3.2006.

MEDIAN RETURNS

You will see from the random list of values above that the median is simply the halfway point, equivalent to the upper quartile. It is that individual fund which sits at the halfway point of the sample population. Again, this is an important point since many confuse it with the average (or mean, as it is properly called). There are those who suggest that the median is a good expression of private equity returns to adopt on the basis that if one is choosing from a set number of funds each year (the sample population) then the median represents what one is most likely to end up with. Personally, I do not agree with this proposition.

Firstly, it assumes that we will be making just one selection, whereas in reality one would be making several. We will be discussing later just how many funds one needs for a properly balanced portfolio, but it is certainly more than one (even from each category) in any one vintage year.

Secondly, just as the upper quartile measure ignores the spread within the upper quartile itself, so the median will underplay the effect of any particularly low (but also, and more to the point, high) values. As we will see later, particularly with regard to venture funds, it is these few very high values that we are seeking to capture and the median simply does not reflect this.

Thirdly, any good professional fund investor will be looking to invest consistently from amongst the upper quartile. Of course this cannot be guaranteed, but with experience comes judgement and a high quality Fund of Funds, for example, would be looking to have at least two-thirds of its fund picks end up in the upper quartile (I used to be a partner in a firm which had approximately a 70% success record over a 20-year period). Taking the median as any sort of guideline in these circumstances is plainly misleading.

Finally, there are some sample populations, European venture being the most obvious example, which contain a lot of very small funds, so small in fact that they simply would not be considered for investment purposes by any institution. The median will take all of these very small funds into account and treat them in exactly the same way as a large, institutional grade fund, which is again clearly misleading.

AVERAGE RETURNS

I am a firm believer in taking upper quartile returns as the appropriate measure because I believe they most closely approximate to what an individual investor may expect in practice provided that a reasonable degree of professional skill is exercised. The two main reasons for this are:

1. That a competent investor will be able to select pretty consistently a good two-thirds of its funds from within the potential upper quartile.

2. That since the upper quartile measure marks only the bottom of the upper quartile but gives no indication of the top (which may be five, or even ten times higher) then it is likely to be a conservative estimate of what may be achieved.

However, there are unfortunately many in the investment world who view private equity as an asset class with grave suspicion, and point to any attempt to use upper quartile returns as some sort of marketing confidence trick. This is not entirely their fault in that if they have been brought up on a diet of quoted investments then this would of course seem correct. It is, however, their fault in that they should be willing to dive into the private equity performance figures in detail and get a grip of what lies behind them rather than turning automatically to the median or average figures.

It is therefore a matter of necessity also to look at the figures on an average performance basis, if only to have the answers to these sorts of objections readily to hand. However, one encounters an immediate statistical problem here which I hope will be obvious in the light of what we have already been discussing. An average, or mean, is calculated by adding up the individual returns and then dividing them by the number of individual observations (i.e., the total number of funds in the sample), thus:

$$\mu = \frac{\Sigma r}{n}$$

where μ (the Greek letter mu) is the arithmetic mean (the average), r is the return of any individual fund, and n is the number of funds within the sample population. For those who may not have met it before, Σ (the Greek letter sigma) simply means "the sum of"; in other words, it denotes adding up all the individual returns.

Can you see the potential problem here? Where our sample includes a large number of very small funds, we are giving them the same weighting that we would accord to a very large one, regardless of the fact that they would not be deemed to be of institutional investment grade, and that they will generally (the very small ones anyway) create very low returns.[2] The very large funds, conversely, are likely to have

---

[2] Such a discussion lies beyond the scope of this book, or at least of this chapter, but many such funds are government inspired/related (either at national or local level) or attached to universities or research institutes. In all such cases, "investment" in companies is likely to take place on a basis that is not strictly commercial, i.e., perhaps with the objective of supporting a particular line of research, or promoting new companies in a particular area rather than with a view purely to investment gain.

attracted money entirely from institutional investors, and may in many cases have been the only funds within the sample that such institutions were prepared even to consider.

Clearly, then, we are faced with the need to create a measure that satisfies the "average fetish" but still gives the best realistic guide to returns that we can manage. This is done by calculating a capital weighted average:

$$\text{CWA} = \frac{\Sigma rc}{\Sigma c}$$

where CWA is the capital weighted average, and c is the capital raised by each individual fund.

This may seem complicated, but in fact it is not. All the formula is telling you to do is first to multiply the return of each fund by its committed capital, then add all these values up, and then divide the resulting total by the total amount of committed capital.

Given the availability of the necessary figures then this can easily be done for any sector within private equity, indeed some of the industry data providers actually calculate it for you. There is one surprising omission, however. Believe it or not, there is no CWA available for private equity as a whole, i.e., the whole asset class on a global basis. When I was preparing my last book[3] I got around this by calculating it for myself based on the published fundraising figures by vintage year, and I will be performing that same exercise again in this book when talking about private equity returns generally.

The disadvantage of such a method is the converse of its attraction. If you are looking at private equity as a whole, where the size of small but successful venture funds may be swamped by large but relatively unsuccessful buyout funds, then is this really a valid way of looking at things? Similarly, does it really matter to an LP if she is invested in one fund of $5 billion and one fund of $50 million, provided that the size of her commitment to each is $10 M? Surely as far as she is concerned they will each make an equal contribution to her overall return?

I think these questions suggest their own answers. If you are looking at the performance of the industry as a whole, or of individual sectors within it, then a Capital Weighted Average can be a sensible way of doing this, provided you bear in mind how it has been calculated and

---

[3] *Multi Asset Class Investment Strategy*, already referenced.

thus what it is telling you. However, I think I have already made it clear that I would personally always prefer the upper quartile as a performance indicator. If, on the other hand, you need specific information for specific purposes then you have to be intelligent about what figures you prepare, and where possible these should match the individual requirements of a particular investor. In the above situation, for example, you might choose to create an average of the funds in which you have actually invested weighted by the relative sizes of your commitment to each.

POOLED RETURNS

Pooled returns attempt to address the same issues as Capital Weighted Average returns, but in a different way. Here, all the funds are combined and treated as if they were one giant fund, and the IRR of the pooled cashflows is calculated. Obviously large cashflows, whether positive or negative, will have a disproportionate effect, just as the returns of a large fund will have a disproportionate effect within a Capital Weighted Average. The advantage of a pooled return is that it probably most closely approximates to how an individual investor will measure the performance of her private equity fund programme.

Pooled returns are open to exactly the same objections as Capital Weighted Average returns, as to which please see above.

MULTIPLES

While compound returns have been universally accepted (at least within the industry itself) as the appropriate measure of performance, there is, however, a totally different way of looking at private equity returns which is rapidly gaining ground. As we have seen, private equity funds may be thought of as a series of individual cashflows, and IRRs are of course usually the best way of measuring these. But IRRs have one practical drawback. They measure the return which is earned on money while it is invested in a project (in this case an investee company), but they take no account of the length of time for which it remains invested. Why is this relevant?

The difficulty of maintaining an IRR increases dramatically with each passing year. Remember that an IRR is a measure of compound return, which means that the return must at least compound itself with each passing year in order to stay the same. By way of illustration, let

Table 2.3 IRR table

Effect of 25% compounding on $100

After *n* years	1	2	3	4	5
Amount	125	156	195	244	305

us look at the rate of change of $100 compounding at 25% a year (Table 2.3). Note that an investment only has to double over 3 years to produce a 25% IRR, but must treble over 5 years to achieve the same result. Incidentally, I have chosen these figures deliberately since 25% is usually the minimum target transaction IRR to which any private equity manager would admit, and 3 years and 5 years may be thought of as the typical holding periods for buyout and venture funds, respectively. In other words, the target money multiple for a buyout firm could be thought of as 2×, while for a venture firm it would need to be 3× to produce the same IRR.

There is thus an implicit trade-off between the three-way relationship of holding period, IRR and multiple which needs to be understood by any investor entering the private equity arena. A venture fund will keep your money for longer, but will need to deliver a higher money multiple than a buyout fund, which may give you each of your drawdowns[4] back in roughly 3 years on average. Right at the end of scale will be secondary funds, which we will be considering in detail later, but suffice it to say that they tend to return money in the shortest time of all, and thus may be expected to produce a reasonable IRR but a relatively low multiple. The sophisticated investor will understand these differences, and use them to their advantage in planning and managing their private equity fund portfolio.

Mention of investors brings us rather neatly to the other point about the trade-off between IRR and money multiple. As we shall be discussing in more detail later, it is very difficult indeed to get money to work quickly in a private equity fund programme, both because funds draw down their money over several years and also because you can only commit a small part of your allocated capital every year if you want to achieve proper diversification by time. Given the way in which private equity funds operate, it is also difficult to keep your money at work; as

---

[4] Not strictly true, of course, since I am not taking any account here of drawdowns for fees.

we have just seen, a buyout firm may actually be using each tranche of capital drawn down for 3 years or less.

Since it is difficult for an LP both to put capital to work in the first place and also to keep it at work, it is strongly arguable that a money multiple is a much more meaningful measure than an IRR. Certainly it is more desirable as a target. Consider for a moment the position of an LP who has an allocated capital of $500 M but currently only has about $75 M actually invested (far from impossible in the early years of a programme). If that LP is offered a choice between earning 35% on some capital for 3 years or 25% for 5 years, which do you think they should take? The answer is 25% for 5 years, since you have to consider what the alternative use of those funds might be. Sadly, most LPs do not have any proper arrangements in place for dealing with uninvested private equity allocations, and even if they did they would hardly be of help in the situation I have just outlined.

The truth is that most investors will only be able to earn either a bond or money market return on such money. Therefore, the rational investor would accept any rate of return that is higher than that. That is the reductio ad absurdam, of course. I am not suggesting that in practice an LP should be satisfied with a private equity return of, say, 9%. If that is all that is on offer then changes within the GP base are clearly indicated. However, this does make a very important point, namely that you cannot and should not consider the returns of any asset class in a vacuum, but only in the context of the total circumstances of the individual investor in question.

This raises another interesting point, to which we will return. Private equity is unlike any other asset class, and one of the distinctions is the big difference that will usually exist between allocated capital and invested capital. The only other asset class that has this to any real extent is property, and there one has a myriad of indirect vehicles and derivative products to consider for interim investment purposes. Thus it could be argued that all private equity returns are in a sense artificial, since they are calculated on invested capital rather than on the totality of the private equity allocation. Of course, once one has a mature programme this argument loses much of its force, but even then there will always be a difference between the two.

The issue, though, is not that the stated returns are artificial, but simply that one needs to understand the distinction and take it into account in one's planning. If you believe that you can make an allocation to private equity one day and instantly start earning a private equity return on your entire allocation, then you are bound to be sorely disappointed. If, on the other hand, you accept that the private equity return is a target towards which to work, and make plans as to how to deploy the uninvested capital to advantage in the interim, then you will within a reasonable time be getting close to your goal. Private equity is a long-term asset class, and is suitable only for long-term investors. This point was widely ignored by new investors who came into the asset class during the bubble period, and then found it easier to blame the asset class for their poor performance rather than their own mistakes.

Enough theorising, however. Let us examine which multiples we can use for practical purposes in analysing private equity returns. I am here going to restrict the discussion to analysing private equity fund returns. We will be looking in detail later at how we can analyse the performance of individual buyout transactions and use this to build a model of an entire fund. I mention this at this stage only because we shall be meeting some other types of multiples there, and I do not wish this to confuse matters. So, to be clear, the following multiples apply to funds, not individual company investments.

Distributed over Paid In (DPI)

This does exactly what it says. It compares the total amount of money paid out (distributed) by a fund to its LPs to date against the total amount of money paid into the fund by LPs. This is the best possible multiple to use for measuring the performance of a fund once it is at the end of its life, since it shows the performance relative to *all* money paid in, i.e., money that has been used to pay fees as well as money that has been invested in companies. All too frequently, GPs try to fob investors off by showing them the multiple to *invested* capital, which is not the same thing at all. Recognising this, most American GPs will attempt to recycle some of their early realisations rather than distributing them to LPs, thus creating a higher multiple, but European GPs have been slow to catch on.

However, DPI is not a good measure in two situations. First: where the fund is not yet either at the end of its life, or so close to the end and so nearly fully paid out that it makes little difference. Second: where a fund has failed to invest all its capital. Here there will have been an excessive draining of fees, and the LP, having allocated the money to this fund, will have been unable to use it within another fund of the same vintage year. For this reason, I would personally favour a multiple of Distributed over Committed Capital. This is commonly abbreviated as DCC.

Paid In to Committed Capital (PICC)

This multiple is of little value in assessing returns. It simply shows how much money has been drawn down, and thus how much remains to be drawn down in the future. This multiple is of most use in the secondary market, which we will be considering later.

Residual Value to Paid In (RVPI)

This is really the other side to the realisation ratio. It shows the current value of all remaining investments (companies) within the fund expressed as a ratio to the total amount paid in to date. This is obviously most useful as a measure early on in the life of a fund before there have been many distributions, in which case it will largely reflect to what extent portfolio companies may have been revalued. It is also one of the measures that will be used when looking at an LP interest in a fund on the secondary market.

The disadvantage of residual value as a measure is that it may give a misleadingly low return expectation, particularly early on in the life of a fund, because companies are typically sold for more than their current valuation, especially in the case of buyout funds.

Total Value to Paid In (TVPI)

This is one of the most useful ratios, and indeed one of the most useful measures of all for evaluating private equity fund returns. Total value adds together both the residual value and the distributions to date. It is obviously subject to the same possible drawbacks as RVPI early in the life of a fund, but if you are going to use a ratio based on paid in capital, then for my money this is the one to use. For those who believe that multiples give a better idea of fund returns than IRR, then the TVPI will be watched very carefully as the fund nears the end of its life, and compared with the same ratio for other funds of the same vintage year.

Incidentally, this is also a very good measure for looking at the different return expectations (and indeed requirements) of venture funds as against buyouts. Remember that we discussed the trade-off between

Table 2.4   Upper quartile buyout and venture returns; IRR/multiple trade-off

Fund type	IRR	TVPI
Early stage venture	16.7%	2.29
Mega buyout	15.8%	1.52

Source: Thomson Financial (VentureXpert).
Note: Figures are for all relevant US funds within the VentureXpert database from inception to the first quarter of 2006.

IRR and multiple? Well, if we look at all the US funds in the Venture-Xpert database, we find the results in Table 2.4. Not quite a perfect illustration of the principle, but good enough, I think. Because venture funds have longer holding periods, then they have to generate higher multiples to earn roughly the same IRR.

VALUATION

The valuation of a private equity fund is as much an art as a science, and if one thinks about what it represents (the net present value of a stream of future cashflows which are uncertain both as to timing and amount) it is difficult to see how it could be otherwise. Notwithstanding these difficulties, however, it is an exercise which players in the second-ary market have to undertake on a daily basis, and we will be looking later at how they go about this.

From an accounting point of view, and also for the purposes of industry benchmarks, the value of a fund is usually taken as being the combined current values of the fund's remaining investments. While this is a convenient procedure, it should be recognised that, like many accounting measures, reality has been sacrificed on the altar of con-sistency. It seems ironic that in many countries accountants force pension funds to discount future liabilities to arrive at an artificial present value which goes up and down wildly with prevailing interest rates, and yet are not prepared to go through the same exercise for the future assets (cashflows) of private equity funds.

Therefore the stated accounting value of a fund will never actually represent its true value, as any attempt by an LP to sell an interest in a fund will quickly show. It may be too low or too high, but it will never be the real value.

Things are less certain in the USA than they are in Europe. This is because there is one area of private equity in which Europe leads the way, namely valuation guidelines; indeed, the earlier form of the EVCA guidelines (which are broadly the same as the BVCA guidelines) had been in place for many years until they were changed recently. All European funds now adhere to these, and many European LPs, through the medium of the LPA or a side letter, make it a legal prerequisite that they should do so.

The original European guidelines were clear and capable of very precise im-plementation. With regard to write downs, for example, a GP was left with little discretion. If a company significantly failed to achieve a budget target then it *had* to be written down by 25%, and each time that a further budget is missed then a further 25% write down was made. The NVCA guidelines in the USA are much woollier; it says instead merely that a valuation "should be reduced if a company's performance and potential have significantly deteriorated". There is ample scope here for any GP who does not want to reduce a valuation; "should" is not the same thing as "must", and how "significant" does "significant" have to be? There again, who is to say that a company's potential has diminished just because its current performance has?

To make matters worse, many American GPs do not even officially adhere to the NVCA guidelines, and when you add this into the existing mix of creative non-compliance great inconsistencies can occur. I remember that towards the end of the bubble period a firm in which I was a partner had invested in three venture funds all of whom had participated in the same round of financing in the same company. At year end, one of them valued the company at $960 M, one of them valued it at $480 M and the third one had written it off to zero. More worrying still was the fact that two of these funds had the same audit firm.

Whatever the case, official valuation figures will tend usually to understate the true value of a private equity fund, particularly in the middle period of its existence when it is largely fully invested, since it is harder to write companies up than to write them down (some European buyout funds traditionally simply keep all their companies at cost unless something goes wrong with them, in which case they write them down according to the EVCA guidelines). In other words, the valuations of the underlying companies themselves are likely to be under-stated.

Note: we will be examining the new EVCA guidelines in more detail later.

FEES

I hope it will be obvious from what I have been saying about private equity returns being calculated as the IRR on cashflows that they will always be stated net of fees, expenses and carried interest. This is because the IRR is calculated on money going into the fund (which will include money drawn down for payment of fees and expenses) and money distributed out of the fund (from which carry will already have been deducted where appropriate). Thus private equity benchmark returns will always be net of all fees and other management remuneration.

This is a very important point since the returns of many other asset classes (in particular quoted equities) are frequently quoted before fees, e.g., calculated on the increase in value of the relevant index or portfolio. Therefore, whenever you see private equity returns being quoted against other asset classes, not only should you question whether they are vintage year returns being compared with vintage year returns, but also whether the figures for the other asset class are stated before or after fees.

TIME-WEIGHTED RETURNS

Before we close this chapter, I must say something on the subject of time-weighted returns because these are sometimes quoted as a performance measurement and there is considerable (and understandable) confusion as to what they represent. In particular, it is not well understood how these differ from IRRs.

A time-weighted return is calculated by taking the returns of different periods and calculating their geometric mean. The geometric mean sounds complicated but really isn't. It is generally recognised as the best way of calculating an average of percentage rates in different periods. It is simply the nth root of the product of all the values, where n is the number of values. In other words, the geometric mean of a series of 26 valuations would be found by multiplying them all together and then finding the 26th root. In formulaic terms, it would be:

$$\sqrt[26]{(v_1 v_2 v_3 \cdots v_{26})}$$

Let us forget the formula and the maths, however, and concentrate on what is actually being calculated in practice. Effectively what we are doing is finding the average of the returns in each year of a fund's life, and it is this that in my view renders time-weighted returns completely inappropriate as a measure of private equity fund performance, since they completely ignore the time value of money. For a time-weighted return, it is irrelevant whether a return of, say, 85% is made in year 1 of a fund's life or in year 10, which is of course ridiculous. Private equity is a cashflow business. Private equity funds represent nothing except a stream of cashflows and the time value of money is paramount. The only proper measure of a stream of cashflows is an IRR.

So, how did time-weighted returns come to be used at all? Well, for those who are old enough to remember a time before computer spreadsheets, calculating IRRs could be a laborious process, and in the days before electronic calculators could be more laborious still, requiring the use of slide rules or logarithms and repeated "trial and error" attempts. A time-weighted return was much easier to calculate since all you had to do was look at one page of your list of tables (the roots).

The other reason was that they were already in use in the quoted markets. Here there is at least some sense to them, since money can be moved in and out of the control of managers, or in and out of different stocks, at any time by investors and thus an average return is quite acceptable. If timing is out of the manager's control then there is no point in calculating a compound return over time. The real pity is that these came to be called "time"-weighted returns in the first place, since "time" is the one thing to which they specifically do not apply. For this reason, artificial though it seems (logically it would seem to be the other way around!) IRRs have come to be called "dollar-weighted" returns in private equity circles.

Time-weighted returns are a perfect example of how many intelligent and well-educated people are capable of completely failing to understand how private equity returns operate. Hopefully they are now of largely historic interest, but they continue to be quoted among the various industry benchmarks and it is important that you should understand what they represent since it is all too easy for the unwary to confuse them with IRRs. Understand them, yes by all means. Use them? No. Not ever. Not under any circumstances.

SUMMARY

- Private equity returns are measured on a compound, not an annual basis. It is essential to remember this when comparing them with the returns of other asset classes.
- The returns of any private equity fund will be negative in its early years as money is paid into (drawn down by) the fund before any

money is paid back (distributed) by the fund as investments are realised. In due course, there will be a moment when the value of inflows exactly matches the value of outflows, at which point the IRR of the fund to date will be zero. This effect is known as the J-curve.

- Returns are measured on a vintage year basis, i.e., from the year in which the fund was formed to a specified date.
- The best measure of vintage year returns is the upper quartile. However, scepticism and suspicion from outside the industry frequently force the adoption of other measures. If so, it is most important that the measure adopted is a Capital Weighted Average, rather than an average or median return.
- The upper quartile figure states the performance of the individual fund at the bottom of the upper quartile, not the pooled performance of all funds within the upper quartile. It gives no indication of the range of returns contained within the upper quartile, which can be huge.
- Multiples can also be a valuable measure of private equity fund returns. Most useful is Total Value to Paid In (TVPI) which measures both the distributions received to date and the residual value of the remaining investments. However, this figure is only really meaningful towards the end of a fund's life. There is a direct trade-off between IRR and multiple, with a longer holding period (such as one typically encounters with a venture fund) needing to result in a higher investment multiple in order to generate the same IRR.
- Valuation guidelines differ between the USA and Europe. The European ones are more certain in their drafting, and more rigidly applied. However, in general, all private equity funds will in normal market conditions tend to under-state the true value on exit of their current investments.
- Time-weighted returns are misleadingly so-called since in fact they do not take timing into account at all. For this reason, they are largely meaningless and should be avoided. Because of this anomalous terminology, IRRs are often referred to as "dollar-weighted" returns within the private equity industry in order to distinguish them from "time-weighted" returns. Time-weighted returns are calculated as the geometric mean of all the funds' annual percentage returns.

3
Buyout

I will be dealing separately with the issue of valuation, how buyouts work, how and why buyout returns are generated, how these may be measured and analysed, and how we might go about modelling buyout activity. However, before discussing the "how" and the "why", we must turn our attention to the "what". What is buyout? What is a buyout firm? Can anyone do it? If not, what are the barriers to entry into the buyout industry?

As we saw earlier, while it is very difficult to arrive at a definition of buyout that will cover every transaction we are likely to see, it is possible to advance various general characteristics even though in many cases we will also have to acknowledge some specific exceptions. However, before we turn to those aspects which tend to distinguish buyout from other fields of private equity activity, I think it would be useful to set out the different types of buyout transactions that can occur.

TYPES OF BUYOUT TRANSACTIONS

MBO

The classic buyout has always been an MBO or management buyout. In its purest form, this involves the executive team who are managing a particular business activity buying it out from the parent company. This was the bedrock of buyout activity in the UK, for example, in the early to mid-1990s, with the management team typically appointing one of the accountancy firms to act for them, drawing up a business plan and pitching the deal to selected buyout firms. The management team would be required to put their own money into the deal, usually having to borrow in order to do so, but they were rewarded with "sweet equity" issued at preferential rates and ratcheted to pre-agreed performance targets.

While still common, this pure form of MBO has become less prevalent, since the increase in fund sizes and thus target transactions sizes has made it increasingly difficult to find businesses which are not either (1) too small or (2) have already been bought out. I do not wish to labour this point, or to suggest in any way that we have seen the last of the old-style MBO (not least because what is or is not a "mid-market" fund is constantly being redefined), but inevitably with the rise of the mega-deal then many transactions which would previously have been classified as MBO would probably now more properly be described as "LBOs" or "take privates" (see below).

MBI

The Management Buy-In evolved from the MBO. It is similar in just about every way apart from the nature of the team or, viewed another way, apart from the way in which the deal initially comes together.

The key difference is that instead of the management team of a business getting together to buy it, a team is put together to buy another company operating in the same sector. This may be because they have tried to buy their own business and been rebuffed by the parent company, or because they wanted to buy it but it was sold to a trade buyer instead.

Pure MBIs are rare, and there was much hearsay evidence back in the 1990s that they tended to perform less well than MBOs. Most buyout firms maintain a small team of industry-specific executives who work with them in much the same way as an entrepreneur in residence operates inside a venture firm, helping with due diligence and deal sourcing but with the clear expectation of leading the management team if a transaction comes to fruition in their own sector. However, strictly speaking these deals tend usually to fall into the BIMBO category.

BIMBO

As the acronym suggests, these deals are a combination of an MBO and an MBI, where outside executives are grafted on to the existing executive team in order to facilitate a buyout. In truth, many buyout transactions probably fall into this category if one applies the definition strictly. This could range from taking on a finance director for a small buyout to supplement the existing financial controller, through the return of a recently departed CEO to a team to whom he is well known, to the effective acquisition by a senior industry figure of a business along with its management team.

LBO

There is a great deal of overlap in these buyout definitions and in truth most practitioners probably never stop to think about where their current deal falls in the spectrum, and probably wouldn't care anyway. For the writer, though, it is important to try to analyse the sector as fully as possible and if this occasionally causes the reader some confusion then I can only apologise.

LBO stands for Leveraged Buyout and in a sense all buyouts are LBOs since "leverage" is simply the American word for "gearing", and all true buyouts will involve the use of some acquisition debt. In the past, this was more an issue than it is today, since there were in most jurisdictions restrictions on the "giving of financial assistance", i.e., the use of the target company's own assets to secure acquisition debt. However, legal reform and the growth of more sophisticated cash flow financing have made these issues largely redundant.

Today an LBO has two main connotations which help to distinguish it from other buyout types, but I stress that these are both imprecise and subjective. The first is that it suggests a buyout which has not been initiated by a management team, either external or internal. Typically today buyout deals will be initiated by the seller appointing an investment bank to prepare a company for sale, and buyout firms entering the fray alongside industrial purchasers. The second is that it suggests a transaction where the target company is large enough (or may well be a group of companies) that no single business activity is involved, but rather a range of them. In these circumstances, it may be convenient to think of an LBO as being equivalent to an industrial acquisition, but with the acquirer just happening to be a buyout firm (or, more frequently these days, a consortium of buyout firms).

Take Private

Again, there is obviously potential for overlap here, but a take private is, as the name suggests, a buyout of a public company removing its listing in the process (or very shortly afterwards once various formalities have been complied with) in order to transform it into a private company. As we will examine later, there is considerable scepticism in some quarters as to whether such deals can produce the sort of returns to which investors have become accustomed in the past, but this is a development which has really been forced upon the buyout sector by the inexorable rise in fund sizes, and thus in target transaction size.

Various arguments are advanced in favour of such transactions. There may well be situations, for example, where very aggressive restructuring is required and it is felt that this might only be effectively accomplished out of the glare of publicity and away from the rigid reporting regime to which public companies are subject.

Roll-up

This used to be much more popular than it is today, largely I suspect because much larger fund sizes make it a less viable proposition. Basically one targets an industry which is highly fragmented, buys lots of small operators and puts them together. The attraction of such an approach is that not only is it possible to increase profits exponentially by better marketing and management and economies of scale, but the resulting larger entity will merit a higher earnings multiple, thus resulting in an upward valuation curve rather than a straight line.

OTHER "BUYOUT" ACTIVITY

I am placing development capital deals in a separate category because if one strictly applies the various characteristics to which we have already alluded in outline, they are clearly not buyout transactions at all. The key feature of a development capital deal is that voting control will not pass to the buyout firm, although some measure of negative control can be granted by reserving the right to veto certain decisions, e.g., relating to capital expenditure, dividends and executive remuneration.

The lack of a majority shareholding also has profound implications for the financial structure of the deal since it will usually not be possible to use an acquisition vehicle/target company model where the accounts can be consolidated and the interest on acquisition debt can be set off at the holding company level. Thus it is frequently not possible to use any debt finance at all.

The development capital deal has largely fallen from favour in the Anglo-Saxon environment (although there are some notable exceptions – firms such as Summit Partners have successfully practised development capital transactions in the USA for many years). Ironically it is in continental European countries, where more primitive commercial legal systems have traditionally made difficult the sort of disguised control provisions which development capital requires, that the model has proved most resilient. In France, for example, it was until quite recently not possible to issue different classes of shares, or to obtain specific performance of a share option agreement, yet it is probably still the case today that many more development capital transactions take place in France every year than true buyouts.

The theoretical drawbacks of development capital are fairly obvious. In practice, the most serious have been the diminution in returns caused by the lack of the debt layer, and the difficulty in forcing an exit against the historic owner of the business who is most reluctant to put his baby up for adoption.

In truth, the continued strength in development activity in continental Europe probably has more to do with cultural than practical concerns. In most continental countries, particularly France and Germany, control investing is viewed with grave suspicion, as is the use of acquisition debt. Since these are the two main components of buyouts it is perhaps understandable that hardly a month goes by without buyout firms (particularly those which are viewed as British or, worse still, American) being lambasted by left-wing politicians as "vultures" or "locusts".

Before leaving development capital it is worth noting a further branching of terminology. These deals are usually categorised by the firms which pursue them as either "money in" on "money out", which will I think be fairly self-explanatory. A "money in" deal is where the private equity firm buys new shares to inject money into the business, thus helping it to grow, usually in certain specific and pre-agreed ways. For this reason such deals are sometimes referred to as "expansion capital". A "money out" deal is where the owner sells some of his (because it is almost always a man) existing shares to raise money for himself. In truth, most deals have an element of both because few firms are willing to countenance a deal which is wholly "money out".

There is yet a further type of transaction with which a buyout firm might get involved, and although I hesitate to discuss it here since it has featured to date more in late stage venture funds than in buyout funds, here is probably as good a place as any since, like development capital, it too defies precise classification. It is a category of deals that have come to be known as PIPE (Private Investment in Public Equity) and occurs when a particular investment instrument is created within a public company that may offer a private equity-type return. Typically, while the company's equity is quoted the instrument itself is not. In some circumstances (though there are significant potential regulatory problems here, particularly in Europe) it may be a prelude to a take private. There have been relatively few such deals to date, but with more and more money coming into the industry it is possible that there may be more in future.

ESTABLISHED BUSINESSES

In contrast to venture, which deals with small companies at an early stage of their life cycle, sometimes even total start-ups, buyout practitioners are concerned with established companies which are usually in either the late growth or mature stage of their relevant product life cycle. There are sound business reasons for this. As we will see shortly, buyout transactions usually incorporate financial structuring that requires cashflow to service debt. Companies which are at an earlier stage of the life cycle are typically cash-hungry, requiring to grow quickly so as not to lose ground on the competition. They may also exhibit what would to a buyout firm be unacceptable levels of market risk, or even product risk, thus raising the possibility that the firm may actually fail.

Growth companies are attractive because they offer the opportunity for increased earnings which are one of the three main drivers of buyout returns. However the choice of the right place on the growth curve, neither too late to lose out on the potential for increased earnings, nor too early to generate sufficient free cashflow, is an extremely delicate one, and an area where experience may confer a considerable competitive advantage. As for the risk of outright failure, this is one which no buyout firm can afford to contemplate. As we will see when we come to consider the buyout fund model and the nature of buyout returns, there is little room in a buyout portfolio for companies which fail to return their invested capital. Thus it is likely, indeed even desirable, that they should err on the side of caution and this is an area where the new entrant may well hit problems, either through inexperience, or through pressure to invest at a time of deal flow paucity.

Mature companies are attractive because they will have become "cash cows", throwing off cash from well-established business activities which have lost the capacity for rapid growth. In a strategic corporate portfolio as envisaged by the classic Boston Consulting Group matrix, these will support the cashflow requirements of the "stars", which need to grow at least as quickly as the competition just to stand still in relative terms. In a buyout portfolio, these companies' cashflow can be channelled into servicing debt and even paying off loan principal. This means both that relatively high levels of gearing can be used initially, and that the company can be recapitalised periodically while it remains within the portfolio, using new debt to replace equity being returned to the fund.

These "recaps" are a significant contributor to buyout returns, but their prevalence and importance has not always been properly recognised outside the industry. For example, they have become hugely controversial in the world of PFI and public/private partnership financing, where they have been attacked by left wing politicians. This points to a fundamental difference of outlook amongst the participants. The politicians focus on the public project being financed, whereas the private sector finance providers are naturally looking for a private equity type return, and recaps often offer the quickest way home to this particular goal. Because recaps allow capital to be returned to investors early, i.e., before any formal exit has been achieved in respect of the underlying company itself, they can have a substantial impact on the compound rate of return used to measure private equity performance, since this focuses on the time value of money and here cashflows are being dragged to an earlier point on the timeline.

There has from time to time been talk of buyout firms moving to an earlier stage of company development for their investment focus. Such talk was prevalent at the time of the technology bubble, with some buyout firms looking at pre-IPO funding rounds for venture companies, and some even looking at a number of internet start-ups, frequently at the urging of their LPs. Fortunately, however, the vast majority of the buyout sector held their discipline and the amount of money actually invested in such deals was small. In retrospect it may seem strange that such a discussion should ever have taken place at all. The skills of buyout and venture managers are demonstrably different, and aimed efficiently at the types of companies in which they respectively invest. To attempt to cross between the two seems to make little sense, yet so strong was the pull of the new and the feeding frenzy which overtook investors everywhere that there was a serious danger that many buyout firms could have been pulled totally off course, and it is to the great credit of the sector that these siren calls were largely resisted.

In the context of the day-to-day terminological confusion between venture and buyout it is this concentration on established businesses rather than on nurturing new and young ones that is the most commonly misunderstood. I hope that for anyone who has read this chapter, the reference to buyout firms coming together to mount a multi-billion dollar bid for an international industrial conglomerate, or public utility as "venture capitalists" will in future be seen as the basic factual error which it is.

Incidentally, the inexorable growth in average size of buyout funds has led to questions of just how many established businesses will remain as fresh pickings for buyout firms. This is actually a more valid concern in the USA than it is in Europe. In Europe, industrial consolidation and rationalisation is generally at an earlier, or at least less-developed stage than it is across the Atlantic. Almost whatever business sector one examines (telecommunications, banking, etc.) will show many more individual operators in an economy of roughly equal size. Historically this has been partly due to political reasons, every country, or sometimes even region, wanting its own airline, bank, brewery, etc. However, the buyout firms would argue that even in the USA the problem is less pronounced than might be thought. The growth in buyout fund size effectively drives a self-perpetuating cycle in which more capital becomes available for investment, allowing larger and larger deals to be attempted. We have probably now reached a stage where no company in the world is too large to be safe from the attentions of the buyout industry, and this obviously in turn raises interesting questions as to the interaction of private equity with quoted markets in years to come.

DEBT

It is the use of debt finance that most obviously distinguishes buyouts from other private equity transactions such as venture and development capital. However, for the sake of completeness, I should point out that (1) venture companies can be partly financed by trade credit (e.g., from suppliers of equipment) which from a strictly accounting point of view would be classified as "debt", and that the very late stages of venture financings can include convertible instruments that may be structured as loan notes and (2) that although it is difficult to inject acquisition debt into development capital deal structures it is not impossible (though usually inefficient from a tax point of view).

For the purposes of this book I am attempting to provide a simple model for explanatory purposes wherever possible but let us be clear from the outset that buyout transactions are structurally very complex indeed, frequently with many different layers of debt, and that no two are the same. Indeed, it is in such structuring that a lot of key buyout skills lie, and in the ability to obtain advantageous terms from banks through a course of dealings over the years that we find a key barrier to entry for new buyout firms, or at least a source of competitive advantage to the established players.

We will be examining in a different chapter exactly how buyouts work, and can be modelled, but let us simply note at this stage that there are three main types of debt with which we need to be concerned.

First, and this is often overlooked, there is the exiting debt that will already be present within a business for working capital purposes. Because the target company is usually going to be viewed on a consolidated basis with the acquisition vehicle (often referred to as "Newco"), banks will take into account the totality of all debt that is to be present once the deal is completed. Thus a company which already has high levels of operating debt will be less attractive as a buyout target, whereas one which has low levels of debt, and possibly even a cash pile, will be highly attractive.

Buyout firms will usually seek to reduce the level of operating debt within a business once they have acquired it. Since operating debt finances the working capital cycle then this may logically be reduced in any one of three ways: lower stock levels, fewer debtor days (i.e., the number of days taken on average for debtors to pay their invoices) or more creditor days (the opposite). Lower operating debt requirement will mean that the bank may be persuaded to issue more acquisition debt in its place, thus enabling some equity to be released back to the buyout fund as part of a recapitalisation.

The second type of debt is straight acquisition debt, which is often referred to as "senior" debt because it will take priority in repayment and on any liquidation of the company to other types of debt in the buyout structure. This will usually have some measure of security, though typically these days this will normally take the form of a floating charge over the company's assets in general rather than a fixed charge over specific assets (since these will frequently be sold off and leased back where necessary to free up cash). There will also be covenants in the loan agreement which will strictly control what the company can do with its cash, though some of these can be to the benefit of both parties; a cash sweep would be a good example.

The third type of debt is variously referred to as "convertible" or "mezzanine", though a caveat should be entered at this stage in that in America "mezzanine" can also refer to pre-IPO funding of venture companies. In its buyout sense, "mezzanine" simply means the layer of debt which sits below senior debt and, in contrast, is usually both convertible and unsecured. The derivation of the term is clear: it is a financing layer which sits between the two floors of the structuring house – debt and equity. Indeed, it shares the characteristics of both.

Mezzanine financing has developed into a specialist area of its own, with dedicated funds being raised to operate in the space, and with senior debt providers being increasingly interested in providing the mezzanine element of a deal as well. Sometimes one bank or, in the case of a very large deal, a consortium of banks will combine to underwrite the whole financial requirement and will then seek to sell down parts of it, like a bookie laying off his bets, either horizontally (i.e., asking someone else to provide the whole of a particular layer of mezzanine) or vertically in "strips".

EARNINGS

We will be looking at earnings in detail when we come to see how buyout transactions are put together, and valuations arrived at. Suffice it to say at this stage that the presence of earnings within a company will usually point to any private equity transaction in respect of that company being a buyout or a development capital deal. However, as so often in private equity there are a couple of exceptions which should be noted.

Some late stage venture companies may have earnings. This is actually not a real exception at all but rather the result of people having traditionally spoken of "earnings" when what is really important is cashflow. Venture companies may have earnings but will almost certainly still have negative cashflow because they need to plough all their earnings and more back into the business in order to fund rapid growth. Buyout companies require cashflow to service debt and while it is often conveniently assumed that for an established business earnings (at least at the operating level) may be a good proxy for cashflow, this is not always the case.

It is also necessary to consider the case of turnaround situations, which I hesitated to describe as a different category of transaction in their own right since they are frequently executed by buyout firms and viewed in much the same way as their other transactions.[1] However, as we will see when we look at valuation and modelling, they can pose significant problems and are generally undertaken only with extreme caution, and even then only when significant sector expertise is available.

SIZE

Here there is much that is controversial and much that is self-evident. Self-evident is that the average size of buyout funds has risen steadily on both sides of the Atlantic. Since there are only two ways in which this extra capital can be deployed (either doing more deals within a fund or doing bigger deals within a fund), and since the time and resources required to execute a large deal are in many cases similar to those required to execute a small one, then unsurprisingly the average size of buyout transactions has also risen quite explosively.

We shall be looking in detail at the whole issue of fund size when we discuss how to analyse a buyout firm but we should note here that the rapid and explosive rise in buyout fund size has changed dramatically the sorts of deals which get done. We will see in a later chapter how European buyout returns were at their best in the early to mid-1990s. This was a time when fund sizes were fairly small and firms were for the most part looking to pick off individual subsidiaries of public companies or, better still, medium-sized owner-managed companies. This market was characterised by various factors.

Firms were able to seek out deals proactively, and to agree exclusivity with a vendor once the target had been identified. This was particularly prevalent at the time in countries such as Germany[2] and Sweden, and it is no accident that it is in these countries that firms such as Doughty Hanson, IndustriKapital and Nordic Capital made their early stellar returns. Today this is no longer the case, with any deal of any size being put through a controlled auction process.

Target companies frequently had low levels of gearing, particularly owner-managed companies, which could be very debt-averse. This

---

[1] As with just about everything one can say about private equity, I do not pretend this to be universally true. There are some firms who specialise in turnaround situations and do nothing else. However, they are generally few in number and small in fund size, and in the interests of space if nothing else, I have decided not to consider them separately.

[2] There was at the time no phrase in the German language for "shareholder value".

facilitated the use of quite aggressive acquisition debt programmes. To be fair, this was also a time of imagination and innovation within the buyout community; it was in the mid-1990s, for example, that we saw the first European buyout ever to be financed by a US bond issue (Doughty Hanson was the firm in question). Today this is hardly ever the case; indeed, operational gearing is sometimes kept at a high level deliberately simply to deter any acquisitive thoughts by third parties.

These companies frequently also had a layer of management effectively missing since in the case of an owner-managed company he was accustomed to performing most of these functions himself and, in the case of a subsidiary, they were usually performed at the holding company level. Thus one might find a financial controller where a finance director was required, and so on. By replacing this missing layer the skill-base of the business could often be dramatically increased, thus facilitating both revenue and earnings growth. In addition, working capital practices had normally not been the most stringent, and extra cashflow could be squeezed out to service and retire debt.

What I have just described was a legendary golden age of European buyout activity, a happy hunting time when great returns could be made; funds frequently returned well over three times their capital to investors. These conditions no longer apply, and buyout firms have had to hone their skills to squeeze out value in other ways.

There are those who claim that in large part this transition has been forced upon the industry by the rise in fund sizes, which in turn make it unrealistic to pursue smaller companies (Bridgepoint, who execute a large number of transactions within a fund, are a notable exception, but most buyout firms have been driven to doing roughly the same number of deals as before, but of a correspondingly greater size). However, many firms have been loath to admit this openly and thus we have the rather silly spectacle of some billion dollar funds claiming that they are "mid-market". Of course, it is entirely possible that the definition of what is or is not "mid-market" may have changed significantly, but it is difficult to believe that if the mid-market could be efficiently served by a fund of no more than about $250 M a few years ago then it can equally well be served by a fund at least four times that size today. Given the effect of gearing, one might be talking about a difference in enterprise value of the target companies between about $25 M and anything up to about $200 M.

It may be convenient to adopt the classification used by Venture-Xpert, since we shall be using their figures to look at the performance of buyout funds later. They currently class anything over $500 M as "large" and anything over $1 billion as "mega". With due respect, I cannot help feeling that these definitions have been overtaken by events, but I will happily adopt them as a matter of convenience. They would classify $250 M to $500 M as "medium", and anything less than $250 M as "small". My own view of the mid-market would, as I point out above, probably only extend about halfway into their "medium" classification, but I do not think that we will do any undue violence to the concept by accepting a $500 M fund size as its upper limit.

The search for the mid-market in private equity today, in the USA as well as in Europe, is beginning to resemble the quest for the holy grail; everybody wants it, but many are beginning to wonder whether it actually exists. A common pattern is to see a first time fund raise a relatively modest amount and then, driven by the LP feeding frenzy created by mid-market fever, raise some multiple of that 2 or 3 years later. Thus the ultimate irony is that many LPs will not invest (because many have blanket bans against first time funds) when the firm is genuinely able to pursue mid-market opportunities, but will invest when it is no longer able to do so (and, perversely, that very inability is created by LP behaviour).

A cynic might say that the buyout industry today is like a clothes shop which only stocks one size – large. However, buyout supporters would say that the ability of buyout activity to include even the world's largest companies has forced them to become more competitive and to give more regard to shareholder value. This is undoubtedly true, and there is now talk of "jug" (juggernaut) funds of perhaps $100 billion, from whose reach no company in the world would be immune. My own view is that the industry has become something of a victim of its own success, though most European investors have been very slow to realise this. In 1998, for example, over 50% of the money raised by funds managed in the UK was contributed by American investors, and nearly 75% by foreign investors in total.[3]

Be that as it may, we are clearly caught up in an upward spiral of fund sizes. For example, let us look at two typical buyout firms, one from each side of the Atlantic: Permira and Blackstone (see Table 3.1).

We see from these figures that the fund size of each firm has increased by a factor of about 15 in the period in question, but that European fund

---

[3] Report on Investment Activity, British Venture Capital Association, 2000.

Table 3.1   Buyout fund size in the USA and Europe

Fund	Permira ($M)	Blackstone ($M)
I	1 000 (1997)	810 (1987)
II	3 850 (2000)	1 300 (1993)
III	6 400 (2003)	4 000 (1997)
IV	14 000* (2006)	6 500 (2002)
V		15 000* (2006)

* Target.
Note: Calculated at $1 = €0.78.

size has grown much more quickly as Permira raised their first fund only in 1997 (when they spun out of Schroders) while Blackstone raised theirs as long ago as 1987. Consequently, Permira's fund size has grown 15 times in less than 10 years and over only four fund cycles. This is a particularly good example to take since Schroders (as they then were) and Apax used to be seen as very high quality players in certain specialist sectors within the mid-market,[4] but both now have been driven to large deals by the increase in their fund sizes.

A recent article[5] confirmed what one had already suspected: by mid-2006, private equity firms accounted for more than 15% of M&A activity worldwide. Nor will things stop there. We have already mentioned the possibility of "jug" funds which may grow as big as $100 billion, and this raises important issues for investment generally which lie beyond the scope of this book. What happens when a significant portion of the world's quoted equity has been taken private by private equity firms? Just how much money can the buyout industry absorb before cost-adjusted returns regress too closely to quoted indices? What happens if a whole generation of senior buyout managers, made wealthy by large management fees, retire more or less together leaving a large amount of capital in less experienced hands? Yes, these questions are alarmist, but they are currently being asked and it would be wrong of me not to record the fact.

CONTROL

As we have seen already, control is the one element which really does distinguish buyouts from other forms of private equity activity. Indeed,

---

[4] Apax also used to do true venture deals within the same fund as its buyouts.
[5] *The Times*, 4 July 2006.

in certain quarters the phrase "control investing" is virtually synony-mous with "buyout". Control will almost always take the form of having a majority of the issued shares in the company. However, it is possible to have a minority holding yet have a majority of the votes, either because certain shares have weighted voting rights or because other shareholders are contractually bound to vote with the buyout firm in respect of at least part of their shares. This varies from country to country, though. In some countries there can be legal difficulties about enforcing these sorts of agreements and one can also encounter an unwillingness on the part of the buyout firm to be seen to be throwing their weight around.

We have also referred already to negative control. This is where a right of veto is reserved over certain decisions, typically executive sal-aries, share dividends, capital expenditure, borrowing, and changes in business activity. At one time these too could be difficult to enforce since in many cases they rest on the legal device of a different class of shares and not all countries allowed the creation of these. Now, though, these problems have largely disappeared. In the days when the classic MBO was the norm, the question of negative control was key, and a delicate balance had to be struck between allowing the management team the freedom to run the business and protecting the interests of the equity investor (the buyout fund), particularly if things did not run to plan. The right to dismiss some or all of the executives was obviously the classic sticking point in these negotiations, and was frequently resolved by the adoption of pre-agreed performance milestones, usually in the form of management budgets and earnings projections.

While the advantage of being able to control the day-to-day opera-tions and key staffing of the target may seem obvious, the real benefit of having control is the ability to exit the investment exactly when, and how, one wishes. Since this may be less obvious, it may perhaps be helpful to set the historical perspective which one used to find particu-larly in continental Europe. Here, where non-control investing used to be much more prevalent than control investing, the former holding company or owner-manager of the firm would frequently remain as a significant, sometimes even a majority shareholder. While day-to-day disagreements could hopefully be resolved under the negative control procedures, the real fun would begin when the end of the private equity investor's target holding period (usually 3 years) approached.

At this point, the owner-manager would be faced with the prospect of having to sell his remaining shares and finally retire. Often, this would be something which he had been unwillingly deferring for some time, and perhaps he would have been persuaded into the private equity deal in the first place only by the lure of generating some free capital. For a holding company, they might have been prepared to bring a junior partner into the business, but the prospect of the company now being bought by someone who might introduce restructuring and redundancies in a town where they still saw themselves as the moral guardians of local interests might look a very different kettle of fish. If the prospective purchase was foreign or, even worse, American, then the problem was compounded many times over.

While there were exit provisions in the original contract, private equity firms would be loath to enforce these as they wanted to be seen as a friendly partner with whom to do business in that country by other prospective sellers, and in any event there were usually no legal precedents available to give guidance as to exactly to what extent a local court might be prepared to grant enforcement of these novel provisions in favour of a foreign "vulture capitalist". One could thus be treated to the spectacle of private equity firm and fellow shareholders dancing an increasingly distracted minuet around each other to the rival themes of exit, delay and possible compromise.

It is difficult to over-emphasise how important an issue this was for the private equity industry, at least in Europe. I once headed in a team which was attempting to create an operational risk model for assessing buyout and development capital transactions and factors such as the lack of control were key. A transaction which was (1) a minority deal, (2) in a continental European country and (3) purchased from an owner-manager who remained involved with the business could expect to score very highly (i.e., badly) compared with, say, a classic MBO in the UK where the buyout firm controlled over 90% of the shares.

Other aspects could be difficult without overall control, too. Owner-managers, for example, are usually debt-averse and so their businesses are frequently cashflow-inefficient from a strict financial theory viewpoint. They will also often have irrational attachments to certain business activities or product lines which may prevent these from being eliminated or rationalised when logic would otherwise demand this. Above all, they will often resist the introduction of high quality senior management, especially a CEO to take over the day-to-day running of the business.

Happily, time has moved on and there is today general recognition that the interests of all parties must be adequately protected, and that control investing can and should be the norm. However, history is cyclical and I now see exactly the same sorts of issues which plagued continental Europe in the past rearing their heads anew in developing private equity areas such as Asia and Latin America. For those in such places who are willing to listen, the European experience has some valuable lessons.

BARRIERS TO ENTRY

As the buyout market has matured and developed, the question of barriers to entry has become a frequent topic of discussion. There is general acceptance that as it has matured, the market has become more "perfect" in financial theory terms. There is much less scope for exclusive, proactively sourced deals (indeed, virtually none at the top end of the market). Pricing and valuation data is much more widely available. Most vendors are now much more sophisticated when it comes to dealing with private equity purchasers than they were 10 or 15 years ago. Both Europe and North America are now covered and served by a very competitive and efficient investment banking sector.

This is not all bad news for the private equity industry. The other side of the coin is that private equity buyers are now widely accepted as an established part of the landscape and indeed at least two or three of them are routinely included in the list of potential purchasers to whom every "book" is sent. In most countries, any perceived stigma which may once have attached to selling a business to a private equity firm has now largely dissipated. Indeed, some governments have willingly embraced private equity consortia as a means to privatise certain utilities (the Italian government being one obvious example).

So what does all this mean for new entrants to the market? For, defying strict business school theory about the undesirability of entering a mature market, that is exactly what teams regularly attempt to do. In many cases, of course, these will not be first time funds strictly so-called since they may represent a breakaway from one or more established firms.

I think the answer to this question depends upon exactly what the new entrant is seeking to achieve and, in particular, on what part of the market they are seeking to address. I have alluded already to the vanishing mid-market and I think this point is particularly relevant here.

As the larger firms get even larger and move to target bigger and bigger deals, they leave something of a vacuum behind them. The classic private equity fund economic model (certainly the theoretical ideal) is for the GPs to be motivated by carry, with the management fee simply covering their operating overheads. In very simplified terms, this is an essential element of what you will often hear referred to as "alignment of interests" in the GP/LP relationship. However, it would be idle to suggest that this has represented even an approximation of the real situation in the buyout arena (venture is a different matter) for some years. In practice, firms are driven by the lure of larger pro rata management fees to raise larger and larger funds and this in turn necessitates them moving to target larger and larger deals in order to deploy the extra capital. Yes, LPs will to some extent be able to reduce the percentage fee rates on larger funds, but such is the bargaining power of the best buyout firms (because of the weight of the capital trying to crowd into each new fund) that usually at the end of the day they manage to achieve a significant fee increase overall.

There are some honourable exceptions here. Some firms offset fees and incidental income which they may receive from portfolio companies, and/or bear the cost of aborted transactions in such a way that the net fee impact on LPs can be significantly reduced. However, it is undeniable that there are many buyout professionals on both sides of the Atlantic who have become very wealthy on management fee profits, and while they are to be congratulated as successful businessmen, this is a long way from what the ideal private equity fund model envisages.

This rather lengthy digression has been embarked upon simply to explain the dynamic which pulls buyout firms inexorably towards larger fund and deal sizes. I know of one European buyout fund whose fund size increased by a factor of 25 in just two fund cycles. Therefore if one was sitting down as a strategy consultant logically to plan how a new private equity firm might best enter the market, a mid-market focus would seem to present the most attractive option.

This does occasionally happen and despite the fact that a mid-market focus normally requires a highly localised geographical approach (usually single country within Europe) these offerings are rightly regarded as highly attractive in principle, though one always has to balance the "first time fund" factor against the attractiveness of the market niche. Indeed, many investors have a blanket ban on first time funds and while they would argue that this is a sensible precaution to minimise risk, my personal feeling is that a blanket ban goes too far and prevents investors from being able to take advantage of the occasional "nugget" that survives rigorous due diligence.

So for a mid-market firm the main barrier to entry is the first time fund factor. At the time of writing (Summer 2006) the mid-market is understandably viewed as a "hot" sector, the only argument being over exactly how to define it. If a team can overcome the "first time fund" issues then they have a very good chance of attracting funding. Once having done so, they are likely to find rich pickings, since the bulk of the buyout capital available will be targeted at much larger companies than they are seeking. This is probably a classic example of a more extreme version of the 80/20 rule (we will encounter something similar in venture in a different context): probably about 95% of available buyout capital in Europe and North America combined is targeted at no more than 5% of total companies by number.

For a team attempting to enter the large buyout sector (and at the risk of putting my head on the chopping block I would certainly categorise any fund size of at least $1 billion as "large", and possibly less depending on the geographic focus[6]), the issues are very different.

We have already touched on the issue of dealflow. These days almost all deals will go through the investment banking network and the vendor will normally stipulate that no more than three or four potential purchasers of each type, including private equity houses, should be included. Thus, the ability to feature on the investment bank's "hit list" is key and will be largely determined by a track record of past transactions. Any new entrant is thus likely to be in danger of hanging around the edges of the feeding tray, either trying to persuade an established player to adopt them as a consortium partner, or being left the crumbs which everyone else has rejected.

An element of these relationships which is often overlooked is that it is these same investment banks who will be pitching for the job of arranging exits for the buyout firms from their companies, either by way of sale or (more usually, since often the buyout firms will frequently handle their own sales) IPO (flotation). One would not wish to suggest that there would ever be any overt connection between the two, but human nature being what it is then an existing and/or potential relationship with a buyout firm for IPO work is likely to weight heavily with an investment bank when selecting a list of addressees for their next book.

---

[6] As always with private equity there are exceptions. A firm such as Bridgepoint raises a large fund but undertakes a large number of transactions, and is therefore probably still mid-market despite its fund size, but this is very much the exception rather than the rule.

Similar issues will apply to the question of debt. Contrary to popular opinion, there is only so much acquisition debt available in the buyout market, and banks will be constantly adjusting their position as the year progresses by syndicating with other banks to make sure they will be able to meet their commitments should more deals than anticipated actually complete. Thus, not only are they unlikely to be eager to finance a new buyout firm where they may be in competition with an established one (since they will judge the established one to be the more likely to emerge as the eventual winner) but this may well be reflected in the terms and gearing offered. Since these are key factors in the relative performance of buyout transactions then banking relationships in general are likely to prove a difficult obstacle to overcome.

There is too the question of raising capital in the first place. I do not wish to suggest that this is an insuperable obstacle, since new players do in fact successfully enter the buyout arena almost yearly. However, it must be the case that if an investor who has a finite amount of money to commit is considering the rival attractions of an established player and a new entrant then they are likely to favour the established player, particularly if they have an existing arrangement with them. In fact, the situation is likely to be even more depressing for the new entrant since the investor may already be faced with a difficult choice between two firms, both of whom they like, but both of whom they cannot accommodate within their cashflow constraints.

SUMMARY

- It used to be possible to classify most buyouts neatly into categories such as MBO, MBI, etc. but today the situation is more complex, perhaps because the average buyout is much larger than used to be the case.
- A buyout transaction will always involve an established, profitable business though the latter condition may obviously not apply in the case of a turnaround transaction in respect of a troubled company.
- A buyout will invariably involve the use of debt. Indeed, today's financial engineering solutions for buyouts will often involve various different layers of debt, ranging from straight senior debt secured on assets of the company to pure cashflow lending with equity kickers (mezzanine).

- Buyout properly so-called will always be control investing. Development capital may be distinguished from buyout on this ground and also because it may be much more difficult, for legal and accounting reasons, to introduce significant acquisition debt.
- Cashflow is key to buyout transactions, since success depends on the ability to service debt, and as much debt as possible.
- Recapitalisations (recaps) offer an alternative to an exit where the exit window may be temporarily closed or where cashflow levels may have exceeded expectations. Recaps can have a huge effect on buyout returns, a fact which is not widely appreciated.
- The VentureXpert definition of a mid-market fund ($250 M to $500 M) may happily be adopted, since this will make it much easier to work with the available figures, though my own estimation would be a little lower. Even adopting this definition, genuine mid-market funds are becoming rare compared with 10 years ago, particularly in Europe.
- The main sector-specific barrier to entry for a new buyout firm is to break into the dealflow channel, much of which is now largely controlled by a relatively small number of investment banks. This is true even moving down the size scale, though it becomes a less serious problem as the number of intermediaries handling smaller deals becomes larger.

4

How to Analyse Buyouts

My aim in this chapter is to explain how buyouts actually work. Not so much how they are put together – we have already covered that in Chapter 3 – but what drives their returns and how people actually make money out of them. Once we understand this, we will be in a position to move on to discussing how to analyse a buyout fund. In that last sentence you will already have absorbed one key point, probably without realising it. All private equity fund analysis should be "bottom up"; in other words, it is only by analysing the individual transactions which comprise it (and knowing how to) that one is able to analyse the fund itself.

Of course, the manager of the fund will have carried out its own financial analysis of the deal before entering into it and it can be very instructive to ask to see this if one is in the process of actually performing due diligence on the private equity firm concerned. The analysis will model the price to be paid for the company, taking into account how this is to be financed, the length of the period for which it will be held, the exit price and the repayment of restructuring of any financing in the interim. This will produce a modelled transaction IRR. This can be instructive both in terms of what target IRR the firm is willing to accept (are they aiming too low?, are they just desperate to put money to work?, are non-commercial considerations at work?, etc.) but also in terms of how realistic you feel their various assumptions are (are they assuming an increase in multiple?, what level of gearing are they prepared to accept?, what debt finance terms are they expecting?, etc.). These are just a few of the many small pieces of the jigsaw which build up to give you a picture of a buyout firm.

By the way, the paragraph above is deliberately and necessarily simplistic. In practice there will be much more to the modelling process than this. A wide range of possible scenarios will be considered and a range of possible outcomes produced. For example, relatively small changes in the financial engineering of the deal can have a large impact on the final result. However, a detailed study of this would require a book all to itself, and would go well beyond the scope of the present publication. The purpose of this book is to explain the basic principles of buyout analysis. The good news is that once armed with a thorough understanding of these, there is no limit to the sophistication of the model you choose to build.

It will hopefully come as something of a relief, therefore, to hear that there are really only three main drivers of buyout returns: earnings, multiple and leverage. Actually there is of course a fourth (time) but as we will be dealing in compound returns this will automatically form part of our calculations. It needs to be borne strictly in mind, however. The time value of money is an enemy as well as a friend. It is the mouse in the larder of your portfolio, nibbling away at the cheese of your returns. The longer you are forced to hold a company for the same multiple, the lower your IRR will be. The sooner you can exit it, the higher your IRR will be.

EARNINGS

Again I must begin with a short terminological detour. The word "earnings" is used in many senses. While it is generally synonymous with "profits", I have actually heard it applied to turnover (American: revenues), particularly with regard to venture companies. So let us be clear from the start; we are talking about earnings in the sense of profits: the turnover of a business less its costs of doing business. Even here, however, there is considerable confusion, since there are various different types of "earnings".

The way in which the word "earnings" on its own is usually used in financial circles is in the sense of that profit which is available for distribution to shareholders, i.e., after deduction not just of the operating costs of the business but also after taking into account tax, interest and depreciation. This is often referred to as "net profits", "the bottom line", "profits attributable to shareholders" (UK) or "earnings available to common shareholders" (USA).

Note however that even this measure can be misleading, since it can be heavily influenced by one-off items that are nothing to do with profits generated by the company's ordinary course of business, such as a notional gain on the sale of an asset in excess of its artificially depreciated accounting value. Notwithstanding, this is the figure usually used to calculate earnings per share and thus the PE ratio (the price of a share over its earnings per share, or the value of a company over its earnings).

There are problems in any event with using this number for buyout analysis purposes. The financial engineering which goes into a buyout will almost certainly dramatically alter the overall debt structure, and thus the level of interest payments. So far as possible, the buyout firm will want to ensure that all available earnings are used to service acquisition debt, so as to keep the amount of equity finance required to an absolute minimum. Thus, is it really meaningful to be looking at earnings after interest? Similarly, because loan interest payments will normally be tax deductible, the buyout structure will normally also dramatically reduce the amount of tax payable. Thus, is it meaningful either to look at earnings after tax?

Also, as we have seen, earnings take into account things such as depreciation and will usually not therefore be the same as cashflow. Because of the need to service debt, it is actually the level of cashflow with which a buyout firm will be most concerned, and if earnings are not a good approximation, then their value for analysis purposes is highly questionable.

In the light of all these drawbacks you may be wondering why we are concerning ourselves with earnings at all. Alas, private equity, like politics, is the art of the possible and there are frequently trade-offs to be made between what is sub-optimal yet possible and what is optimal but not possible. Briefly, there are generally speaking no publicly available and universally consistent or comparable measures of earnings save those which we have already discussed. Thus one of the very few ways in which we can look at the price paid or realised for a buyout company as against the valuation of a comparable quoted company is by means of a PE ratio. As a matter of practice, therefore, it is very difficult to build any such functionality into a buyout model unless we have resort to it.

Which PE ratio should we apply? If the transaction is a "take private" then of course we have an obvious answer: the PE ratio of the company itself in the period leading up to the transaction taking place. Yet even here there can be problems, especially if the deal has elements of a turnaround about it, in which case the last available profits may be historically low. Similarly, as we have already discussed, the figures could be influenced by non-cashflow items (such as depreciation) or even non-business earnings items, such as profits made on the sale of assets, or the proceeds of a law suit.

Where no such continuity between quoted and private company status is present, we are forced to take either the multiple of a comparable quoted company or that of the sector within which the buyout company would reside were it itself quoted. The former is open to charges of subjectivity and inconsistency, which can be particularly grave if there is a large range of multiples within the sector, or if there is no directly comparable quoted company of a similar size or scope as that of the buyout company. Bear in mind, too, that PE ratios can be influenced by things as diverse as the perceived quality of the management team, its level of gearing, its degree of exposure to overseas earnings, or its attractiveness as a bid target.

Sector multiples appear to make more sense. At least here there is the advantage of consistency, and variation within the sector is smoothed out to a certain extent. Here the two main potential drawbacks are either where the buyout company is for some reason much more attractive than the quoted sector (perhaps because it is enjoying higher growth than otherwise comparable public companies), or where there is confusion or ambiguity about which sector a company might fit into. For example, suppose a company is using proprietary computer technology to make available film previews via the internet and cable. Is it media, IT or telecoms? In many cases there is no clear answer and it is left to the individual company itself to suggest its own classification (in which case they will obviously choose that with the highest sector PE ratio!).

So, as with so many aspects of private equity, by all means take full advantage of all the available data, but be aware of what lies behind it and of what allowances have to be made for it being possibly unreliable or even occasionally misleading. If it's any consolation, when a PE ratio works for analysis purposes then it can work very well. If a buyout fund were to take private a public company at a 35% premium to its PE ratio, and there was no obvious indication that the company was artificially lowly rated, then this would clearly raise some very obvious issues as to valuation.

EBIT

An EBIT ratio would appear to be a better bet. EBIT stands for Earnings Before Interest and Tax, and thus would seem to address some of the above issues. Certainly buyout firms are understandably suspicious of PE ratios being used for analysis purposes by investors, and have a stated preference for the EBIT ratio. The two problems with this have already been touched upon.

First, it still does not take account of things like depreciation, which can be significant if a company has recently spent heavily on new equipment. Second, the EBIT figure is not usually readily publicly available (though it can be calculated from a company's accounts) and is thus difficult from the point of view of plugging a number directly into a computer model.

In the past, I have sought to address this issue by assuming that EBIT will be a pre-stated percentage of earnings, and thus if one has one figure one can calculate the other. This is far from ideal, but is probably an acceptable compromise. At least it delivers consistency of treatment across the whole database population. Also, if a buyout firm knows that you are going to calculate a possibly erroneous EBIT figure anyway, then it is remarkable how keen they can become actually to provide you with the correct figure!

A word of warning, though, for those who choose to try this approach. Please bear in mind that levels of tax and interest differ with location and currency, as do those of capital allowances, so you cannot just take a particular figure and apply it universally, even within the same region. There may, for example, be a significant difference between Germany and the UK.

EBITDA

Earnings Before Interest, Tax, Depreciation and Amortisation is claimed to be a pure cashflow measure since it excludes non-cashflow items such as depreciation, etc. In other words, it eliminates the effect of both financial structuring and accounting policy and decisions. However, this is not strictly true. While EBITDA is a better indicator of likely cashflow than any of the other earnings measures we have been discussing, it does not take into account things such as required capital expenditure or working capital. Of course, a purist would say that this point is well understood and that all EBITDA is supposed to be is a "top line" entry from which to start your cashflow calculations.

EBITDA is an earnings measure that was more or less invented by the buyout industry in the late 1980s, initially in the USA and then in Europe, as they were looking for a measure that could specifically indicate the ability or otherwise of a company to service certain levels of debt. Such was its effectiveness that it began to be adopted by industrial companies, especially those that were burdened with high asset values and consequently high depreciation numbers stretching over long periods.

While this lies outside the scope of the book, you should be aware that dangers abound in trying to use EBITDA for normal company valuation purposes. Since it is a non-GAAP measure it is not governed by universal accounting conventions and companies are thus largely free to include or exclude what they like, even changing the way in which they calculate it from one period to the next.

For buyout purposes its obvious advantage is that it mirrors exactly how a buyout firm will look at a target company. As we will see later in this chapter, leverage, or debt, makes a huge difference to buyout returns and a buyout professional will be primarily concerned in their analysis with how much acquisition debt a company can support. Its disadvantage is the same as for EBIT: one cannot just pick up the FT and find a company's EBITDA figure or indeed multiple. Thus one is forced back onto the PE ratio for most basic modelling exercises, though there is nothing to stop you adopting the rough rule of thumb approach which we came across when discussing EBIT. However, please be aware that there is even more margin for error here, since EBITDA will be very significantly affected by the age and value of the company's assets.

A buyout firm will typically be happy to reveal an EBITDA multiple to its LPs, and while this is fine for analysing the deal itself, it is largely valueless unless one has some comparable EBITDA figures for similar companies. It is here that the modelling process is likely to break down (unless you are lucky enough to have access to some analysts' research on the relevant sector) and you will find yourself being forced back to the sector PE ratio as a default value.

EARNINGS GROWTH

Earnings growth is the holy grail of buyout investing; the ability to grow the profitability of an investee company is the one thing that every LP looks for when selecting a buyout fund, and it is accordingly something at which your analysis should look very carefully indeed. I think the importance of this speaks for itself. If a buyout firm can grow the earnings of a business, then they have a good chance of being able to make money on the sale of that business in any market conditions. Consequently, many buyout firms will claim to have "sector expertise", and have experienced senior industrial executives available as advisers, or even to go into companies and run them. Some, such as Apax and

Permira, go further and subdivide their firm into a number (usually about five) of sector-specific teams.

The best buyout returns are made when all four of the buyout factors: earnings, multiple, leverage and timing, all work together, but if one was forced to choose just one of these then earnings would be the one to achieve. Apart from anything else, increased earnings will often present an opportunity to recapitalise a company, as to which see below. However, there is often a trade-off here which is not fully appreciated. A buyout firm will often be at least as focused on growing the cashflow of a business ("freeing up working capital") as on earnings, and often earnings growth will come at a price; it may be necessary to buy new equipment, for example, or to grow the workforce to expand into a new area. This requires money. Specifically it requires working capital, and portfolio decisions within a buyout firm are therefore complex ones, especially as time's wingèd chariot will always be hovering overhead. Should we view this as an investment to turn quickly, in which case we forget expensive expansion which will have no effect on short-term earnings, or should we invest judiciously because we believe that we can grow the earnings significantly over a 3- to 4-year period?

In fact, the decision will often be even more complex than this, since the firm will also have to consider the shape and timing of their portfolio as a whole, the remaining capital and likely cashflows of the fund within which the company sits, and market conditions. There is, for example, little point in deciding to turn a company quickly if exit conditions are currently unfavourable. There may be the possibility of merging the company with another, or selling off individual business units. There may be monopoly (US: anti-trust) considerations to worry about. There is the situation of, and relationship with, the providers of mezzanine and senior debt, etc. I trust that even this brief survey will be enough to convince you that there is much, much more to the skill set of a buyout firm than just buying a company, loading it up with debt, and sitting back for 3 years to see what happens.

An obvious question here is "how should we treat inflation?". The answer is that it probably doesn't matter so long as you do it consistently across your model to all buyout funds. You can either ignore it completely or apply it to earnings by index linking them to something such as the RPI of the country concerned. This is of more importance when analysing historic returns, some of which were made in times of very high inflation.

MULTIPLE

We have mentioned various types of multiples already, so let us be clear what we are talking about here. We are considering earnings multiples, in other words that multiple which is applied to whatever measure of earnings we care to adopt in order to reach the price agreed to be paid for the company. At the risk of stating the obvious, the resulting valuation will always be the same. What will be different in each case will be the multiplier and the multiplicand:

$$\text{Earnings} \times \text{Earnings multiple} = \text{EBIT} \times \text{EBIT multiple}$$
$$= \text{EBITDA} \times \text{EBITDA multiple}$$

For example, if a company has been bought for \$200 M, and we know that its earnings were \$15 M and its EBIT was \$25 M, then the earnings multiple will be 13.3 and the EBIT multiple will be 8. The valuation number is fixed, the various earnings measures are given, while the other numbers (the multiples) are variable.

An obvious way in which buyout firms can make money is to sell a company at a higher multiple than that at which they bought it. This is the private equity equivalent of a free lunch. Even if you do not manage to increase the earnings of a company at all, you will still make money. There are two possible reasons for this, largely depending on whether the company was bought in an imperfect or a perfect market.

Multiple Increase in an Imperfect Market

In financial theory, a perfect market is one where all investments are equally accessible to all investors, and all investors have full and equal knowledge of all relevant information. Arguably, there is no such thing as a truly perfect market, but it is certainly the case that some markets are less perfect than others.

If a company is bought privately, i.e., otherwise than through a market on which its shares are publicly quoted, in principle this will always be a transaction on an imperfect market. It is true that this distinction is blurring, chiefly because any private transaction of any appreciable size will now be subject to some form of auction process. However, there are limits to such openness. Only a certain number of potential purchasers will be admitted into the process, which usually means that only two or three buyout firms will be included in the list of possible buyers to whom the book is sent. Another issue, less prevalent than before but still discernible, is where a potential buyer will be preferred because of nationality, or some other such quality (for example, a bank may not wish to sell a subsidiary to another bank). This used to be a particular problem in France, where most large companies were at one time para-statal and when occasionally one had to be disposed of because it could not be propped up for any longer there used to be earnest talk about "finding a French solution". This gave rise to the term "French auction", which meant an auction in which the highest bidder is not guaranteed to win and where the auction may be reopened so that the preferred bidder can be given an opportunity to match the other bidder. There were also instances where trifling technical irregularities in the bid document, or issues which had not even been raised during the offering stage, were used to disqualify particular candidates.

There are some instances where the transaction has clearly been bought in imperfect market conditions, and we will see in a later chapter how such conditions dominated buyout returns in Europe in the late 1980s and early 1990s, for example. Let us simply note for the present that any company which is bought on an exclusive basis (i.e., where the vendor agrees to deal only with one particular purchaser) will by definition be "imperfect".

In such circumstances an increase in multiple may occur simply because the company in question has been bought on a lower multiple than it should actually enjoy. This may seem unlikely to a contemporary reader, but it must be remembered that the buyout environment has changed dramatically in recent years, not least because of much higher average fund sizes. So has the deal environment in many countries. In Germany and Italy, for example, only a small number of companies were actually quoted compared with the UK, and even then these would usually contain a blocking family interest (such as still exists within BMW, for example) making the company immune to takeover, and thus meaning that it would be quoted on a lower multiple than should be the case anyway because of the absence of a bid premium.

Given that the average German vendor 15 years ago was also obsessed with secrecy, and a desire not to be seen to be making a large profit on a financial transaction,[1] then it will become more credible, I trust, that

---

[1] The German language at this time contained no word or phrase meaning "shareholder value". This absence may be instructive in understanding the attitude adopted by many German corporate groups at the time.

buyout firms could and did regularly buy companies effectively at an undervalue. In these imperfect market conditions, an increase in multiple could be achieved simply through listing the company in due course, at which time it would simply be acquiring the multiple that should probably always have been applied to it in the first place.

Market conditions were reflected in the analysis procedures of buyout firms at the time, which would always include at least one scenario in which the exit multiple would exceed the entry multiple. Significantly, multiple increase is no longer routinely assumed in buyout analysis.

The other way in which multiple increase can occur is by the business being made more attractive in some way (perhaps by selling off a mature business unit and retaining an exciting, high-growth one) or even just bigger. Large companies generally command higher multiples than smaller ones, which opens up the interesting prospect of company value being an upward curve rather than a straight line. Roll-ups are a very good example of how this may be exploited. I remember one instance in Italy during the early 1990s when a small road haulage company was bought and no less than about 18 subsequent acquisitions were bolted onto it.

Of course there comes a size beyond which multiple increase is unlikely to occur, and it is almost certainly the case that the "mega" (>$1 billion) funds have reached this point with regard to the size of company which they need to target. So, apart from rare instances where it may be possible to reposition a company into a different sector which commands a higher multiple, then this sort of increase is in future likely to be of benefit only to the mid-market.

Without wishing to muddy the waters, it may be both convenient and apposite to think of these two types of multiple increase as "beta" and "alpha" in quoted market terms.[2] The way in which a multiple goes up and down with the market is systemic, just like the sort of "beta" return which will be earned by buying the market index. The other way is something which it is open to the manager (buyout firm) to control, influence or create and thus represents an additional, non-systemic source of return. As with all investment manager selection, it is this sort of "alpha" return in which one is particularly interested.

---

[2] I am of course aware that these terms can unfortunately be used in a number of different ways. For example, Beta can be used as a measure of the volatility of any one stock against a market portfolio, and there are different connotations again when considering the analysis of investment managers. That is why I make the point as lightly as possible, but I do think it is an interesting analogy.

Multiple Increase in a Perfect Market

For our present purposes, it is generally safe to assume that any company which has been taken private has probably been bought in perfect market conditions. The same can probably be assumed for the sake of argument where a large company has been taken through an auction process. However, the possible reservations set out above must always be borne in mind.

In such conditions, there are only two ways in which a multiple increase can be achieved. Before we examine these, though, please bear in mind that any increase at all will be much less likely if a company has been taken private, since in order to buy it in the first place the buyout firm will have had to pay a premium to the quoted multiple (varying with time and market conditions, but typically anywhere between about 15% and 30%).

The first and most obvious is where there is a general increase in company valuations resulting in higher earnings multiples. In strict theory this should only happen in periods of falling interest rates (if you look at earnings multiples the other way round you can view them as a means of implicitly discounting the future value of a company; if the risk-free rate falls then so does the rate by which you should discount the company's future value, resulting in a higher present value and a higher earnings multiple), but unfortunately for financial theorists markets do not always behave so rationally. A general increase in multiples can be indicative of nothing more than a need to justify higher valuations brought about by a period of irrational exuberance (in which case it is probably a good time to be selling rather than buying).

General market change can be quite dramatic when it happens. For example, if one looks at the S&P500, its overall PE ratio was about 17 in 1968, had fallen to about 7 by 1975, and then remained fairly low before accelerating steadily throughout the 1990s to hit a peak of over 40 in 2003, but has since fallen back to less than 20 again. Thus something like a 1998 vintage year buyout fund, which would hopefully be selling high around the 2003 peak, will probably turn out to be a good performer. While a 2002 vintage year buyout fund, which would have been buying high for its first couple of years, may well turn out to be the opposite.

In passing, I should warn against reading too much into quoted multiples when it comes to the analysis of private equity returns in general. Many very clever people have tried to find trends and correlations between patterns of quoted and private equity returns and have largely failed. The reasons are partly that private equity funds invest across long periods, and therefore tend to be largely unaffected by short-term public market movements (unless they are extreme and part of a larger phenomenon, such as the collapse of the technology bubble) and partly that people's pricing expectations do not move strictly in line with current multiples, but lag them by as much as a year or two. If a vendor is told in a certain year that he can sell his business on an EBIT multiple of 12, then he is going to hold onto this expectation even if in the following year the appropriate sector EBIT multiple may have declined to 10. Thus, buyout firms are often unable to take full advantage of periods of low multiples because by the time vendors' valuation expectations have started to adjust, multiples are usually on the rise once again.

LEVERAGE

Leverage, or the use of debt to help finance an acquisition, is sometimes also called "gearing" and this is a very good way in which to think about it. If an engineer adds an additional (smaller) gear wheel to an existing one, then he knows that by so doing he is increasing the number of times the spindle attached to the smaller wheel will rotate relative to the rotations of the larger one, thus increasing the speed of the whole mechanical process involved. If a buyout professional goes in for financial engineering, this involves, in its simplest form, adding debt into the financing mix to increase the impact of the underlying equity. So it is quite apt to think of debt as an extra gear wheel, which does not affect the performance of the equity (just as the smaller gear wheel does not affect the speed of the larger, original gear wheel), but does greatly increase the impact which it is able to have on the overall return of the transaction, just as the smaller gear wheel enables the large one to have a much greater impact on the speed of the process.

The principle is simple and well known. If a business is bought for \$100 M and sold for \$150 M 3 years later, and is financed entirely with equity, then the equity return will be a money multiple of $1.5 \times (150\text{M}/100\text{M})$ and the equity IRR will be just under 15%. Replace half of the equity with debt, however, and the equity multiple becomes $3 \times (150\text{M}/50\text{M})$ while the equity IRR increases to about 44%. See how dramatic is the effect that leverage may have, and now imagine what might happen if you could replace not just half the equity with debt, but 90% of it. (Just to satisfy your curiosity, the multiple would now be 15× and the IRR would be over 145%.)

Such "thin" financing structures (i.e., having very little equity compared with the amount of debt involved) are the dream of buyout firms and I have seen many over the years, but the opportunities to employ them are becoming less, partly because most businesses today will already have quite high levels of operating debt (if only to make a takeover or buyout a less attractive prospect!) and partly because some countries are pursuing tougher and tougher "thin equity" tax rules under which it can be difficult to make loan interest fully deductible.

We have discussed senior debt and mezzanine in outline already, and I do not propose to go into this any further, since this is a book about private equity, not financial engineering. Suffice it to say that this is a very complex area, and that the financial structure of a buyout will almost always be far more complicated than the simplistic debt/equity/mezzanine breakdown that I have used for illustrative purposes. There may well be different levels of senior debt and mezzanine. There will almost always be a separate working capital facility. There may be factoring of invoices, or other trade finance such as operating leases. There may be sale and leaseback of certain assets. Certainly there will always be a separate strip of sweet equity for the management team. However, in complexity lies opportunity, and in financial engineering we find a way in which an experienced and skilful buyout team can exploit both their financial expertise and their standing with financial institutions to add significant value to a deal.

RECAPITALISATION

Recapitalisations or "recaps" are a very significant but little appreciated contributor to buyout returns. Essentially, all that happens is that where the finances of the company have improved to the extent that they have been able to pay down part of the debt, and/or will be able in the future to support a larger burden of debt, then the company is recapitalised. Some or all of the equity is released back to the buyout fund and replaced with debt. Again, the process can be much more complex than I am here describing, but what is important for the purposes of this book is that you should understand the effect which a recap has rather than exactly how one might go about it.

By releasing some or all of the equity back to investors the fund is now essentially "there for nothing". The effect is twofold. First, a positive cashflow is pulled into the reckoning early (i.e., well ahead of the exit event which would otherwise have triggered it), thus boosting the IRR. Second, the multiple which will be made on eventual exit is enhanced.

In the past, recaps were usually resorted to when the exit route was blocked, as can happen, for example, when the IPO window is closed, and/or at times of depressed public market valuations. For this reason, little understood by those outside the industry, the returns of 1997 and 1998 vintage year buyout funds will not actually be as bad as had originally been feared. Finding themselves in danger of being stuck with investments for 5 years or more, most buyout houses went in for recaps fairly heavily between about 2000 and 2003.

However, so successful has the technique proved that many buyout houses now look for recap opportunities within their portfolios as a matter of course (in London, CVC were one of the pioneers of this approach).

It is worth noting in passing that the technique has not been well received when used in public/private partnership projects such as PFI in the UK. Many left wing politicians have not yet fully accepted the idea of private financing being used in public sector situations, and there have been vocal protests at the use of what is after all a standard private equity technique when applied to things like hospitals. Full discussion of PFI-type financing lies beyond the scope of this book (although it is arguably a form of private equity), but I believe the paradox of politicians wanting to attract private equity into public projects but being unwilling to accept the sort of returns which are expected, and the techniques required to achieve them, throws into question the whole future of such funding. In the UK we have already seen the government repeatedly delay a decision on the Saint Bartholomew's Hospital ("Barts") project for no apparent reason other than backbench unrest.

It follows from all this that whatever buyout model you create must be capable of handling recaps. In other words, you cannot just assume that a buyout will be an entry transaction and then an exit transaction 3 years later. You must be able to accommodate changes in debt and equity levels, and map all cashflows involved.

TIMING

We noted at the beginning of this chapter that time was the fourth buyout driver, but one that rarely needs to be considered explicitly since it will be an automatic operator in calculating the IRRs with which we measure private equity performance. However, it is worth just running through this very quickly to be sure that the different implications of timing are properly understood.

First of course there is time in the sense of absolute time – the day, the month, the year, etc. Market conditions will vary from one year to another, both in the public markets and with respect specifically to private equity, even at the fundraising level. For example, healthcare might be popular one year and the German mid-market the next. How should one change one's behaviour to adapt to these changing conditions?

The short answer is that you shouldn't. Market timing is one technique which can be almost guaranteed not to work in private equity, and it is not difficult to understand why. If I raise a healthcare fund today I am going to be making investments for at least the next 3 years, and am likely to be selling any companies over a period starting in about 4 years' time and going out perhaps as far as 12 years into the future. How can I or anyone else possibly know what conditions are going to be like in 3 years' time, let alone 10 or 12? Market timing simply is not possible, and if you ever hear anyone at a conference saying anything such as "now is a bad time to be investing in buyout" or "we have gone overweight in telecoms because we really like the sector" then you will know that you have stumbled across someone who understands nothing about private equity.

At whatever level you are investing in private equity (company, fund or Fund of Funds) it is imperative that you put your money to work steadily year after year. We shall be looking at this in more detail in a later chapter, but there is an important lesson to be learned here. Diversification should occur naturally in any private equity investment programme (largely as a result of the number of underlying companies) but of all the different types of diversification, by far the most important is diversification by time. If you are properly diversified across vintage years then the returns of the good times will more than compensate for the occasional bad times.

If, on the other hand, you choose to "blow your wad" in less than a single year on a portfolio of almost exclusively internet-biased US venture funds, as many did in 1999/2000, then you cannot be heard to complain if things go disastrously wrong. Sadly, human nature being what it is, they do complain, and vociferously at that. It is apparently easier to blame an entire asset class for some supposedly inherent defect than to admit that you got things hopelessly wrong.

Then there is time in the sense of the life of a fund, or a fund pro-gramme. This has probably already been dealt with in the comments above about diversification by time. If you are running a buyout fund you must keep your discipline and make your investments roughly equally over a 3-year period. No matter how attractive the prospects you may see in year one, you must maintain your discipline. Then, once the investment cycle is complete, there will begin the period in which you look first to develop your companies and then to harvest them. This is an art in itself. Which companies should you select for the investment of more time and money to help them grow, and which should you look to sell quickly? Can the former maintain their IRRs over longer periods? Will the latter contribute enough to the eventual fund multiple?

So finally we have come specifically to the question of the holding period of each individual company. As we noted earlier, length of holding period is the continuum along which the IRR/multiple trade-off operates and every buyout professional will be acutely aware of it at all times. As a rough rule of thumb, a buyout fund will generally expect to hold their companies for an average of about 3 years, and a venture fund for about 5. If your analysis suggests a longer average holding period then you should be vigilant about finding out why this is, and what effect it has had on IRRs and multiples.

MODELLING AND ANALYSING BUYOUT FUNDS

Now we are ready to start pulling together what we have been discuss-ing. Allow me first of all to introduce the concept of enterprise value. This simply means the total value of the business, or the price which is paid. The equity value is the amount of equity which has gone into the deal, so:

$$\text{Equity value} + \text{Debt} = \text{Enterprise value}$$

The concept of enterprise value is central to any buyout model. This is the amount of money for which any business is actually sold and which, after repayment of outstanding debt, will belong to the shareholders.

I am using "equity" and "debt" here as if they were homogeneous generic expressions but if you bear in mind all that we have already covered you will realise that you will have to distinguish between different classes of equity (usually the management's sweet equity and then the rest) and various layers of senior debt and mezzanine. Convertible shares (US: convertible stock) should typically be treated as mezzanine. However, remember to treat any convertibles or other mezzanine which is provided by the fund as opposed to outside sources as part of the fund's investment in the deal when calculating the fund's total return. It is fine to calculate the mezzanine and the equity returns separately if you wish, but in practice, LPs will only be concerned about the total return. After all, the mezzanine is usually just taking the place of equity which the fund would otherwise have been compelled to subscribe.

At the top level of analysis, however, the four values which are essential to our workings are enterprise value, earnings (whichever measure you choose), earnings multiple and debt. The debt figure will be the total of all non-equity financing and will include all mezzanine. In other words:

$$\text{Enterprise value} - \text{Equity value} = \text{Debt}$$

These figures need to be captured both on entry (purchase) and exit (sale or IPO). As already noted, the model must also be able of accommodating interim cashflows such as recaps, but this can happen separately on a time period-based model. The important part of the buyout model is analysing the performance of one buyout fund against another.

There are some obvious things that can be done, all of which can give clues to how a buyout firm operates, any strengths or weaknesses which it may have, and any problems which it might be encountering. Average leverage, and average holding period, are two examples. These and other values can of course be combined and/or calculated across more than one fund to give a picture of a firm's total history.

Average leverage will be:

$$\frac{\Sigma \, \text{Debt}/n}{\Sigma \, \text{Enterprise value}/n}$$

expressed as a percentage, where n is the number of companies. However, where a fund has one or two very large transactions then it may be more meaningful to take the capital weighted average, particularly if they have either unusually low or unusually high levels of gearing.

Average holding period is best calculated by number of quarters, and will simply be:

$$\Sigma \, \text{Holding period}/n$$

The interesting part though is to see how we can analyse how a buyout firm is adding value to its investments. In particular, to what extent can we identify the "alpha"-type elements of earnings growth or non-systemic multiple expansion?

A couple of important points need to be made here before we begin. First, if you are planning to take inflation into account then this is where you need to do it, by indexing the earnings over the length of the holding period. Second, the mathematical purists amongst you will notice that there is an element of double counting about some of the calculations. This is acknowledged and deliberate.

The problem is that you have two variables (earnings and multiple) in operation independently and it is impossible to arrive at figures which add to 100% without a little bit of jiggery-pokery. To complicate matters still further, the level of debt will act as a gearing factor on both multiples, and may also change itself during the lifetime of the transaction. This is a problem on which I have worked alongside some very clever mathematicians, including one from Harvard and one from Trinity College, Dublin, yet none have thus far been able to arrive at any final conclusion.[3]

So I have adopted a simplistic solution which works, at least in terms of adding up to 100% and in mitigation I would say only that if and when anyone finds a better solution I will happily and gratefully adopt it. As you will see when you consider the basic algebra that follows, the effect of multiple expansion should logically be calculated on the "going in earnings", otherwise there is always going to be an element of double counting. However, if you do that, you are left with an awkward sort of remainder which does not seem to fit logically anywhere and ends up getting ascribed to the effect of debt (since this is the only other way of dealing with it).

The other valid objection is that the algebra understates the effect of debt. Strictly speaking we should calculate the transaction twice, once as it actually occurred and once on a notionally debt-free basis and then compare the difference in the two results. Strictly speaking, yes, if we wanted to look at the total effect of debt, but we don't. We want to analyse one buyout against another, and all buyouts are going to have high levels of debt, so it is artificial to exclude it all together. Remember we are calculating the level of gearing for each deal and it will be easy to check for correlation between high debt levels and high transaction returns.

---

[3] For the mathematically curious, this is similar to Foucault's famous "three bodies" problem.

However, having considered such arithmetical niceties, let us now ignore them and get on with the algebra.

Let: Impact of Earnings Increase $= A$
       Impact of Multiple Increase $= B$
       Impact of Debt $= C$

       Going In Earnings $= E1$
       Going In Multiple $= M1$
       Going In Debt $= D1$
       Exit Earnings $= E2$
       Exit Multiple $= M2$
       Exit Debt $= D2$

For each portfolio company:

$$A = (E2 \times M1) - (E1 \times M1)$$
$$B = (E2 \times M2) - (E2 \times M1)$$
$$C = D2 - D1$$

Each can then be expressed as a percentage of the total, e.g.

$$\left(\frac{A}{A + B + C} \right) \times 100$$

I am deliberately keeping this all at a very straightforward level, since I want to make sure that the basic methodology is understood. Once it is, the only limit is your imagination! You might choose to analyse returns by deal source, country, transaction size, fund size, or any one of a myriad other considerations. For the moment, let us look at a worked example just to make sure that everything is clear.

Let us assume that a company with earnings of $10 M is bought for $80 M, thus on an earnings multiple of 8. It is held for 3 years and then sold for $117 M, by which time its earnings have increased to $13 M, and so the exit earnings multiple is 9. The original purchase price is funded by $70 M of debt and $10 M of equity. Let us look at two different scenarios: one where there is no change in the level of debt during the holding period, and one where $20 M of debt is paid off at the end of year 2.

Scenario One

Going In Earnings	$10 M	Exit Earnings	$13 M
Going In Multiple	8×	Exit Multiple	9×
Enterprise Value	$80 M	Enterprise Value	$117 M

Capital Structure:		Capital Structure:	
Equity	$10 M	Equity Value	$47 M
Debt	$70 M	Debt	$70 M
Enterprise Value	$80 M	Enterprise Value	$117 M

Gain ($47 M − $10 M) = $37 M
Money Multiple ($47 M/$10 M) = 4.7×

IRR	Yr0	Yr1	Yr2	Yr3
	−$10 M	0	0	$47 M
68%				

Contribution of Earnings Increase ($13 M × 8) − ($10 M × 8) = $24 M
Contribution of Multiple Increase ($13 M × 9) − ($13 M × 8) = $13 M
$37 M

Contribution of Earnings Increase = ($24 M/$37 M) × 100 = 65%
Contribution of Multiple Increase = ($13 M/$37 M) × 100 = 35%

Scenario Two

Going In Earnings	$10 M	Exit Earnings	$13 M
Going In Multiple	8×	Exit Multiple	9×
Enterprise Value	$80 M	Enterprise Value	$117 M

Capital Structure:		Capital Structure:	
Equity	$10 M	Equity Value	$67 M
Debt	$70 M	Debt	$50 M
Enterprise Value	$80 M	Enterprise Value	$117 M

Gain ($67 M − $10 M) = $57 M
Money Multiple ($67 M/$10 M) = 6.7×

IRR	Yr0	Yr1	Yr2	Yr3
	−$10 M	0	$20	$67 M
124%				

Contribution of Earnings Increase ($13 M × 8) − ($10 M × 8) = $24 M
Contribution of Multiple Increase ($13 M × 9) − ($13 M × 8) = $13 M
Contribution of Debt Decrease ($70 M − $50 M) = $20 M
                                                                    $57 M

Contribution of Earnings Increase = ($24 M/$57 M) × 100 = 42%
Contribution of Multiple Increase = ($13 M/$57 M) × 100 = 23%
Contribution of Debt Decrease = ($20 M/$57 M) × 100 = 35%

SUMMARY

- Fund analysis must be "bottom up", i.e., modelling the individual buyout transactions in order to build up a picture of the fund as a whole.
- The four drivers of buyout returns are earnings, earnings multiple, debt (leverage or gearing) and time.
- Buyouts are measured both by IRR and by money multiple. Be aware that there is an inherent trade-off between the two over time.
- When modelling buyouts, pseudo-cashflow measures such as EBITDA are the closest to what buyout firms themselves will use, but lack of consistency and public availability of such figures will usually drive the modeller back to earnings and PE ratios.
- The ability to grow the earnings of a company is the most highly prized of buyout firm abilities, and your analysis should focus on identifying this. Be aware, though, of the effect of inflation, especially when modelling returns from the late 1980s and early 1990s.
- Multiple increase can be thought of as both systemic (beta-like?) and non-systemic (alpha-like?). The latter is obviously preferable and, like earnings growth, represents a highly desirable buyout firm expertise.

- Debt plays a key role in the generation of buyout returns, operating as gearing to enhance equity returns. The way in which different layers of debt and mezzanine can be structured into a deal is a complex subject and requires separate study.
- Timing is largely implicit in buyout returns, since they are calculated by a time period-based measure (IRR). However, there are some explicit considerations which will impact on decision-making and returns, such as the stage of a fund's life cycle, and prevailing market conditions.
- The effects of earnings increase, multiple increase and debt reduction can and should be broken out and analysed.
- Other key factors to capture and analyse include the gearing ratio, length of holding period, type of deal (MBO, MBI, etc.), deal source (proactive, auction, etc.), country and fund size.
- Given the mathematical complexities introduced by multiple variable, some degree of algebraic simplification is required. However, once the basics are grasped, there is no limit to the complexity of model which may be created.

5
Buyout Returns

Having examined how buyout returns are generated, and thus how they may be analysed both within a single fund and also by comparison between different funds, it is time to look at what returns the asset class has actually generated, and how we should view these.

US VERSUS EUROPEAN BUYOUT

For many years during the 1990s there was an axiom "buyout in Europe and venture in the US" which was often used to express investors' instinctive belief as to where the best returns were to be found. We will be looking at venture returns in a later chapter, so let us focus for the time being on the buyout part of this maxim. The belief was that European buyout returns generally out-performed US buyout. Well, let's take a look at the figures (Table 5.1).

As you can see, the axiomatic view seems to hold water. For every vintage year save 1993 and 1998 the European upper quartile figures are significantly higher. Of course, there are those who argue that looking at upper quartile figures is inherently undesirable for all sorts of reasons, not least that one is looking at the returns of a single fund. However, the Capital Weighted Average figures tell a very similar story save only that here it is the 1999 rather than the 1998 vintage year return that is less good.

Remember please that we are looking here at vintage year returns, that is the compound return to date (in this case 30th June 2006) of all qualifying funds (i.e., US or European buyout funds as appropriate) that were closed ("born") in that year. It may be easier to see the relationship between the two sets of figures if we set them out as graphs (Figures 5.1 and 5.2).

Each graph shows broadly the same story. You will see from Table 5.3 on page 104 that there is a significant difference in the TVPI (money multiples) generally, particularly the Capital Weighted Average and particularly after 1993. "Significant" both in range (in 1994 for example) and in effect, since it is generally multiples that drive IRRs, rather than

Table 5.1   US and European buyout returns; IRR by vintage year (%), calculated to 30.06.2006

	US CWA	US UQ	Euro CWA	Euro UQ
1990	10.90	12.50	8.50	19.40
1991	10.00	13.90	14.50	21.50
1992	24.40	29.70	28.10	32.30
1993	21.60	26.10	17.60	22.80
1994	16.80	21.60	42.50	49.20
1995	11.70	13.60	44.10	20.30
1996	6.10	10.40	18.60	22.90
1997	9.50	10.70	12.30	24.10
1998	0.70	12.50	5.40	11.50
1999	6.80	9.60	2.80	11.00

Source: VentureXpert.

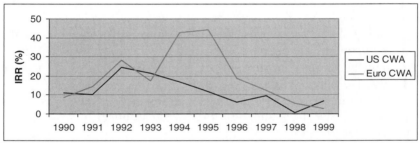

Source: Thomson Financial VentureXpert.

Figure 5.1   Buyout returns to June 2006 by vintage year, Capital Weighted Average IRR

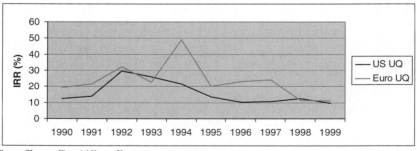

Source: Thomson Financial VentureXpert.

Figure 5.2   Buyout returns to June 2006 by vintage year, Upper Quartile IRR

vice versa (there is more than 89% correlation between the CWA TVPI during the 1990s and the CWA IRR for the same period). The difference in buyout returns between the USA and Europe can clearly be traced to this fundamental difference.

In Europe in the early and mid-1990s there were various funds which achieved at least 3×. I do not say that this was a regular occurrence, but it was far from rare; I can remember several instances off the top of my head. With US buyout funds, as with European funds today, that simply did not happen. By about 2000 expectations were for buyout funds to achieve about 1.9×, while today I would go even lower than that for the mega funds.

We shall be looking later at the phenomenon of falling buyout returns. For the time being, let us focus on the difference between these historic European and US figures and try to think of some possible explanations for the difference.

BUYOUT SKILL BASES

Let me dispose of one possible suggestion very quickly. There is absolutely no difference between the quality of the skills and expertise of buyout professionals on either side of the Atlantic, neither has there ever really been, certainly not during the period we are discussing here, although it is broadly true that buyout activity (certainly in any real volume) started in the USA and then spread to Europe via the UK. Nearly $50 billion had already been raised by US buyout funds prior to 1990, compared with perhaps as little as $6 billion in Europe,[1] but there were by that date a number of very active and very professional European buyout firms based in London such as BC partners, Doughty Hanson, Duke Street, CVC, Permira, Apax, Cinven and Candover,[2] while in Scandinavia both Industri Kapital and Nordic Capital commenced operations in 1989.

The skills involved in operating as a buyout professional are profound, and can confer a significant strategic advantage, and while I

---

[1] My own calculations based on Thomson Financial's VentureXpert system, which may slightly under-state the European figures for this early period, as not all European buyout firms registered their data in those days.

[2] For the sake of convenience, I have used the present names of all these groups. Doughty Hanson were previously CWB Capital Partners, Duke Street were born out of Hambros European Ventures, CVC were originally part of Citibank, and Permira were previously part of Schroders.

would be the last to belittle them, many of them are essentially financial in nature, which is why buyout firms favour young accountants when they recruit entry level personnel. For anyone with a good level of financial education these skills can be learnt and quickly developed. Of course there are others, such as the ability to source deals, and when and how to exit them, which require considerable judgement and experience, but these too can be learnt. Suffice it to say that I have never heard it suggested by anyone that during the 1990s European buyout houses (at least the major, independent ones – those attached to continental European banks may well have been a different story, but these were frequently practising development capital rather than buyout anyway) had lower levels of professional skills than their US counterparts, or indeed vice versa. So, whatever the reason for the differing levels of returns, we need to look beyond the firms themselves, at the broader environment within which they were operating. We also need to be alive to what lessons this may have for us when looking at buyout conditions today.

IMPERFECT MARKETS

The most frequently heard explanation for the very high European buyout returns of the early and mid-1990s was the "imperfect markets" issue to which I have already alluded in an earlier chapter. US markets, both public and private, so the argument goes, were much better developed by 1990 than their European counterparts, certainly so far as continental Europe (that is, Europe excluding the UK) was concerned. Thus the ability to source a deal proactively and be able to transact it on an exclusive basis was still very much alive in Europe at a time when it had already largely disappeared in the USA, certainly in respect of a business of any real size.

Like all generalisations, this one is largely true. Nobody would deny, least of all the private equity firms involved, that a lot of the buyouts in countries like Germany and Sweden in the early 1990s fell fairly and squarely into this category. They were rarely put through any sort of auction process, the vendor was frequently either a family owner or a socially embarrassed local corporate group, and as a result they were often bought for values which in retrospect seem generous to the purchaser. However, on the other side of the coin, it should be remembered that these businesses were usually subject to all sorts of restrictions which would simply have been unfathomable to any US purchaser, such as the extreme difficulty in some countries (legal, political and cultural) of any significant rationalisation involving redundancies and/or plant closures. The continental socio-economic model at that time, even more strongly than today, held that a company existed to provide employment and retirement security to the local community at least as much as to make a profit for shareholders. German companies in the 1980s, for example, were customarily ranked on their turnover (sales revenue) and their number of employees, not on their profits (the figures for which, by the way, were not usually publicly available).

Thus, this combination of historical circumstances might be thought of as a sort of "happy hunting time" during which buyout firms were able to conclude difficult but attractive deals largely undisturbed. However, these conditions were largely confined to Scandinavia and German-speaking Europe. Countries such as France and Italy, for example, were largely untouched by large buyout activity at this time, although this changed as the decade progressed and, indeed, one of the most spectacularly successful buyouts of all time took place in Italy (the Yellow Pages deal, the chief beneficiaries of which were BC Partners and Investitori Associati).

US buyout firms were perhaps slower than they might have been in trying to access this particular honey-pot, an interesting parallel with US venture firms, who have also been very slow to seek deals outside their own immediate geographical environment.[3] It was only in the late 1980s that the large US buyout firms began to set up European operations, and even then these were frequently staffed largely by Americans at senior level, with all investment decisions being taken in America by Americans. This is often cited as a reason why they found it very difficult at first to access deals in continental Europe, particularly those which had a political element (which so many did), but in fairness I believe this was a product of deep anti-American sentiment, particularly a suspicion (often unfounded, but not always) that what the American firm was after was a quick turn, after mass asset sales and redundancies, and would have happened anyway. Whatever the case, it is certainly true that American firms largely missed out on these early opportunities and this would thus definitely be one plausible reason for the difference in historic returns.

---

[3] Though this is easier to understand in the case of venture capital, since hands-on company building skills are best exercised face to face.

EARNINGS MULTIPLES

Thinking back to our discussion about the drivers of buyout returns, it would be instructive to look at how the different drivers might have contributed to the historic situation, but I must enter an immediate caveat here. This sort of information is available, in so far as it exists at all, only within the buyout models of professional Funds of Funds and other sophisticated LPs. The private equity industry does not handle the concept of transparency very well; indeed, there are some US venture firms who insist on strict secrecy from their LPs on pain of possible expulsion from their funds. They believe that they have all sorts of good reasons for this (chief among which is the problem of performance data falling into unsophisticated hands which do not, for example, understand the effect of the J-curve, or the difference between annual and compound returns), but with respect I disagree.

Investors today expect transparency across all asset classes and are entitled to get it. There are legitimate concerns among GPs that data may be compared across firms in ways which are not fair and consistent, either because it has been prepared on different bases in the first place, or because the analysis systems used by individual investors make different assumptions, or categorise information in different ways. Buyout firms, for example, can be extremely sensitive about the way in which gearing ratios or earnings multiples are calculated, and as to the attribution of particular deals to particular individuals within the firm. However, these legitimate concerns can be addressed given goodwill and professionalism on both sides, and it is a huge pity for those of us who take a genuine interest in the analytical side of the industry that there is so little data available with which to work.

The fact that underlying data is not available is a major stumbling block, but not a complete impasse. There are ways in which we can imply or infer the action of buyout drivers, so let us do the best we can with the information at our disposal.

As we discussed in an earlier chapter, there is a relationship between quoted earnings ratios and those which are applied to private equity transactions. While this link exists, let us remind ourselves of its limitations. It works well when a public company is being bought, as the company will have its own irrefutably relevant multiple. However, even here one hits problems immediately, since the buyout house will be thinking in terms of EBITDA, which may paint a very different picture to the "earnings" used for the PE ratio. When the transaction is anything other than a take private, there will be arguments about the comparative factors (size, growth, business activities) and there will also be a time lag between publicly quoted sectors changing and private company vendors' pricing expectations making a similar adjustment. In some cases this latter phenomenon may be so extreme that the vendor will simply refuse to sell at any reasonable price, no matter how irrational such behaviour may be given his own particular circumstances or those of the company.

Even taking all this into account, however, we can at the very least say that private equity multiples are heavily influenced by publicly quoted PE ratios, and that accordingly any rise or fall over a period (particularly if it was a fairly steady rise or fall, so as not to confuse people's valuation expectations too much) in the latter would almost certainly be reflected in the former.

As you can see from Figure 5.3, the PE ratio of the FTSE index, which we may take as a proxy for the European buyout industry since it is likely to be the index to which they would turn first, rose steadily during the 1990s, and so one would expect the earnings multiples available for buyout transactions to have risen steadily as well. The only problem with this analysis is that the comparable US ratios also increased steadily throughout the 1990s, and so US buyout funds should have been equally able to profit from rising earnings multiples as their European counterparts. The fact that they apparently did not (or, at

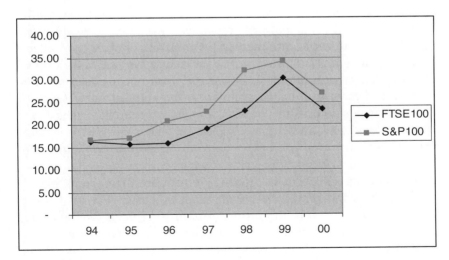

Figure 5.3   PE ratios 1994–2000, FTSE100 and S&P100

least, not to the same extent) suggests that while there must logically be some force to this argument, it is at best a partial explanation.

In fact, if one tries to measure the correlation between the FTSE PE ratios for the period 1994 to 2000 against first the Capital Weighted TVPI for European buyout funds and then the Capital Weighted IRR for the same vintage years, one arrives at figures of −78% and −77%, respectively (running the same figures for US buyout gives a broadly similar result: −75% and −70%, respectively). In other words, not only is there no correlation, but there is a strong negative correlation.

It therefore seems more logical to ascribe at least a part of the assumed multiple increase in the European arena to "imperfect market syndrome". If one is buying on a multiple that does not fully reflect the value of the business on a public market, and subsequently disposes of it either by floating it on a public market or by selling it semi-publicly in a way in which the public multiple will be used as a comparator, then this clearly opens up the potential for greater gain.

One specific situation merits discussion, since it had a major influence on the returns of a number of London-based buyout funds in the mid-1990s. The Conservative government decided to privatise the railways and chose to do so by offering the various individual companies into which assets and routes had been bundled for sale by tender, rather than offering their shares on the stock exchange as they had done in previous privatisations such as British Telecom. The Labour opposition, unable to halt the process because of their (then) minority in parliament, threatened to compulsorily repurchase the companies when they returned to power. Because the various transactions were thus subject to a huge amount of political risk (a general election was in the offing), this was reflected in the price, as was the government's determination to be rid of them well ahead of any possible political interference by the then opposition. In the event, compulsory repurchase ideas were quietly abandoned after Labour's election victory in 1997, and the buyout firms involved had anyway already been able to sell the companies on almost at once for greatly enhanced prices (geared by substantial amounts of debt) and reap rewards that were almost embarrassing even by the standards of the private equity industry. City of London humour being what it is, the various participating funds (who included Candover and Charterhouse) promptly became known collectively as "the Great Train Robbers", a reference to a famous and highly romanticised (such accounts conveniently ignore the fact that the train driver later died of his injuries) British crime which caught the public imagination in the 1960s.

I mention this because these various railway deals had a huge impact on the returns of various European buyout funds, both because of the gains that were made[4] and also because the holding periods involved were unusually short, thus boosting IRRs as well as money multiples. This should be borne in mind when looking at 1994, since Candover and Charterhouse both had 1994 vintage year funds.

The 1995 figures are also a little strange, particularly since the Capital Weighted Average is so much above the upper quartile fund. There is one specific issue which needs to be pointed out here, although I am not sure exactly how great an effect it had. Apax raised a fund in 1995 which was scheduled to invest in both venture and buyout deals (as was their practice then) but because of the way in which the VentureXpert funds database works, this whole fund was classified as a buyout fund, which means that the 1995 vintage year European "buyout" returns include the results of some very successful venture investments, such as Autonomy, Dr Solomon's and QXL Ricardo. I mention this for the sake of completeness, but it is unlikely to be a significant factor. Though less than $2.5 billion was raised for European buyout that year, Apax V was only a $300 M fund. It may actually be more of an issue for the 1995 European venture figures, which presumably do not benefit from these companies being included.

EARNINGS GROWTH

Earnings growth can come about in three ways. First, there is the growth that would have occurred naturally anyway from higher revenues (perhaps as a result of a new product coming on stream) or lower costs (for example the removal of the sort of hidden costs that often accompany family ownership). Second, there is growth caused by the effects of inflation. Lastly, there is the sort of "alpha" earnings growth to which we alluded in an earlier chapter which is brought about by the specific actions of the buyout group.

Without underlying data of the necessary complexity we can only attempt conjectures here. The first type of growth can probably be

---

[4] An equity investment of £70 M in Eversholt, a rolling stock leasing company, allegedly turned into over £450 M: "Red faces over rail privatisation", *Sunday Times*, 1997.

discounted as a distinguishing factor, since logically it would have occurred to the same extent in both the USA and Europe. Indeed, given that the USA led the way into the intensive computerisation of business processes which occurred during the 1990s then, if anything, I think this factor should have favoured American rather than European returns. However, I think there may have been significant differences in both the other two areas.

The 1990s began as a high inflation decade in Europe, particularly in the UK (less so in countries such as Germany, where it was held in check by high interest rates to the ultimate detriment and effective collapse of the European Monetary System) but ended as a low inflation decade. Thus, some argue, there was a period during the early 1990s when inflation could have played a key role in earnings growth, which would mean that the glory day returns of 1994 and 1995, while still very impressive, may actually be slightly less so than they appear to be. However, I do not wish to overplay this; high inflation was much less of a factor in continental Europe than in the UK (though the UK at the time accounted for about half of all European buyout activity by value).

In fact, if one looks at the official UK government figures (the various different measures for the Retail Price Index) it is clear that this can have had little real effect on proceedings. With the possible exception of 1995, inflation can have had little impact on the stand-out vintage years in question, and if it was a significant factor then one would have expected the vintage year returns for 1996 and 1997 to have been similarly boosted, which they weren't. Thus, I am inclined to dismiss inflation as a factor which could provide any significant explanation.

The second factor is in my judgement much more likely to have been significant. Companies bought from family vendors, and even some which had been owned by public companies had pursued a deliberate policy of keeping earnings in check, usually by aggressive asset acquisition programmes, in order to avoid as much as possible high rates of taxation. This was a particular problem in Germany, where the real cost of unification on a one-to-one basis between the Deutschmark and the Ostmark had been badly under-estimated (or perhaps just swept under the carpet at the time for political reasons). So this was one reason why it might have been quite easy to increase earnings.

Another was the condition which afflicts most owner-managed companies, namely a missing layer of management. Regardless of what titles are in use, there tends to be a Financial Controller rather than a Finance Director, for example, and a similar situation in all the other disciplines. Often simply replacing this missing layer of management can yield quite spectacular results.

Yet another has been referred to obliquely elsewhere in this book. In Europe, the process of industrial consolidation which took place in the USA in the 1960s and 1970s had been delayed, and arguably still has not been properly completed 40 years later. In part this was due to national and local pride; every country wants its own airline, and every town in Belgium and Germany wants its own brewery, and preferably two or three. In part it was also down to the heterogeneous nature of Europe itself, a factor which is often overlooked by Americans, who find it difficult to conceive of a situation where you can drive a few miles down the road and be confronted by a different language, currency and legal system, together with completely different cultural mores and purchasing habits; the "white sausage/black sausage" border in Germany is perfectly real, for example, even though it is not marked on any map.

That being so, it was frequently possible to buy a company and put it together with another business in another country, or spin individual business units off for such a purpose, something that would probably have been politically impossible for the previous owner even to contemplate. Indeed, sometimes this possibility was explicitly discussed at the time the original buyout was done, and the vendor kept a stake in the business precisely to derive some financial benefit from this when it happened.

Because the consolidation process was still in its infancy, the size of the business units involved rarely gave rise to any serious monopoly (anti-trust) problems. Compare and contrast that with the situation today, where much larger fund sizes have led to much larger transaction sizes, which in turn frequently raise significant legal and regulatory issues whenever any merger is contemplated.[5]

---

[5] In some cases, where a utility has been purchased, or where a business may have monopoly-like issues, government pricing restrictions may also be in force. This was a factor, for example, in the UK Yellow Pages deal in which Apax participated.

LEVERAGE

In a sense, leverage, inflation and interest rates are all inter-related. Monetary policy in Europe in the early 1990s was to attack high inflation with high interest rates. Such an approach will in turn prompt low earnings multiples, since the perceived risk-free investment return, and thus the discount rate applied to future cashflows, is high. So, in a sense it is a case of what you gain on the swings you lose on the roundabout as far as buyout funds are concerned.

At the beginning of the 1990s one could look to inflation to flatter one's earnings growth, and buy on low earnings multiples. However, high interest rates made aggressive leverage difficult, or at least very expensive. By the end of the 1990s, Europe (particularly the UK) had become a low inflation, low interest rate environment with plentiful debt available at reasonable prices,[6] and much higher earnings multiples than 10 years previously.

Thus, one would expect there to have been a change in the relative impact of the buyout drivers over the course of the decade in Europe, with earnings growth and multiple expansion playing a large part early on, but diminishing towards the end of the period, perhaps with gearing levels rising. As I have said already, it is a great pity that this information is not freely available, in which case we would be able to know for sure rather than having to guess, but these seem reasonable assumptions to be drawing.

If so, then this is one area where some of the difference could be explained. The USA did not experience anything as extreme as the British conditions, and in particular neither inflation nor interest rates ever got as high as they did in the UK. So, this might explain some of the differential early in the decade. The fly in this particular ointment, however, is that because US interest rates were typically lower, then it should have been that much easier to gear companies up with debt. However, this might in turn bear out one's instinctive view that earnings growth and multiple expansion have a higher potential to influence buyout returns than does the effect of some extra leverage. I do not wish to labour these points, since we are here forced into the realm of pure speculation, but they are important issues which one should bear in mind when analysing buyout returns.

---

[6]The actual economic cycles within Europe were different, particularly as between the UK and Germany. Generally speaking, the UK went from low growth to medium/high growth, while the German economy did much the opposite, but that is much less relevant for our purposes.

There is one extra point that falls to be made about leverage. With the rising transaction values brought about by larger fund sizes, the amount of acquisition debt available at any one time is not infinite. Remember that, at least in the early stages, there may be two or three different buyout funds (or, more usually these days, consortia of buyout funds) chasing a particular deal, and each will need to have its potential funding firmly in place before making a formal offer (indeed, this is usually a specific requirement of the sale process). Thus, if there are a number of large deals in the market at any one time, and particularly if the bidding process in respect of most of them has not yet been narrowed down to one preferred purchaser, then the banks which habitually supply this acquisition debt start to come under pressure, and may have to start tweaking their terms to regulate supply, or even deciding not to proceed with a particular deal (these days there are also some fairly sophisticated underwriting and syndication techniques entered into between banks). Having the stature, credibility and track record to ensure that you are the bidder proceeded with rather than the bidder who is dumped by the banks, is in fact a significant but little recognised strategic advantage.

FUND SIZE

We have already noted the phenomenon of rising buyout fund sizes and conjectured whether there may be some connection between fund size and return. This may be of particular interest for the period under consideration, since there was a stark difference between Europe and the USA.

The average size of European buyout funds raised between 1990 and 1999 was less than $250 M, whereas for US buyout funds raised during the same period it was nearly $370 M.[7] To throw this into starker contrast, US buyout funds raised a total of $348 billion during the 1990s, while only $66 billion was raised in Europe. In other words, the American buyout industry was trying to put over five times as much money to work during the 1990s as were their European counterparts in an economic block of roughly equal value. Given that by common consent there were more potential buyout companies in Europe at

---

[7] All figures in this chapter are taken or calculated from Thomson Financial's VentureXpert system unless specifically stated otherwise.

this time [since industry consolidation in just about every sector was well behind that in the USA, thus meaning there were a larger number of (generally smaller) players in each case] then I think this factor is significant.

It is not just that American GPs had more money to put to work (which would raise obvious implications that they may have been less price-sensitive, since they could afford to be less choosy in the face of greater competition) in total, and the Europeans less. It is also that the vast majority of European buyout capital was being targeted at what we would today call the mid-market. There were only 14 mega funds (more than $1 billion fund size) raised in Europe before 2000, whereas there were 85 in the USA. During the 1990s, the amount of capital raised by mega funds in the USA fluctuated between 11% and 55%, whereas in Europe it was zero for five of the years in question (Table 5.2).

Table 5.2　The impact of mega fund capital in Europe and the USA 1990–1999

Europe

Year	#Funds	#Mega	Total capital ($M)	Mega capital ($M)	%
1990	21	0	2 588	0	0
1991	21	0	1 376	0	0
1992	10	0	1 201	0	0
1993	14	0	1 518	0	0
1994	20	1	5 186	1 779	34.31
1995	20	0	2 474	0	0
1996	29	1	7 753	2 038	26.28
1997	38	4	13 489	7 240	53.67
1998	50	5	16 787	10 380	61.83
1999	49	3	14 033	5 485	39.09

USA

Year	#Funds	#Mega	Total capital ($M)	Mega capital ($M)	%
1990	74	1	9 101.20	1 015.50	11.16
1991	36	1	7 889.70	1 944.50	24.65
1992	64	4	14 120.10	4 855.00	34.38
1993	76	2	18 413.00	3 151.40	17.12
1994	105	5	26 087.70	6 524.80	25.01
1995	111	10	32 999.60	14 404.70	43.65
1996	102	4	26 791.20	6 746.10	25.18
1997	128	14	57 101.10	28 147.00	49.29
1998	183	22	88 312.70	46 288.70	52.41
1999	141	22	67 483.80	37 205.50	55.13

Of course we have to keep things in proportion. We are talking about a smaller sample size in Europe, because of a younger and thus smaller industry. Even by the end of the decade, the number of European buyout funds is less than was the case in America at the beginning of the decade (although the difference is less pronounced than it seems, because of the absence of some European funds from the VentureXpert population). However, there is no getting away from the fact that we are talking about lower average fund sizes and very significantly less total capital in Europe than in the USA. There was also markedly less incidence of mega funds in Europe during the 1990s (the figures pick up after 2000). Since we are clearly also looking at higher vintage year returns in Europe, let us dig a little deeper and see if it is possible to establish any specific connections.

You will see from Table 5.3 that it looks as though our suspicions were correct. Here we take four main measures of return: money multiple and IRR (both Capital Weighted Average and Upper Quartile in each case) and measure the correlation in the vintage year data series against the same series for average fund size and total fund capital.

Let's look at the American figures first. Here there is a very clear and very strong negative correlation with every return measure against both our fundraising figures. If average fund size is bigger one vintage year than the year before then it is highly likely that any of the return measures will be lower, and the same holds true for total capital raised.

For European funds during the same vintage we see the same relationship, although the degree of negative correlation is lower, significantly so when measured against average fund size. I suggest that this merely reflects the lower incidence of mega funds in Europe during the 1990s, which we have already noted above.

In both the USA and Europe then the message seems to be that fund size and capital availability are the enemy of returns; the more the capital available for investment, and the higher the average fund size then the lower the returns of that vintage year are likely to be. In Europe, at least, there has been a strong connection between growth in the two capital measures. As a matter of interest, let us look at what has happened to buyout fundraising in recent years (Table 5.4).

You will see that in Europe since 2000 both total capital and the percentage of the total represented by mega funds have more than doubled, while in the USA the total has increased by nearly 50% while the mega fund percentage has remained broadly the same. In other

Table 5.3 Impact of average fund size and total capital on buyout returns by vintage year 1990–1999

Year	US buyout					European buyout				
	CWATVPI ×	UQTVPI ×	CWAIRR (%)	UQIRR (%)	Avg. size ($M)	CWATVPI ×	UQTVPI ×	CWAIRR (%)	UQIRR (%)	Avg. size ($M)
1990	1.80	1.72	10.90	12.50	123	1.45	1.77	8.50	19.40	123
1991	1.46	1.96	10.00	13.90	219	1.70	2.07	14.50	21.50	66
1992	1.94	2.38	24.40	29.70	221	2.54	2.88	28.10	32.30	120
1993	2.05	2.21	21.60	26.10	242	1.99	2.42	17.60	22.80	108
1994	1.56	1.96	16.80	21.60	248	2.78	2.95	42.50	49.20	259
1995	1.46	1.87	11.70	13.60	297	2.19	1.89	44.10	20.30	124
1996	1.24	1.49	6.10	10.40	263	1.78	1.96	18.60	22.90	267
1997	1.37	1.35	9.50	10.70	446	1.57	2.13	12.30	24.10	355
1998	1.01	1.56	0.70	12.50	485	1.22	1.55	5.40	11.50	336
1999	1.28	1.30	6.80	9.60	479	1.10	1.37	2.80	11.00	287
Correl. avg. size	−0.71	−0.66	−0.57	−0.44		−0.35	−0.28	−0.29	−0.09	
Correl. capital	−0.74	−0.67	−0.65	−0.47		−0.63	−0.56	−0.53	−0.43	

Source: Own calculations, primary data from Thomson Financial's VentureXpert system.
Note: "Correl. capital" is the calculated correlation with total buyout fund capital raised for that region in that vintage year (not shown).

Table 5.4 The impact of mega fund capital in Europe and the USA by vintage year 2000–2005

Europe

Year	#Funds	#Mega	Total capital ($M)	Mega capital ($M)	%
2000	72	7	23 088	7 946	34.42
2001	50	5	26 500	17 917	67.61
2002	44	5	19 233	10 592	55.07
2003	37	3	23 660	15 620	66.02
2004	35	11	15 603	5 864	37.59
2005	56	7	53 576	38 714	72.26

USA

Year	#Funds	#Mega	Total capital ($M)	Mega capital ($M)	%
2000	150	29	93 577	63 738.60	68.11
2001	120	24	76 173	47 027.40	61.74
2002	119	10	37 795	14 293.80	37.82
2003	98	11	53 468	33 544.50	62.74
2004	146	21	85 447	47 199.50	55.24
2005	174	31	139 184	99 766.80	71.68

Source: Own calculations based on data from Thomson Financial's VentureXpert system.

words, in the USA the impact of the mega funds appears to have reached a plateau some years ago, while in Europe it is only now finding its appropriate level. Thus if there is any difference in returns due purely to the performance of mega funds relative to the others, then one would expect this to have a roughly similar impact in both Europe and the USA from now onwards.

This also means that if our above hypothesis about the inverse relationship between average fund size and returns is correct, then European buyout returns are due to decline steadily towards the sort of levels being achieved in the USA. In fact, there is some evidence to suggest that they may actually cross over.

I haven't shown it in any of the above figures, largely for reasons of space, but if we look at the period 1990–1999 more closely we find that in America there are only two years out of the sample when the Capital Weighted Average IRR is below the average, whereas in Europe there are six. This suggests that the larger funds have done better in the USA relative to Europe, and thus that as the impact on total returns of the larger funds in Europe grows, we can expect total European buyout returns to diminish disproportionately. The figures are given in Table 5.5 for you to judge for yourself.

Admittedly this is a pretty rough and ready indicator, particularly as European mega funds can have had no impact at all on five of the years in question, but I suggest that the figures in respect of the last four years of the decade (when they undoubtedly *did* have an impact) may be significant. There is another way in which we might be able to check this theory, and that is by looking at the returns since inception of different sizes of buyout fund in each region. In Table 5.6, the pooled return refers to treating all the constituent funds as if they were one giant fund and then calculating the IRR of the total cashflows.

The US figures show a steady decline in returns as fund size increases. The European figures suggests that there may be a "hot spot" for fund

Table 5.5 Relative impact of mega funds in Europe and the USA, relationship of the Capital Weighted Average IRR to the average

Year	US buyout			European buyout		
	Average IRR (%)	CWA IRR (%)	CWA/Avg. %	Average IRR (%)	CWA IRR (%)	CWA/Avg. %
1990	4.10	10.90	265.85	10.80	8.50	78.70
1991	8.20	10.00	121.95	13.60	14.50	106.62
1992	20.20	24.40	120.79	22.40	28.10	125.45
1993	19.30	21.60	111.92	20.10	17.60	87.56
1994	15.20	16.80	110.53	27.40	42.50	155.11
1995	9.80	11.70	119.39	25.90	44.10	170.27
1996	7.90	6.10	77.22	28.00	18.60	66.43
1997	4.90	9.50	193.88	16.10	12.30	76.40
1998	5.20	0.70	13.46	5.80	5.40	93.10
1999	4.20	6.80	161.90	4.70	2.80	59.57

Source: Own calculations based on data from Thomson Financial's VentureXpert system.

Table 5.6 Pooled and upper quartile returns since inception (%)

	USA pooled	Europe pooled	USA UQ	Europe UQ
Medium ($250M–$499M)	17.5	13.4	21.8	18.3
Large ($500M–$999M)	12.7	18.9	14.7	15.7
Mega (>$1 B)	11.3	−26.8	19.1	−9.3

size, with returns declining both above and below it. Unfortunately it is not possible to investigate this any further with the level of data available, but my instinct suggests that, if so, it is probably somewhere around $350 M to $600 M. Incidentally, this is clear and strong evidence for the existence of the fabled "mid-market" opportunity in Europe, and for the fact that most GPs have now moved well above it.

I would be cautious about reading too much into these figures as far as European mega funds are concerned; 37 out of 55 are 5 years old or less and thus most unlikely, given the effects of the J-curve, to be showing good returns yet. However, they do suggest cause for some concern. After all, at least 11 of the other 18 *are* in meaningful return territory, and yet the maximum recorded IRR so far is just 23%, and I would suggest that this is still more indicative evidence that (1) buyout returns decline with rising fund size and (2) European mega funds have yet to match the performance levels of their US counterparts.

WHAT CAN WE EXPECT FROM BUYOUT RETURNS IN FUTURE?

We have advanced the hypothesis that fund size is the enemy of returns. Let us check this a little more, and then consider what implications this may have for returns in the future.

Let us look again at European returns during the 1990s. First I would like to graph average fund size against the Capital Weighted IRR for same vintage year. See Figure 5.4.

This graph is interesting, but the trendline is somewhat spoiled by the outlier in the top right-hand corner. I wonder if you can guess what this is? Yes, it is the effect of the Great Train Robbers distorting the figures for 1994. Just for fun, let's leave it out and try again. See Figure 5.5.

The trendline is much more significant now, clearly indicating what we suspected, namely that average fund size can have a direct inverse relationship with fund returns.

Now let's take a look at US buyout returns and see if we can discern a similar pattern. See Figure 5.6.

If anything, the trend is even clearer here. So, it looks as if there can be little doubt. In general, a higher average buyout fund size will result in lower fund returns, regardless of whether the buyout activity in question is taking place in America or Europe.

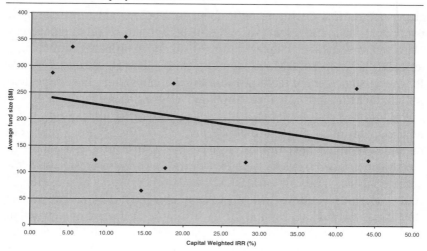

Figure 5.4   European buyout returns 1990–1999 by vintage year

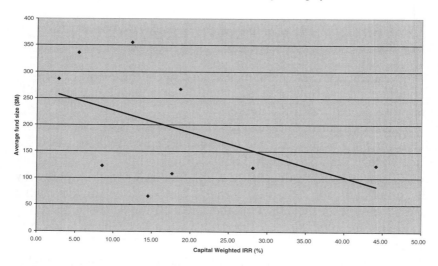

Figure 5.5   European buyout returns 1990–1999 by vintage year, but excluding 1994

Of course, the trendline which we have been adding is an artificial construct, and is intended to give no more than a general indication of likely future returns. Nobody is suggesting that returns are going to head downwards in a straight line until they disappear through the floor and become negative. What *is* being suggested is that the general trend

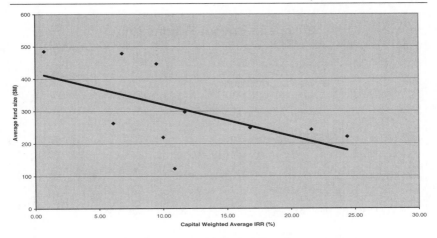

Figure 5.6 US buyout returns 1990–1999 by vintage year

of buyout returns has undoubtedly been downwards, that this downward trend has a direct inverse link to the growth both in individual fund sizes and the amount of capital being deployed by the industry as a whole, and that all three of these trends are likely to continue into the future.

RECENT FUNDRAISING LEVELS

Let us look, for example, at what has happened to buyout fundraising since the end of the period we have been examining, i.e., from 2000 onwards.

To get a proper feeling for the data series, Figures 5.7 and 5.8 show the total amounts raised by the buyout industry in Europe and America for the 10-year period since 1996. You will see that there has been a dramatic increase for Europe, fuelled in large part by mega funds such as the one currently being raised[8] with a stated target of €11 billion by Permira.

In 2005, mega funds accounted for over 70% of the total capital raised in Europe, having been at zero as recently as 1995. It is this dramatic shift in balance (by fund size at any rate) in favour of the mega funds which is one of the most intriguing parts of the ongoing

---

[8] Writing in August 2006.

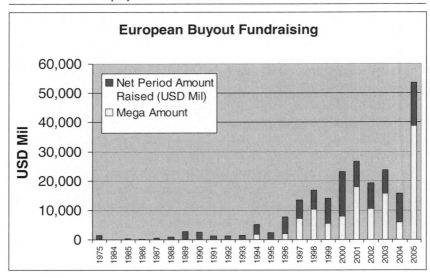

Figure 5.7 Commitments to European buyout funds by vintage year, showing the amounts raised by "mega funds"

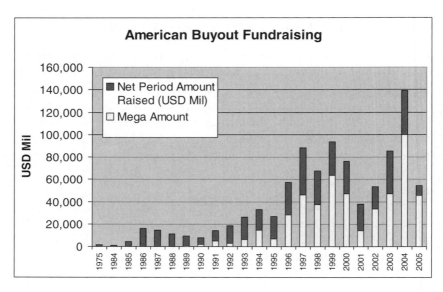

Figure 5.8 Commitments to American buyout funds by vintage year, showing the amounts raised by "mega funds"

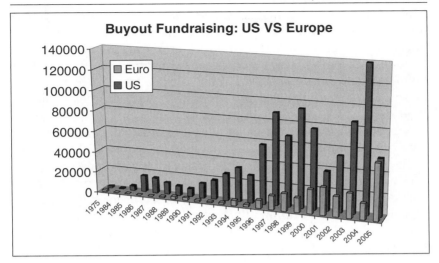

Figure 5.9   Total amounts committed to US and European buyout funds by vintage year

equation. There is simply no precedent to guide us in how this might affect European returns, since it is a very recent phenomenon. However, remember that the available data (which is admittedly largely young and therefore unreliable) seems to suggest that mega funds may not have performed as well in Europe as they have in relative terms in the USA.

Finally, look at the way in which the gap in overall size of the two markets is narrowing both quickly and substantially. It would be logical to expect them to be about the same, since they are operating in economic blocks of roughly equal size, and they appear to be headed in this direction. Given our earlier hypothesis about total buyout capital being another driver of lower buyout returns, then this would seem to sound yet another note of caution about future European buyout returns, at least for the larger funds (Figure 5.9).

SOME CONCLUSIONS AND PREDICTIONS

So, our analysis of the available data strongly suggests that the downward trend in buyout returns is set to continue, but let us keep this conclusion in context. First, I strongly suspect that the downward trend is not a straight line, as suggested by the graphing techniques we have been using, but a curve, and that where the curve bottoms out will have a lot to do with where average fund sizes end up. Also, because of the effect of the J-curve, it may well take 4 or 5 years after it has in fact bottomed out for this fact to become apparent; it may, for example, have bottomed out already, though I doubt it since (at least in Europe) I believe that there is still scope for considerable upward expansion in fund sizes.

Second, I have little doubt that buyout returns will continue to out-perform quoted equity returns (and particularly actively managed quoted equity) on a true cost-adjusted basis. However, in the case of the very largest buyout funds the differential between the two will narrow considerably compared with what we have seen historically. I have in various articles said I think it likely that in future large buyout returns may be no more than about 150 basis points above quoted equities and I am content to stick with this prediction for the present.

Third, we must note the continuing spread of syndication, which will have an ongoing tendency to reduce differentiation amongst fund returns. This has been an issue for some years; for example, as long ago as the late 1990s there were two London-based firms which had co-invested with each other so often that investors began to realise that it was inadvisable to invest with both. More recently, the Philips semi-conductor transaction saw Bain Capital and Apax, who had been part of an unsuccessful consortium, being invited to participate in the equity by the successful consortium of KKR, Silver Lake and Alpinvest. While there have been isolated examples of this before, the extension of syndication across consortia threatens to "commoditise" buyout transactions and reduce still further the chance of stand-out returns by any one firm.

Fourth, and lest it be suggested that I am uniformly negative about the future of large buyout returns, let me say that there are a small number of such firms who have out-performed their peers in the past and will continue to do so in the future. Without mentioning any names, could I advise LPs to look for those firms which have shown the disci-pline to stick with their basic investment model to at least some large degree, limiting their fund size in consequence. Remember, the invest-ment model should drive the fund size, not vice versa. Whenever a buyout firm is looking to raise a new fund which is considerably bigger than their previous one, or looking to close a fund above its original target size, be sure to quiz them very closely as to how their investment model has changed, and why.

Finally, though, let us remember, lest we be accused of spreading doom and gloom about the private equity industry, that we are actually talking about a very small part of that industry indeed. Since the beginning of 2001, funds in excess of $1 billion have made up 44% of the total fund capital raised in the global private equity market, but less than 6% by number. So, even if you have reservations about the returns likely to be earned by the mega funds (reservations which the above analysis would appear to support, at least in part), then you could simply invest in the other 95% of the market, which by the way would have given you well over 3000 funds from which to choose!

SUMMARY

- Historically, European buyout funds have consistently out-performed US buyout funds. In particular, European buyout funds enjoyed a period of significant out-performance in the mid-1990s, with both 1994 and 1995 being stand-out vintage years.
- While no specific underlying data is available, it is likely that earnings growth and multiple expansion were the main drivers of this European out-performance.
- These in turn were facilitated by the existence of market imperfections in Europe, leading to buyout firms being able to buy companies on a proactive and exclusive basis that had largely ceased to be available by the end of the decade. No comparable conditions existed in the USA at any time during the decade.
- The available data strongly suggests that there is a direct inverse relationship between (1) buyout returns by vintage year and (2) both total capital raised and average fund size by vintage year. In other words, if either the total capital raised in any one vintage year, or the average size of the funds raised in any one vintage year is higher than the corresponding total for the year before, then the returns of the funds raised in the vintage year in question are likely to be lower than for the preceding vintage year. Thus a period of steadily increasing fund sizes would seem to signal a period of steadily declining returns.
- Europe was comparatively little affected by the "mega fund effect" during the 1990s, but the European fundraising pattern has changed dramatically in recent years, so that in 2005, for example, mega

funds accounted for over 70% of all European buyout capital raised.

- One must be cautious about drawing firm conclusions, since much of the relevant data is young and therefore unreliable, but mega funds appear to have performed significantly better relative to other funds in their market in the USA than they have to date in Europe.
- It seems likely that buyout returns are in long-term decline in Europe, and that this decline is particularly significant for funds of larger size. The decline is probably a downward curve rather than a straight line and is regressing towards both (1) US buyout returns and (2) quoted equity returns.
- For the larger funds, there is likely to be little difference between US and European returns in future years. The IRRs of such funds currently being raised will probably struggle to out-perform quoted equities on a cost-adjusted basis by more than about 150 basis points.
- There may well be a small handful of firms who are able to out-perform their peers. Logically these will be those who avoid excessive exposure to syndication and seek out deals which can be exclusive to their fund.
- Those who are concerned by the possible low return potential of mega funds should remember that since the beginning of 2001 they have represented less than 6% of global private equity funds, which would leave well over 3000 other funds from which to choose.

6

Venture Capital

WHAT IS VENTURE CAPITAL?

Just as we have already done for buyout, we will now take a closer look at venture capital. What is it? What are the qualities that characterise a venture firm? Can anyone do it? If not, what are the barriers to entry? What are the current issues which concern the venture industry? This will be an important chapter since arguably there is no single area of the whole investment universe that is more widely misunderstood, or more unfairly vilified.

A glance back at Table 1.1 will remind the reader of those things which tend to distinguish venture transactions from buyouts, and it will be useful to bear these in mind. It is time to amplify these very considerably as we look at the types of venture deals and firms that one may actually encounter in practice.

Unlike buyouts, which may be classified broadly by the type and size of the deal, most venture transactions are very similar in their form, while variations in size tend (except during periods of irrational exuberance) to be a function of stage (see below). It is therefore much more useful to categorise them in terms of their sector and stage. However, geography also plays a part, particularly when we look at historic trends (though I believe that this will play much less of a role in the future, and may indeed even become irrelevant as venture capital becomes a truly global industry) and we will need to look in particular at the differences between the traditional "US" and "European" venture models.

I should mention one point before we begin. In Chapter 1 I presented buyout and venture as two distinct and separate entities, and indeed they are. However, as with much of private equity, the truth often lies not in black or white but in the intervening shades of grey. I will be discussing early stage venture capital almost exclusively, partly because it represents what has become known as the classic US venture model, but also because it is the easiest with which to demonstrate the way in which venture deals are actually transacted and developed, and last but not least simply because it is so much fun. However, as we will see, there are firms which quite legitimately specialise in later stage venture and here the rigid differentiations which I laid down earlier begin to creak at the seams a little. For example, the way in which returns can be earned across the portfolio is different (more uniform in the case of later stage, more explosively binary in the case of early stage) and debt can enter the equation. There are specialist providers of venture debt both in the form of equipment finance (although traditionally in the USA this has been handled by the equipment manufacturers themselves) and in the form of working capital facilities for companies which have already become profitable, or at least cashflow positive. I mention this point at the outset for the sake of completeness, but I will not be seeking to labour it, not least because I do not want to confuse the very significant distinctions between what really are two very different investment areas. Witness the fact that it is almost unheard-of for the same private equity firm to conduct both venture and buyout transactions, at least within the same fund (Apax did so until recently, but this is a very rare exception indeed; a very few others, such as Doughty Hanson and Carlyle, have done so but with separate teams and separate funds).

BACKING NEW APPLICATIONS, NOT NEW TECHNOLOGY

Before we begin our detailed look at venture, however, let us clear up one widespread misconception. There is a popular belief that venture capital exists to fund the development of new technology. This is quite simply untrue. Indeed, I am not aware of a single professional venture capitalist who would be prepared to invest in pure technology risk of the "when I switch it on, will it work?" variety. What a venture manager is looking for is someone who is looking to develop a new application of an existing technology, which has itself been tried and tested. They are, in other words, not prepared to take the "when I switch it on, will it work?" technology risk, but they are prepared, if appropriate, to take the "when I show it to people, will they buy it?" market risk.

You will notice that I said "if appropriate". In these two words lie the further level of distinction between what venture capital actually is and what the misinformed believe it to be. Venture capitalists are looking for a new application of an existing technology that addresses a commercially significant need or problem. Ideally, the entrepreneurs will have worked in an industry sector and will there have experienced a particular problem to which they believe they now have the answer; this will, for example, be the classic model of a venture-backed enterprise software company. Unfortunately, many ideas which are put forward for venture funding are technology focused rather than commercially focused. As one former chairman of the Irish Software Association told me a little while ago: "every year I see two hundred solutions in search of a problem". The world is full of engineers who believe they can build a better mousetrap, but it is not the function of venture capital to support their endeavours.

The words "commercially significant" also merit further consideration, since it is here that much of a venture firm's due diligence may take place. If a venture company is to produce the sort of potential returns for its investors that the venture model requires (we will see later that this is about 25 times capital invested) then it needs to be able to grow quickly to a significant size and thus the size of the potential market represented by the identified need or problem is crucial, as is the likely presence of any competitors. The word "size" here not only refers to the totality of the market, but also the number of participants; a product or service for which there may only be a dozen customers worldwide (albeit any customer is likely to be prepared to pay large amounts of money for it) is clearly an inherently riskier proposition than one which can be marketed to tens of thousands.

Given the above, it is unfortunate that such a jaundiced and inaccurate view of venture capital should still prevail. Yes, of course there is risk in investing in venture companies, but given the right investment planning techniques capital risk can be reduced to virtually nothing at the LP level,[1] and given the right mind-set and experience it is actually significantly lower than people may believe even at the level of a single venture fund; I know of one professional venture fund investor who over a period of more than a decade did not invest in a single fund which failed to return its capital. We will look at this in more detail when we consider venture returns.

Historically, this was not always the case, the most obvious exception being drug discovery projects, although the purist might argue that even here this is rarely total innovation, since the research team will frequently be moving onwards or outwards from protein or chemical

---

[1] See *Multi Asset Class Investment Strategy*, already referenced.

combinations which are already known to have certain properties. However, the venture industry, particularly in the USA, has shown an enviable ability to develop and evolve by abandoning anything which does not work well, and even this area has now been largely abandoned, at least in terms of early stage deals. Again, we will look at this point in more detail later, since it is one where geography has a part to play.

Just to be clear, then, there are actually two reasons why professional investors will shun technology creation, as opposed to technology application or development. The first is the technology risk issue. The second is that the research teams involved will usually be preoccupied with investigating a particular scientific area without any particular idea of how this might be applied to commercial uses. It was notable, for example, how little success was enjoyed by the various "nanotechnology" funds which went out fundraising a few years ago.

CLASSIFICATION BY SECTOR

Having disposed of this misconception, let us turn now to examining the different sectors within which venture operates. There are basically three of these: IT, Telecommunications (Telecoms) and Life Science (sometimes called Healthcare or Biotech). Historically a significant amount of venture funding was also directed towards retail products and services (a branded chain of steak restaurants in the USA comes to mind), but I do not propose to consider this further as it is now largely of only historic interest. Of course, many internet-related projects are aimed at the retail market, but I will consider these within the IT and/or Telecoms sectors.

IT

Sometimes just referred to as "technology" deals, these were traditionally divided into "hardware" and "software" (since the technology referred to refers exclusively to computers). However, I must say right at the outset that it is becoming increasingly difficult to distinguish between IT and Telecom deals. These categories were dreamt up two decades ago, when the average PC could have an 8-bit 4 MHz processor and only 64 KB of memory. The computer then was seen as a means of storing and processing information and was typically used for word-processing and spreadsheet work. Today, of course, the computer is viewed primarily as a communication device attached to a global network, and processing and storage capabilities are regarded as commodities, and cheap commodities at that.

So, while I will honour the conventions of venture deal classification for the purposes of this book, please be aware that today the issue is frequently not clear-cut. How would you classify, for example, a new email application for Microsoft Outlook? Or a new development in wireless networking?

In the early days of venture capital, technology deals could encompass the development of a new computer itself, or new computer peripherals (there were repeated attempts, for example, to develop an alternative to the QWERTY keyboard), but it is extremely unlikely that such projects would even rate a meeting with a venture firm these days. There is general acceptance that the basic infrastructure of computer technology is cast in stone, and that the global market is dominated by a handful of immensely powerful players. There is perhaps one exception to this, and it lies in the field of memory. The computer hard disk suffers from a particular problem in that the speed at which data can be moved around and processed within the computer is many times faster (some people suggest by as much as a million times) than the speed with which the disk can be mechanically accessed. This might be thought of as a sort of holy grail of computer design, since even a small improvement could have a dramatic effect on performance. There are currently experiments taking place with different storage media and techniques; however, this probably falls foul of the "technology risk" objections referred to above and is best left to the R&D departments of big computer companies.

These days, hardware deals are more likely to feature chips, data connectors and so forth, although there can be some hardcore production engineering involved as well, such as vacuum automation systems for chip and storage disk manufacturing. It is this hardware section which perhaps strays most insidiously into the Telecoms sector. How would one classify things such as radio baseband processors for wireless networks, or some of the advanced laser components for fibre optic communication? The latter is almost certainly "Telecoms", but the former could really be either.

Software companies can fall into various different categories. First there are the so-called "tools" companies which provide utilities which can be used in the design both of hardware and software (particularly where the latter is object oriented), and also in the construction and operation of systems. Where these are used to diagnose and cure particular operating problems, they are sometimes referred to as utilities.

Second there is the world of integrating software, which has become a very hot area. Banks and financial institutions are a particular market here. Most banks have legacy systems going back many years (dating from the days of green screens!) and have over time bolted on other systems around them, resulting in a huge mish-mash of largely incompatible systems. For most banks it is currently impossible to pull together on screen the full information for any one customer if that customer has a spread of accounts ranging across, say, currency, trade finance, leasing, investments, etc. These will mostly be dealt with separately and in many cases at least two of the various systems will be unable to speak to each other.

This is another "holy grail" area but subject to a large Catch-22. While banks would love to have an integrated system to cope with the demand of new regulatory environments (such as Basel II), they are understandably reluctant to close down their legacy systems and subject themselves to the disruption which we all know attends the introduction of a new computer system, particularly since during any such period of disruption they could hardly avoid being in breach of exactly those regulatory requirements which they were seeking to satisfy. This has in turn led to some innovative proposed solutions in the form of software that can act as a "front-end", making it look as if an integrated system were in place but in fact operating more as a reporting agent, burrowing into each system to extract the required information.

Operating software used to form quite a large part of venture portfolios, but this is another area which has become of largely historic interest since most operating software is now proprietary and the sector is dominated by one huge player, with whom few are prepared to tangle. Kleiner Perkins, one of the most successful venture firms in history, has a maxim "don't stand in the path of an oncoming train", which means "never invest in anything which may compete with Microsoft".

Application software, too, has become less attractive of late. An early success story (Sage, which developed some of the first PC-based accounting packages would be a good example), this has become increasingly standardised, based on the Windows platform and bundled with new computers. There are still opportunities here but they are tending now to be based around the email, chat and contact management spaces.

There were great hopes for enterprise software (i.e., software specially tailored to the needs of a particular industry) in years gone by, but these have been largely unfulfilled, despite some individual success stories. One of the problems here has been industry consolidation, with the number of potential customers in some areas (insurance companies, banks, etc.) shrinking rapidly. At the other end of the scale, where an industry has an almost infinite number of customers, then venture companies have seemed unable to handle the scale involved, resulting in the enterprise software space becoming highly fragmented, with a large number of small players (perhaps a roll-up opportunity for a buyout group?), and copyright piracy has also been a significant problem, particularly in countries such as China.

Where software is being created, particular problems are faced by venture capitalists. The process itself must be rigorously controlled, but a balance must be struck so as not to alienate the individual developers; as a matter of temperament, software engineers tend not to respond well to discipline. At the very least, a daily development log must be maintained (and it is worth considering hiring one individual to do nothing else) so that in the event of the loss of any one developer or batch of code everything can be recreated.

The other challenge lies in successfully marrying "a bunch of guys writing code"[2] with people who can sell the product, and people who can run the business. Too often, one or more of the software engineers will believe that they can fill these roles themselves, and may be allowed to do so by inexperienced or irresolute venture capitalists.

Telecoms

This has probably been the most exciting sector in recent years given first the birth of the internet and then its rapid growth, fuelled in part by the other big factor: fast, affordable broadband. Over the last decade or so we have seen some major technological changes. Analogue communication has given way to digital. Fax has given way to email. Traditional cabling systems have in many cases given way to fibre optics, while even old-fashioned copper can carry ADSL. Data

---

[2] As I once heard software companies described at a venture firm's annual meeting.

communications have overtaken voice conversations on both national and international networks.

Then of course there is the whole mobile world, which was part of the analogue to digital progression noted above and has now spawned both 3G, properly so-called (UMTS) and also GPRS, which is colloquially referred to as third generation but is in reality 2½G. We now routinely use mobile devices to access email and the internet, while wireless technology such as Bluetooth enables machines to talk to each other, and wi-fi creates wireless networks that allow us to use laptop computers to access the internet no matter where we are. Yes, there are problems which have not yet been solved, but for the most part these are now practical, commercial, problems such as the unwillingness of incumbent telcos either to provide fast, affordable broadband themselves or to allow others to do so over their networks, or the stubbornness of operators (including many of the newer entrants) to price wireless broadband as the commodity that it is, rather than as a luxury product. The technical problems have been largely overcome, though much remains to be done in the field of UMTS.

These are all fertile ground for entrepreneurs and thus also for the venture capital community. One particularly popular area of interest (so much so that it became a bubble) was the whole of the optical technology field. There were some exciting successes early on in this area: Chromatis, a metro optical networking company which started life in Israel was bought by Lucent in May 2000 for $4.5 billion in stock, while in the same month Altitun, a Swedish tuneable laser company was bought by ADC for nearly $900 M, representing a multiple of over 80 times the invested capital of its local venture backers. Incidentally, I have deliberately chosen these two examples rather than their many US counterparts since the ability of venture capitalists outside the USA to create home run companies has been largely overlooked. We will look at this in more detail later.

Particular problems to which engineers have turned their attention in the optical field have included the ability to split an optical beam into many different signals without any leakage from one to another, and the need to boost the signal at regular intervals to prevent it degrading. Then there is the whole area of the optical routers and switches which are needed to transform an optical signal into a wire-carried one, and vice versa. In the early days, many companies sought to develop the individual items (tuneable lasers being a good example) which went into these devices; this became known as the subcomponents field. Today, however, companies that look to provide the whole device can be called components companies by way of distinction. I mention this specifically since it is not an obvious use of the terminology – it would seem more logical to call them component and device companies, respectively.

The optical bubble was as devastating in its way as the dot.com bubble, though because it happened in a specialist area with which consumers had no dealing, and which was of interest only to engineers and venture capitalists, it received relatively little publicity. In fairness, the problem was not just too many venture capitalists putting too much money into too many optical companies (though this certainly happened "in spades", as the Americans say). More pernicious was the conduct of the incumbent telcos in both Europe and the USA in denying new operators access to their exchanges. This prevented the new entrants from rolling out the high speed networks for which they were purchasing technology from the venture-backed start-ups, with the result that most of them simply ran out of money and went out of business. Since the telcos themselves were very resistant to the idea of using the new technology (since they could enjoy the position of being able to sell obsolete technology to their existing customers on a monopoly basis at a high price), the venture companies were faced with a nightmare situation of a dramatic fall in the number of carriers, who were the natural customers for their product. Some were able to sell to equipment manufacturers, and this in turn prompted a wave of corporate acquisitions such as the Lucent/Chromatic transaction, but this proved short-lived as the full potential downside of the market crash became evident and large corporations the world over slashed their budgets for R&D or the purchase of new technology. As this last window closed, the optical sector entered a nuclear winter from which it is only slowly emerging.

Another area of interest is mobile telephony, where the Nordic area, and particularly Finland has traditionally led the way. Mobile applications have featured in many venture capital portfolios and there is some geographic variation here; for example, SMS messaging has been rampant in Europe for years, particularly among younger people, but took some time to catch on in America. One showing considerable novelty value was a computer dating application that was beta tested among the gay community in Los Angeles. Having fed your preferences (history does not record what categories there might have been) into the system, the application would track your location and if you were found to be within a certain number of feet of someone whose preferences matched your own then both mobiles would ring simultaneously. Although the traditional set of mobile technology has been the Nordic area, many innovative applications have originated in Israel.

During the period leading up to the collapse of the dot.com bubble some venture firms also backed large systems companies, including businesses which were actually installing and operating high speed metro networks for business customers. However these proved poor investments, as the large amounts of capital required to fund their roll-out could not be justified in terms of the ultimate valuation of the business, so I doubt whether we shall see companies of this type in venture portfolios in future.

Life Science

Life Science has traditionally been divided into two broad areas, although this classification is no longer exhaustive. The first is the drug discovery area, which as the name suggests involves backing research teams who wish to spin out of university laboratories or the R&D departments of large drug companies. This is probably very much the stereotype view of what venture capital is all about on the part of those with no actual knowledge of the area. In fact, as we have already seen, there is very little truth in such an image at all.

The other main area of specialty is usually just called "devices", and as the name suggests dwells on the various sorts of devices which are used in the medical profession, ranging from stents (the tiny tubes inserted into blood vessels during surgery), through diagnostic testing equipment to large, expensive scanners. Perhaps the most exotic variants I have encountered were a pump plumbed into the penis to facilitate erections (this was in the days before Viagra), and what was enthusiastically described as "a flight simulator for dentists" – an artificial replica of the human mouth on which dentists could practise their gentle arts.

As I said, these two areas are no longer exhaustive. The major change has been brought about by the success of the human genome project which, as one leading venture capitalist told me "means that everyone is suddenly playing with a new deck of cards". In addition to pure research projects in the genetic field (usually involving identifying the exact genetic combination which causes a particular condition, and whether this becomes defective in some way which can be reversed, thus forestalling the onset of the condition), there is now specialist genetic software which can greatly speed up this process, as well as assisting drug development by suggesting compounds which are known to have worked (or are close to compounds which have worked) before, and anticipating possible side-effects in time for a line of research to be discontinued early, with consequent savings in time and money.

Another area which has grown up is that of specialist services in the healthcare arena, particularly in the field of testing, analysis and diagnostics. Interestingly, this area has also been of interest to buyout firms, driven in part by the trend for both hospitals and large companies to outsource service provision to specialist third parties.

Life Science investing has increasingly become a tale of two continents. While there is little publicly available data to back this up, apocryphal evidence and my own personal experience strongly suggest that Life Science venture deals have performed better in Europe than they have in the USA, both in absolute terms (i.e., that European Life Science deals have achieved better multiples on average than their American counterparts) and also in relative terms (i.e., that Life Science has generally performed better than technology deals in Europe, with the opposite being the case in America). In fairness to the American venture community, however, it must be admitted that this latter point loses much of its force when one considers that technology venture returns in Europe (at least as recorded in the available industry databases[3]) have been extremely disappointing for the most part. Whatever the case, this has led to a number of developments.

It used to be the case that venture firms would routinely practise both Technology and Life Science within the same fund (this was less universal in America, but still a frequent occurrence). In the USA, however, this practice has been almost entirely discontinued. Publicly, the stated reason for this is usually a desire for focus, and the desirability of all partners within the venture firm to be able to understand and discuss everyone else's deals. Privately, the reason is clear. Rightly or wrongly, Life Science is seen as having under-performed, and the technology-focused GPs want to be free to pursue their business without this perceived drag on their fund returns. Consequently, most venture firms, and that includes just about all the leading ones, have either hived off

---

[3] We will see later that these consistently under-state European venture returns, but this does not change the point I am making here, only lessens its extent a little.

their Life Science teams to become separate firms, or closed them down entirely.

I can remember being at the annual meeting of a venture group in California sometime around mid-2001, when there had been a sudden flurry of interest in Life Science ventures by many LPs, and the GP who was on the podium at the time describing the current situation said "you know things must be bad when Life Science starts to look attractive". I mention this only to illustrate the attitude towards Life Science that is sincerely felt by many in the American venture community.

While it may seem a very sweeping (not to mention somewhat jaundiced) statement, there are a number of very valid reasons behind this attitude, and it may be worth taking a little time to consider some of them.

Chief amongst them is the whole question of the approval process for many Life Science products. The FDA approval process for new drugs and other therapeutic products, for example, can be very lengthy and involve clinical trials lasting years rather than months. Given that a new drug has a limited patent period during which to earn royalties, this has been a major stumbling block to achieving venture-type returns, particularly when coupled with the very large amounts of money which such a venture company typically requires. The combination of a long holding period, high capital requirement and limited income period make it very difficult to justify this as a legitimate venture capital activity, particularly given the extreme product risk involved (it has been estimated that as few as one in every hundred thousand pharmaceutical research projects ever result in a commercially available drug). In truth, "pharma" itself mirrors closely the early stage US venture model, where the occasional home run such as Viagra or Zantac justifies the very many failures and also-rans. However, here much competing activity is carried on by the big pharma companies themselves, and so there is the added complication that as a venture firm you do not even have access to all the potential home runs from which to make your selection. This latter point is often overlooked.

The arguments against other forms of Life Science activity are less clear-cut. There seems no obvious reason, for example, why medical devices, particularly of the external and/or diagnostic variety, which require a very light touch on the licensing tiller, should not have the potential to be successful on a similar scale to other forms of technology projects. While the data is not available to support this, it would be my instinct that what is lacking here is widespread genuine home run potential. An application such as Google, Amazon or eBay can meet needs and change behaviour patterns across the globe. In the early days of chip development a relatively small advance in microchip technology could increase the power and speed of a computer by two, or even ten times. Short of an artificial brain or a functional suspended animation machine, it is difficult to conceive of a medical device that could have a similar impact. Since, as we will see, it is home runs that drive venture returns, then it may well be that this is a major reason why US venture firms have shunned this sector in recent years.

There is another possible reason which is more nebulous, but I think still valid. America has led the world in technological advancement in information technology, particularly in software, applications and hardware bundling (not necessarily chip technology, much of which was developed in the Far East, and certainly not in Telecoms, where much pioneering work was done in Europe). Thus, if one was able to establish a leading position across the USA as a provider of, say, an internet search engine (Google, Yahoo), or operating software (Microsoft) or bundled hardware (Dell), then a position of global leadership followed more or less automatically. In other words, the amount of proactive marketing in different parts of the world that was required in the very early stages of the company's life is probably negligible. That is not to take anything away from the achievements of such companies, which have been impressive on a truly staggering scale; I am simply seeking to draw a distinction.

Compare and contrast this with the position of a young medical devices company, perhaps the one I referred to above which developed a flight simulator for dentists. Almost from the day when they had test product available, they needed dedicated sales people around the globe trying to sell sometimes individual machines to teaching hospitals, wrestling with different languages, buying practices and regulations. That same teaching hospital would probably have bought Windows software for each new computer without even stopping to think about it, and without Microsoft having to make that sale specifically to them. Thus, companies where it is possible to establish a position of global leadership without having to step outside their home market in their early days clearly enjoy a significant advantage, and the companies I have mentioned above have done a great job of exploiting that advantage to its maximum potential.

So, yes, there are some valid reasons why Life Science has lost favour in the USA (although it still has a dedicated following amongst many

LPs), but I would pose two questions to which I do not know the answers, but could guess at the likely outcomes. First, if US technology venture had not been so dramatically successful during the mid-1990s, would the bifurcation in US venture and the relegation of Life Sciences to perceived second place necessarily have happened? Second, if one accepts for the sake of argument that it is no longer possible for any LP new to the asset class to access any of the leading technology venture funds, then which is preferable (in US terms): to invest in upper quartile Life Science, or to invest in second or third quartile Technology?

In Europe, the pattern has been different. Life Science still routinely forms half of the activities of many leading venture firms (Innovations Kapital in Sweden and Sofinnova in France being two obvious examples) and in addition there are some very respected firms who specialise in nothing but Life Science investing (Health Cap in Sweden, currently investing Fund V, is one of the recognised leaders in this field, though multi-stage rather than just early stage). As mentioned above, this is largely because the sector's performance has been viewed in a much more friendly light. It may also have something to do with the fact that most of the world's leading pharma companies are based in Europe, and that perhaps there are thus more spin-out opportunities available; indeed, Actelion, one of Europe's most lucrative venture deals to date (a huge success for Joel Besse and the Life Science team at Atlas Venture[4]) was just such a transaction.

However, notwithstanding these apparent differences it is fair to say that drug discovery deals have been declining in Europe too. In truth, it was probably always difficult for European venture firms, with their small fund sizes, to finance these sorts of undertakings and there is in any event a growing feeling that these projects are probably best left to large pharma companies or university research labs, at least in their early stages.

CLASSIFICATION BY STAGE

We have just looked at one of the two main ways of classifying venture deals, namely by sector. The other is by stage, and this is less clear-cut than the former, since there is considerable looseness of terminology.

---

[4] Actelion went public on the Swiss stock market in April 2000, just 2 years after its first venture financing round (there were only ever two) at a valuation in excess of $800M, reputedly gaining its venture backers a money multiple in excess of 200×.

Table 6.1 The venture universe by sector and stage

Life Sciences	Telecoms	IT
Seed	Seed	Seed
Early	Early	Early
Mid	Mid	Mid
Late	Late	Late

Venture deals, unlike buyout deals for the most part, will enjoy successive rounds of financing, and the point in the company's development when each of these rounds occurs will determine whether such a round is, for example, "early" or "mid". Certain venture firms specialise in different stages; thus a late stage firm might only invest for the first time in the fourth or fifth round, while a seed firm will tend to invest heavily at the beginning and then seek subsequently to invest the bare minimum necessary to maintain a significant equity position (at least in Europe, where the availability of seed capital is severely limited).

At the risk of stating the obvious, the valuation of the company will typically rise with each successive round as its perceived risk decreases, and thus in theory the gains available to the venture capitalists involved will correspondingly diminish. It is a classic example of the relationship between risk and reward.

Broadly, the venture world divides by stage into seed, early stage, mid-stage and late stage. Thus, the venture universe might be thought of as a grid (Table 6.1).

Let us take a look at each stage in turn, and we need to be quite clear what we mean by the relevant term in each case.

Seed

This term is particularly corrupted in Europe, where a lot of venture capitalists claim to be "seed" investors who are really nothing of the kind.

The word "seed" carries very strong implications of a total start-up, and in my view that should be the sense of the word adopted by the industry as a whole to avoid confusion. However, while this is broadly true, industry practice also recognises as a "seed" round one which occurs very early in the life of a company but not quite at the outset if there has been an "angel" round to fund the actual start-up.

An angel round is one put together by angel investors, i.e., investors who are not professional venture capitalists, and there are important differences in practice and possible consequences between the USA and Europe relating to angel rounds which merit a separate section on this below.

I must apologise for the confusion that this introduces into proceedings, not least because it can have a knock-on effect so far as the classification of subsequent rounds is concerned. However, this confusion is not of my making and I am simply trying to clarify as best I can the obfuscation that industry practice has created. There are many venture firms who claim that a "seed" round is the first one in which at least one professional venture firm participates, even if this happens a year or two into the life of the company. While every situation is different, and it is hard to lay down universal rules, I have problems with this definition.

I agree that in general the first round in which a venture firm participates will be a seed round (particularly in America). However, where there has been a long period between the start-up of a company and the first institutional round (as is frequently the case in Europe) then I do not believe that this is a proper use of the term, and I would much prefer the phrase "A Round" to be employed. How long is too long? Well, definitely if a company is generating revenues and probably even if they have test product out with alpha or beta customers. The word "seed" implies the very early stages of a company's existence and we must not lose sight of this.

So I would suggest the following as an answer to the question "was this a seed round?". In any particular case:

- Where the company is a genuine start-up: definitely.
- Where the company has yet to produce its product or service in even alpha testing form: probably.
- Where a company has product in test: probably not.
- Where a company is generating revenues, no matter how small: definitely not.

As the story of seed funding unfolds, differences between European and US practice become very stark. It is probably not going too far to say that with a very few honourable exceptions there are actually no European venture firms who are pursuing genuine seed stage opportunities. To understand why this is, I am afraid we need to take quite a lengthy excursion into the US venture model.

THE US MODEL

As we will see in a later chapter, so far as historic returns are concerned then venture is the mirror image of buyout; not only have American returns been better, they have been quite dramatically better. This has given rise to an impassioned debate about whether there is something intrinsically superior about the way in which US venture firms do business, or whether environmental factors produced a "happy hunting time" in US venture in the same way that they may well have done in European buyout. We will be examining this debate later, but suffice to say for the moment that the answer, as usual, is "some of both", but we must at this point examine the former of these points, since we cannot sensibly discuss seed funding unless we understand what the US model is.

There are a number of components to the US venture model, and although they interact to the point that they form a cohesive whole, we will look at each of these in turn for ease of discussion. They are (1) a focus on the seed stage, (2) a home run mentality and (3) "value add".

Seed Stage Focus

As we will see shortly, two of the things which US venture capitalists look to do is to achieve as high a money multiple as possible and to add value in actually building a company alongside an entrepreneur. Both such things are facilitated by trying to invest wherever possible at the seed stage. This boosts the chance of being able to achieve a high money multiple (because one is getting into the company at the lowest possible valuation) and also allows the venture capitalists to build the company from day one in the way they believe it should be built, rather than getting involved at a later stage and possibly having to unscramble unsatisfactory arrangements that may already have been put in place.

In order to increase the possibility of sourcing quality seed stage dealflow, and also to increase the chances of being able to work with experienced company builders in that seed stage dealflow, many US venture firms adopt an "EIR programme". This is an intriguing and exciting process which has not as yet been widely copied in Europe. It consists of finding three or four experienced entrepreneurs (who have preferably been backed previously by the firm in successful ventures and are now "going round again") and designating them as "entrepreneurs in residence" (EIRs). They are encouraged to spend time in the firm's offices talking to start-up teams about their ideas. The aim is partly that they might be able to join one of these teams (probably to lead it) if they like the idea sufficiently, but this is more the province of so-called "venture partners". The real objective with an EIR is that he should be persuaded actually to start his next company right there in the venture firm's offices, using their facilities and in full discussion with the GPs and with every expectation of being funded by them. This process is called "incubation" and is very different from the way in which the term is used in Europe, where frequently all that is provided is a glorified business centre, with little hands-on support.

While it is difficult to be certain, since no performance figures for individual funds are publicly available broken down by stage, there is a general belief that it is seed stage funds which have consistently scored the best returns in the USA. This is borne out by the available industry figures. We will be looking at this in more detail in a later chapter, but let us glance quickly in passing at the TVPI figures for US venture since inception broken down by stage (Table 6.2).

You will see that this shows roughly what one would expect, with the fund's money multiple declining slightly the later the stage at which its investment focus lies. I appreciate that these differences may seem slight in view of the possible difference in the perceived risk of each stage, but they tell only part of the story, since the real excitement of venture returns lies at the upper margins. The best ever early stage fund recorded by VentureXpert had a fund multiple of over 28×, while the most successful late stage one enjoyed a multiple of 14.6×; the best balanced, i.e., multi-stage fund was in the middle as one might expect at just over 16×, and I think that these figures present a much more potent view of what might be expected.

Table 6.2 US venture returns by stage; TVPI since inception, 1969 to 2005 inclusive

Stage	Capital Weighted Average	Upper Quartile
Early/Seed	1.57	2.56
Early	1.58	2.29
Balanced	1.47	2.23
Late	1.42	2.09

Source: Thomson Financial's VentureXpert.
Note: "Balanced" refers to funds which invest at all stages.

Home Run Mentality

This phrase is bandied about continually when discussion turns to American venture practice, but often with little real understanding of what lies behind it. Briefly, as we shall be discussing in more detail in the next chapter, US venture returns have been dominated by a small number of very big winners – the home runs. Publicly available evidence is sketchy, but leading US venture capital Fund of Funds manager Horsley Bridge released into the public domain some years ago their analysis of their own database (which is generally recognised as being the best in the industry), which was that slightly less than 5% of all companies by cost produced 80% of returns by value, and as these conclusions have been widely quoted and never challenged I think we may safely adopt them.

A difference which has often been claimed to exist between US and European venture capitalists (with much justification, in my view) was that American GPs recognised this and adapted their approach accordingly, whereas European GPs did not. I do not want to get drawn into this discussion too deeply at this stage, as it is one we shall be having in the next chapter, but let us note for our present purposes that this involves trying to grow every company in which they invest into a very large company, instead of just a medium-sized company, and not considering for investment in the first place any company which does not appear to have this potential. It also follows that, unless they have lost confidence in a company, they will resist the temptation of an early exit, preferring to "swing for the fence".

"Value Add"

This is an American phrase that would perhaps be more elegantly expressed as "added value". It describes that ability of American venture capitalists to get closely involved with a company's development on a hands-on basis, using their own personal knowledge and contacts gained in many cases when they themselves were an entrepreneur who had founded a start-up company. It is key to the US venture model, and is the one element of it which has in general been undeniably largely absent from European venture activity. When an American entrepreneur tries to attract the attention of a venture firm he is not going there primarily for money, but for the first-hand operating experience of its GPs. A European entrepreneur, by contrast, will be desperate for money from any source, since there is much less of it available for early stage companies in Europe, and will not expect operating experience to be on offer.

THE US MODEL COMES TO EUROPE

Since we are dealing with the US model at this point, it is only fair to point out, since it does actually impact on the question of stage preference, that while the above distinctions between US and European venture were largely valid on a historical basis, they are becoming less so with every passing year. There are an increasing number of European venture firms who recognise the merits of the US model and are making great efforts to apply it in Europe. This will be of particular relevance when we come to consider venture returns in later chapters.

Why European Venture Capital Firms have Avoided the Seed Stage

If you do not have the first-hand operating experience to bring value add to the party then the picture changes dramatically. From being viewed as an area of opportunity in the USA [because you can (1) get in at a low valuation and (2) build the company as you would like it to be from day one], it is viewed as an area of risk in Europe and thus an area to be avoided, rather than sought out. "Come back when you've got some customers" is a commonly heard refrain, according to the first-hand accounts which I hear from entrepreneurs.

Incidentally, it is here that a lot of the confusion over terminology arises. There are some European firms who are honest enough to say "we don't do seed", but there are many others who seek to portray the image of being very early stage investors without having either the skills or the inclination to do so, and they do this by calling what are essentially A Rounds "seed". I can only repeat my own belief, which is drawn from many years of practical experience, and let me phrase it very carefully: in my experience there are almost no independent, professional venture firms in Europe who offer genuine seed round funding. There are a very few who do, and I happily acknowledge the fact, but they are very, very few in the context of the industry as a whole.

CLASSIFICATION BY STAGE, CONTINUED

Early Stage Investing

We discussed above the difference between "seed" and "early". I take "early" as meaning a genuine A Round together with a possible B Round if the A Round was very small and/or very early in a company's life, and/or the B Round quickly followed the A Round. As with so many aspects of private equity this is an art not a science, and instinct and experience are probably more important than scientific analysis.

It is at early stage that the bulk of European firms enter the fray. In fairness, it makes comparatively little difference in valuation terms, as shortage of capital ensures that there is usually little difference between the pre-money valuation of a company in the early stages of its life and the post-money valuation of the preceding round, but in the USA it can make a dramatic difference.

Mid- and Late Stage Investing

The skills required for a later stage venture investor are different from those needed at early stage, and start to approach those that one might find in a buyout firm. Financial analysis becomes increasingly important, and technology skills and sector knowledge less so. Debt can also enter the picture, either by way of working capital facilities (if the company has the cashflow to justify it) or by way of equipment financing (which might actually be present from a very early stage of the company's existence in some circumstances).

Please remember that the term "mezzanine" is often used to describe very late stage (typically pre-IPO) venture investing in the USA, whereas in Europe this term is used exclusively to describe convertible debt, almost exclusively for buyout transactions.

SUMMARY

- The main differences between buyout and venture are set out in Chapter 1.
- Venture can be classified by sector and by stage.
- The three main sectors are Life Sciences, Information Technology ("IT") and Telecommunications ("Telecoms"). The latter two are

frequently referred to together as "Technology" to distinguish them from Life Sciences and the distinction between them is becoming increasingly blurred.

- The main stages of investment are seed, early, mid and late. Again, the distinction between them is frequently blurred and they can mean different things to different individuals. In particular, the usage of "seed" and "early" is often confused, especially in Europe.
- Historic returns in the USA have been driven by a small number of very large winners, which are referred to as home runs. Strictly speaking a home run is any investment that returns the entire committed capital of the fund which invests in it at least once, but in practice it has come to mean any investment that returns over 25 times its capital ("25×").
- It is believed that amongst the leading US venture firms, about 5% of companies by cost generate about 80% of returns by value.
- The traditional US venture model recognises this and preaches (1) a focus on investing as early as possible, preferably at the seed stage, (2) a focus on producing home runs, not medium-size companies and (3) value add, which means the ability to contribute personal company building skills on a hands-on basis.
- The US model has not historically been practised in Europe, but various European firms are now seeking to implement it, and have in fact been doing so for some years.
- European firms have in general avoided the seed stage, which has been seen in Europe as an area of risk rather than as an area of opportunity.
- The skills required for later stage venture investing start to approach those relevant for buyout firms, with financial skills becoming more important and technology and sector experience becoming less so.

7

How to Analyse Venture

We have seen that there are three main drivers of buyout returns: earnings, earnings multiples and the use of debt (usually known as either leverage or gearing, depending on what side of the Atlantic you inhabit). These drivers arise naturally from the way in which buyouts are transacted, and in particular they reflect the underlying financial engineering that can make the difference between an indifferent buyout and a really exceptional one.

As we saw in the opening chapter, venture capital transactions have different characteristics, and operate in a different way (debt, for example, is rarely present, at least in early stage deals). Since the way in which their returns are generated is different, it follows that the drivers of those returns must also be different. So, what do we have to consider when looking at venture firms and their transactions?

THE FUNDAMENTALS

Money Multiples

Let me say at once that removing the debt factor renders the basic arithmetic of venture returns considerably more simple. In very basic terms, a venture capitalist buys shares in a company, hoping to be able later to sell those shares at a higher price, thus generating a profit. It is the relationship of the latter figure to the former (the price originally invested in the company in return for the shareholding) that generates the basic money multiple which lies at the heart of analysing venture returns.

Remember that we looked earlier at the various ways in which the money multiples of funds could be expressed? There are two very important points to bear in mind as we start to consider how actually to use these in practice. The first is that whatever money multiple we decide to use at the fund level, it can only have been generated in gross terms by the money multiples achieved on the fund's underlying portfolio companies. Note that I say "in gross terms" because of course before being made available to LPs there will be payments of management fee and (if and when appropriate) carried interest to be deducted first. The basic principle will always hold true, however. A venture fund, just like a buyout fund, can only ever be a composite of its individual transactions, and this is why we model them on a "bottom up" basis.

The second point is that there is typically only one way of calculating the money multiple which is earned on a company and that is by looking at the actual amount paid out and the actual amount received. Distinctions such as Total Value, etc., have traditionally been accorded little significance at the company level. For the purposes of simplicity, and also with a view to keeping discussion within the proper scope of this book, I propose to accept this view, but allow me to digress very briefly to point out why this might be a slightly dangerous assumption to make.

I say above that the way in which venture returns are made is by buying shares and selling them at a profit. Thus the money multiple is essentially the ratio between those two numbers. All this is true. However, let us consider a couple of different situations where such a measure is either unavailable or potentially misleading.

The first one will become obvious if you stop and think about the way in which a venture fund operates, and about the different ways in which we looked at fund level multiples. What do we do about companies which are current investments within the fund's portfolio, but which have not yet been sold? I do not want to get drawn into a discussion at this stage about how they will be valued, because we are going to look at this in detail a little later, but let us just note for the moment that we assume them to be worth what the venture capitalist says they are worth. Since at the end of the day they are going to be either written off or sold for some amount of money, then little harm is done, since sooner or later we will know the real figure and be able to use it. Thus everything comes out in the wash at the end of the day, but it does mean that both at the fund and the company level we can never be sure of exactly what the final multiple will be until the very last investment is fully exited.

The second one arises from the way in which companies are exited, particularly in the USA. Where a company is sold to a large corporation, then all or part of the consideration for the sale is frequently in shares (stock) of the acquiring company. Where these are readily saleable and do not represent too large a proportion of the total float, then this will not raise any significant issue; the individual vendors can simply sell those shares and pocket the resulting cash. However, there may be legal restraints, either agreed at the time or arising thereafter which can delay things significantly. For example, the acquirer may decide in the coming weeks or months to issue new shares, and this can cause regulatory headaches if a venture firm GP has been welcomed onto the board. Similarly they (and, by extension, their firm) may be barred from dealing in the company's shares at certain times, such as before publication of financial results.

If the portfolio company is exited by way of an IPO, then similar problems can occur with lock-up provisions, particularly in the USA where these may well be regulatory, rather than contractual, in origin. Whatever the case, there may well be a period of considerable uncertainty before all the venture fund's shares can be sold and the final price established. During the rampant equity market conditions of the late 1990s this could actually work to the venture firm's advantage, since the shares would usually be sold for considerably more than their original exit valuation. However, the reverse could also be true; I was personally involved in one venture transaction where the price finally achieved by some investors was only just over 10% of what had originally been anticipated.

So, I am happy to accept the simplistic approach but subject to these reservations. Certainly anyone who wishes to analyse venture funds on a sophisticated basis will be alive to these possibilities. At the end of the day, all that matters is the real number actually achieved, but there will always be those who either do not have the perception to realise this, or the patience to wait for it. In fairness, there will of course always be situations where LPs feel that they are forced to sell an existing interest (a "secondary") for some reason or other, and then of course this becomes a very major issue. We will examine this in more detail when we look specifically at the secondary market.

So, before we move on, let us be quite clear about what the money multiple is at the company level. It is simply the ratio between the total cash invested in a company and the total cash realised by disposing of that interest, no matter how many individual cashflows may be involved. For example, if we pay a total of $2.5 M into a portfolio company and we eventually receive back $5 M then the money multiple will be 2×. It is irrelevant for these purposes how many individual cashflows are involved, or over what period they take place, though this *will* become of great relevance when we move on to look at transaction IRRs.

Valuation

Having touched on this above, let us now turn our full attention to the vexed question of valuation.

"Vexed" partly because this is one of the major reservations voiced about venture returns, partly because very different issues apply in Europe compared with the USA, and finally because it is an issue which is (particularly in the USA) open to much abuse and uncertainty even though this is usually innocently arrived at.

Valuation as an Element of Stated Returns

One hears many reasons (excuses?) for not investing in private equity funds. One of them is that private equity returns contain a large element of illiquid and therefore unrealisable capital gain which is represented solely by a portfolio company having been written up by the GP. Similar accusations are levelled at asset classes such as property (real estate). While this is undeniably true, particularly in the case of venture and particularly in the USA (as we shall see in a minute, different considerations apply in Europe), it completely fails to grasp the true nature of venture returns, what they represent and how they should be used.

As I have pointed out many times before,[1] annual returns are irrelevant when considering how to measure private equity fund performance, not least because one is a hostage to circumstances so far as the J-curve is concerned. All that matters are long-term compound returns over time and, as we have seen, these are conventionally expressed in vintage year terms. IRRs measure cashflows; that is what they are designed for and they cannot operate in any other way. Yes, while a fund is not yet fully divested it is necessary to assume that the current valuation of the existing investments will automatically occur as a cashflow at the end of the period in question, but in what other way could this be handled?

Property returns customarily adopt an annual return approach and break down the return into capital gain and rental yield. There are two problems with adopting this approach, however. First, with private equity, unlike property, an investment is never made with the objective

---

[1] See *Multi Asset Class Investment Strategy*, already referenced.

of creating an income stream,[2] but for generating a capital gain. Second, wherever we are concerned with a closed-end fund (and this applies to property funds just as much as to private equity funds) then any notional but unrealised capital gain is essentially irrelevant as it will sooner or later be realised and become a cashflow back to the investor. So it is entirely appropriate to adopt a cashflow measure such as an IRR to analyse the overall return to the investor.

Private equity funds comprise a stream of cashflows and the true return of a fund can only be measured in retrospect, once all cashflows have been mapped and analysed. Any true private equity professional knows this. Attempts to impose mensural disciplines on a fund which has not yet run its full course may be necessary for periodic accounting purposes, but they will rarely give a true picture of what may actually transpire; certainly they will give little clue to the timing of likely cashflows and it is of course this timing that will have a crucial effect on the final IRR. It is in precisely this area of uncertainty that secondary players seek out value. Thus to criticise the stated returns of half-run funds as containing an element of unrealised valuation is analogous to criticising a long distance lorry driver for being unable to give a precise ETA for a journey of several hundred miles. All he can do is to provide an estimate based on the time he has taken to cover a certain distance to date and his own experience of what sort of road and traffic conditions he is likely to encounter on the rest of his journey. Of course, the closer he gets to his destination in terms of time and distance, the more accurate his estimates will become, and it is precisely the same with private equity funds.

As we will see below, this is in any event much less of an issue in Europe than it is in the USA, and there are measures that one can take to address unrealistic valuations in individual cases.

Differences in Valuation Approach between Europe and the USA

It is generally believed that the venture industry in the USA is ahead of Europe in terms of its development and this is undeniably true in most areas. When it comes to the field of valuation, however, Europe has led the way.

---

[2] Except for certain types of mezzanine investment and even here this rarely tells the whole story.

From the very early days of private equity in the UK, the BVCA operated valuation guidelines which had been prepared in consultation with accounting bodies, and similar guidelines were adopted by EVCA; the current version is now published jointly by the BVCA, EVCA and AFIC. Sadly, the development of subsequent versions has led to less, rather than more certainty.

Briefly, the original guidelines severely limited the ability of a GP to write up an investment, but provided various circumstances in which it *must* be written down by an arbitrary 25%. Note that there was typically no option here; it *had* to be written down by 25% if, for example, it missed its annual budget or other targets by a significant amount, and by further 25% tranches if similar circumstances reoccurred. The new guidelines have replaced brevity and clarity with verbosity and obfuscation. Evidently drafted by committee (a phrase which I have come to think of as almost an oxymoron) they talk at great length about the nebulous concept of "fair value", and while they list a great number of things which "*should*" be considered or which "*may*" indicate a decrease or increase in value", they provide few of the obligatory admonitions that were a hallmark of earlier versions.

There are two particular ironies here. The first is that these new guidelines were apparently prepared at the behest of the LP community,[3] which in my humble opinion beggars belief. Why should any rational LP who may be concerned about the level of venture valuations want guidelines which provide less, rather than more, certainty and more, rather than less, room for subjective manoeuvring by the GP? It may be significant that the working party which prepared the new guidelines did not include a single LP. For example, it would have seemed logical to include at least a couple of the large Fund of Funds managers, but these are conspicuous by their absence.

The second is that, it seems to me, particularly from reading the comments about funding rounds, what the Europeans have done is largely to adopt and reflect prevailing practice in the USA. Yet the difference between USA and European valuation methodology was one of the few genuine strategic advantages which the European venture industry enjoyed, so why throw it away for no good reason?

Be that as it may, it is certainly the case that historically European venture has been subject to a more restrictive valuation environment than its USA counterpart, and in most quarters is perceived as still

---

[3] At least, that is what I was told by a former chairman of the BVCA.

being so. It remains to be seen what will happen in the future, but the new European guidelines certainly loosen the shackles of any GP who wants to exercise a little creativity (sorry, subjective judgement).

In the USA guidelines exist too, but the difference is that these are of a purely advisory nature and many private equity firms do not adopt them. At least in Europe there is now almost universal acceptance that all private equity fund accounts will be prepared in accordance with the guidelines (and indeed this is usually a legal requirement imposed by the LPs through the medium of the LPA – it is most unlikely that any institutional investor would consider any fund which did not so undertake). The US guidelines are prepared by a body called the Private Equity Industry Guidelines Group[4] and published in association with the NVCA. Many of their recommendations are similar to what now appears in the European guidelines, but as these are neither mandatory nor widely adopted, I propose not to devote any further discussion to them.

Variability of Venture Valuations

Variability of valuation has been a particular problem in the USA, though to be fair this became only pronouncedly so during the technology bubble and in its immediate aftermath. To give you a real life example, I was a partner in an American Fund of Funds manager during this period and at one point three venture funds which had participated in the same funding round in the same company had it valued in their audited year end accounts at $960 M, $480 M and zero, respectively. Even more alarmingly, two of the three venture groups involved had the same audit firm (so, a resounding raspberry here for the accountancy profession, I am afraid). This is of course an extreme example, but it does illustrate just how severe a problem this can be. How can the same company be valued at the same time by one venture firm at $960 M and by another at zero? And what is an LP to do when confronted by such wildly differing assessments? Specifically, what figure is the LP to adopt for inclusion in its own accounts (particularly as "ask the auditors" does not seem to be a good approach)?

It was because of cases like this that many American LPs yearned for semi-compulsory valuation guidelines such as Europe already enjoyed, but I think it will be clear from the example given above that

---

[4] www.peigg.org.

it hardly helped matters that the audit community was found wanting. In situations like this surely it is they who should take the lead. Sadly, far from doing so they seemed to go to extraordinary lengths to avoid taking any responsibility whatever, helped in many cases by the terms of the relevant LPA. I served on one advisory committee, for example, where the GPs and the auditors tried to throw the burden of valuation onto the members of the advisory committee, who had no first-hand knowledge of the portfolio at all. Hopefully this is an area where progress will be made in the future. All it really needs is to have a provision in the LPA which says something to the effect: "in the event of any dispute or disagreement as to the valuation of any portfolio company, the auditors' view shall prevail" and then go on to detail what they should or should not take into account.

In fairness, I should point out that there may be perfectly genuine commercial reasons for a GP not to want to write down the value of a company. They may, for example, be in the throes of negotiating a new funding round, or even a disposal of the business. However, when it comes to a question of what value should be placed in a set of audited accounts I would suggest that one may be straying into fairly dangerous territory.

You might be forgiven for wondering why I have focused on this issue when writing about venture, but not about buyout. The answer is that it is rarely anything like so difficult an issue. For one thing, there will almost always be a publicly available earnings multiple (or range of multiples) against which to compare a buyout transaction. This approach is obviously irrelevant for a venture company which is not yet making any profits; there have been attempts to argue for turnover (revenue) multiples such as used to be popular in Germany before cashflow-based valuations caught on, but I would be very nervous of ascribing any scientific basis to this.

Second, the range of valuations within which a company can fluctuate is obviously vastly different, and thus the scope of the problem is dramatically bigger with venture deals. In an extreme case, a venture fund might invest in a company at an initial post-money valuation of, say, \$20 M and see it grow to several billion dollars. The range within which a buyout company will fluctuate is much narrower, unless it is a turnaround, or perhaps unless something dramatic and unexpected happens in its business environment.[5] Thus it probably does not matter

---

[5] This can happen. For instance, CVC bought a business in Spain which had a limited term contract for conducting the Spanish equivalent of the annual MOT check on motor vehicles. Unexpectedly, the Spanish government extended the term of the contract, thus significantly increasing the value of the company. The Great Train Robberies are another obvious example.

too much (at least during the life of the investment) if a buyout transaction has an earnings multiple of 17 attached to it as opposed to 18. It
does matter if a venture company is valued at $960 M as opposed
to zero.

Finally, as we saw when we looked at the analysis of buyout funds
and transactions, debt makes a key contribution to buyout returns
and in many cases the enterprise value of a business may not actually
change very much while the equity value could change considerably
(due to acquisition debt being repaid). With venture capital, the enterprise value is the only value which matters (since debt is normally
absent).

Pre-money and Post-money Valuations

Before we move on to discuss the nuts and bolts of how venture returns
are actually generated, it is important that we understand the difference
between pre-money and post-money valuations, since this is a constant
source of some confusion to those new to the asset class.

The distinction is best considered in the context of a single round of
funding for a venture company, and for the sake of argument let us
assume that it is the B Round, and that there has already been one round
of financing (the A Round). The pre-money valuation will be the valuation of the company upon which the B Round is based, while the
post-money valuation will simply be that figure plus the total amount
contributed by the B Round investors. Perhaps a simple example would
be helpful.

Suppose that the venture company is looking for an additional $5M
of funding, and that they agree during the negotiations with the venture
capitalists that they have identified a pre-money valuation of $8M. They
can now calculate how much of the company's equity the new investors
will require:

$$\frac{5}{13} \times 100\% = 38.5\%$$

Thus in principle the new investors will take 38.5% of the equity in the
newly enlarged capital structure. The figure of $13 M is the post-money
valuation (the pre-money valuation of $8 M plus the amount of new
money being introduced of $5 M).

There are three important points to note here. First, I have deliberately given a very simplified example. In reality, things would be much

more complicated than this. Certain investors, such as the entrepreneurs who comprise the key executives of the company, may well have anti-dilution rights which prevent their shareholding from ever falling below a certain percentage of the total. Others, typically those who come into later rounds, will have liquidation preferences (I will discuss these in detail below). There may also be options attached to some of the shares (particularly those of the founders) and these will also be potentially dilutive.

Second, it is important to understand that the same investors do not participate pro rata in each round of the company. In particular, those who participate in the very early rounds, whether as entrepreneurs, angels or seed stage venture capital funds, will rarely have the large amounts of money available which may be required to fuel the rapid growth of a potentially very large company. In any event, seed stage funds will want to keep their money available to participate in other early stage situations, not D and E Rounds. This means that some dilution is inevitable (as we will discuss below) and will be built into their plans from the outset.

Third, it is not necessarily the case that the pre-money valuation of one round will be the same as the post-money valuation of the previous one; far from it, in fact. This uplift in valuation is one of the ways in which early stage investors make their money and, indeed, the main financial argument for investing at an early stage in the first place. In the example I gave above, for example, it is quite possible that the A stage was a $2 M dollar round at a pre-money valuation of $3 M. Thus there has been an uplift from that post-money valuation ($5 M) of $3 M to the new pre-money valuation of $8 M. Thus there has already been an increase in the value of the A Round investors' investment:

$$\frac{2}{5} \times \$5\,M = \$2\,M$$

$$\frac{2}{5} \times \$8\,M = \$3.2\,M$$

Thus, before the possibly diluting effects of the B Round come into play, the A Round investors have already made an unrealised potential gain of $1.2 M, or 60% of their original investment.

Share Classes

To give expression to the various anti-dilution and liquidation preference provisions referred to above, a different class of shares in the company is typically created for the participants of each funding round, with the relevant protection being given effect as what lawyers term class rights (rights attached to a particular class of shares which cannot be varied except with the consent of the holders of that class of shares). Since any one investor may participate in different funding rounds, it is quite possible for them to end up with shares of several different classes in the same company.

By tradition, the shares issued for the A Round are called A shares, the shares issued for the B Round are called B shares, and so on.

Cost and Value

Having had fairly complicated discussions about the nature of buyout returns it may come as something of a relief to hear that when it comes to venture we are concerned with such basic topics as cost and value. This initial view might well be mistaken, however. Once you can ignore the debt factor then buyout returns too come down to little more than this, while the way in which cost and value are built up is actually much more complex in a venture transaction, largely because, unlike the typical buyout, a venture company may go through several funding rounds, all at different values and on different terms.

Cost is of course a fairly straightforward concept. The cost of an investment is what we pay for it, and so we can and do calculate this simply by adding together all the various amounts which have been contributed by any one fund in the various funding rounds of that one company. However, it is important for us to be able to see how that cost figure has been built up, otherwise we will not be able to conduct any meaningful due diligence.

Thus, the "cost" side of your model may well look something like Figure 7.1. Let us just be clear what we are looking at. We are modelling an individual venture fund, and within that we are modelling an individual venture company. This part of the model is showing us essentially how much we have invested to date in that company (our cost), what percentage of the company we currently own in return for that cost, and what percentage of the fund as a whole this investment represents.

Fund Name: Allstar Ventures III
Fund Size ($M): 220
Company Name: Crazy New Venture Inc.
Sector: Telecoms
Business Description: High speed optical routers for metro networking

Round	Pre ($000)	Amount ($000)	Post ($000)	%*	Cost ($000)	Co-investors
A	3000	2000	5000	20.0	1000	Baby Seed II
B	8000	5000	13000		800	California Warriors IV. Baby Seed II

Total Cost: 1800
Fund %:   0.82

*This column is designed to show the *current* percentage of the company's total issued shares owned by the fund. It will therefore need to have something like the following sitting behind it in the model:

Round	#Shares Pre(000)	#Shares Round(000)	#Shares Post(000)	#Shares Taken(000)	#Shares To Date(000)	% Current
A	3000	2000	5000	1000	1000	20.0
B	5000	5000	10000	800	1800	18.0

Figure 7.1   The "cost" side of a venture fund analysis model

We can in turn use the percentage we own of the company to calculate our current value. Assuming that the valuation of the company has not increased since the time of the B Round, we currently own 18% of a company which is valued at $13 M. This values our holding at $2.34, which in turn represents a money multiple of 1.3× on our current cost of $1.8 M.

Is it really as easy as this? Well, no, actually it isn't. We are happily ignoring for illustrative purposes the potentially dilutive effects of any anti-dilution rights, liquidation preferences and options in the hands of either third parties or indeed of the fund which we are analysing. Thus there would have to be yet another level sitting behind our model which calculated the possible effect of these based on the current value of the company. However, we run very quickly into three major problems here.

First, the full effect of them often cannot be properly appreciated until one knows the final exit value of the company. It may be advantageous to exercise options at one value but not at another, for example. Second, this is an extremely complicated process and many investors may well take the view that it really doesn't matter that much, since they will know at the end of the day exactly what cash multiple results and in the meantime they have a roughly accurate figure which is fine for their everyday monitoring and reporting purposes. Third, the information which you need will frequently simply not be available. The exact terms of funding rounds are usually not disclosed save to those who have signed the relevant documentation, and again the vast majority of LPs will neither need nor want the information, nor would they probably know what to do with it if they had it. Thus as a matter of practice most LPs simply ignore this aspect of things and adjust their figures on exit as necessary. Indeed, in my experience, many LPs do not undertake even the level of analysis which you see set out in Figure 7.1 (though it is difficult to see how they can conduct any meaningful monitoring or due diligence without it).

We also need to remember that just as a venture company may have several rounds of funding, so the exit rarely comprises one single cashflow. Either the company will be floated (IPO'd) and quoted shares may be held within the fund (or distributed in specie to LPs) and sold in tranches over a period of time, or the company may be bought for stock by a public company and a similar process will ensue. It is relatively rare for a venture company to be bought for a single cash payment.

Thus our model will have to distinguish between money that has already been distributed to LPs or, to put it another way, value that they have already realised, and unrealised value that is still sitting within the fund as potential distributions that have not yet occurred. Just as the performance of a fund cannot be properly measured until the end of its life, so an individual investment in a portfolio company can only be properly analysed once there is no remaining value (in other words, once the company has been either fully exited or written off).

IRRS AND MULTIPLES

Discussion as to the timing of cashflows brings us rather neatly to the question of IRRs. You may be wondering why we have been talking about money multiples when analysing venture transactions rather than IRRs. Well, the answer is that we look at both, but sophisticated investors have always realised that with venture (and with buyout too, in truth, but that is more difficult as buyout LPs and GPs alike seem obsessed with IRRs) the multiple is what matters. If you can get the multiple right, then the IRR will take care of itself. The same is not necessarily true vice versa. Consider what may happen if a private equity transaction generates an IRR of 60% over a 6-month period. This is all very well, but I am most unlikely to be able then to redeploy that money straight away in another private equity transaction offering a similar rate of return. On the contrary, the most likely outcome is that it will end up invested at a money market rate of return while some alternative use is found for it. We will come back to this point in a later chapter.

The other side of this particular coin, as I have mentioned before, is that if given the choice I would rather have the money invested at, say, 20% for 10 years than 60% for 6 months. To say that what I am concerned about is the money multiple rather than the IRR is simply another way of putting this. As a rough rule of thumb, a venture fund will always be deemed a success if it generates a money multiple of 3×, but will usually not be if it does not. The ability to generate 3× on previous funds is therefore one of the main things you should be looking for when performing due diligence on a venture group, and those who slavishly rank funds purely by IRR will miss this point entirely.

However, IRR is obviously another valuable dial on the dashboard and our model should be calculating this both at the individual transaction level and also at the fund level (which will of course be lower because of the impact of fees and carried interest). Please remember, though, that while the closer one comes to the end of the fund the more accurate IRR is likely to be as a measure of final performance, the early stages of the fund's life when it is still under the undue influence of the J-curve will tend to be much longer for a venture fund relative to a buyout fund because of the longer average holding periods. This measure should therefore be treated with extreme caution during the first 6 years or so of a fund's existence.

Let us look briefly at one or two individual components of our model and then turn to considering how the pattern of venture returns is made up.

Going in Equity (GI%)

This is one of the two factors which make up the cost of any one round and the value of any total investment in a venture company. Surprisingly, many LPs pay little attention to it, given its vital nature. There is little point in having an investment in a successful company unless one is going to be able to claim a major part of the spoils, and indeed, experience shows that levels of equity ownership are a major driver of venture fund returns. This is particularly important given that early stage investors will not be able to invest pro rata in later rounds (and sometimes not at all) and must therefore plan both the level of their initial investment and also their strategy for dealing with the capital structure thereafter with this in mind. Traditionally, the very best US venture firms aim to end up with no less than 20% of a company if at all possible and will typically look to start at around 40% for this reason.

We will be looking at this further in Chapter 9, but consistently low levels of equity ownership are indicative of a firm which is either (1) piggy-backing on other people's deals rather than sourcing their own, (2) attempting to limit their downside by investing in too many companies rather than looking to maximise their upside by concentrating on fewer and fewer potentially successful companies as the fund progresses, or (3) whose fund size is too small to allow them to hold onto a decent equity position once other, larger, investors become involved. None of these are desirable qualities so far as an LP is concerned.

Percentage of the Holding within the Fund

This is another key indicator which many LPs ignore. As we will see in a minute, venture returns are driven by a very small number of very big winners, and there is little point in having a big winner which is not able to make a significant contribution to the overall fund return. As a rough rule of thumb, any one of these big winners (home runs) should be able to return the entire capital of the fund at least once, and since 25× is generally regarded as the hurdle multiple for a home run then this suggests a target of about 5% of the fund, in order to allow for the impact of fees and carried interest.

As we will see when we look at due diligence, one of the key indicators when looking at a venture firm is the correlation between their biggest bets and their biggest winners. Putting a lot of money into poorly performing companies is indicative of bad judgement. Even worse, putting a small amount of money into very successful companies smacks of a lack of home run mentality.

Putting a good proportion of your capital into successful companies, on the other hand, speaks not only of being able to choose the right companies behind which to throw the main thrust of your efforts but also of knowing which companies to kill, and doing so as early as possible.

THE IMPACT OF HOME RUNS

This is the one issue which is fundamental to a proper understanding of venture capital; indeed, it is probably the single most important issue to understand in the whole field of private equity and so would probably justify a whole chapter (if not a book!) to itself. It is also the one issue which has most divided the private equity industry; there are many European LPs, for example, who find the whole concept just too much to stomach.

We have already looked briefly at the "US venture model" and so you will already have an understanding of what a home run is. It is an investment which can return the whole capital of the fund at least once, and a 25× multiple is usually accepted as a proxy for that level of performance.

We also looked in the last chapter at what it means to have a home run mentality, and I do not propose to repeat any of that. What we need to look at here is the impact which home runs have on venture returns. There is an immediate difficulty here in that data on individual venture companies is not as widely available as it is for venture funds, and what data there is tends to be relatively recent in origin. However, the industry owes a huge debt of gratitude to leading US Fund of Funds manager Horsley Bridge, whose US funds specialise in almost nothing but early stage venture, and whose in-house database is therefore almost certainly the best repository of venture company information in the world. While of course they cannot do anything that might identify individual funds or companies, they do occasionally release into the public domain summaries of their data on a "blind" basis, and Figure 7.2 has been widely seen and discussed.

Let us be clear what we are looking at. On the left-hand side of the graphic, I have inserted what I believe to be the roughly typical profile of a buyout fund. At most (I have been conservative) 10% of companies by cost will fail, i.e., fail to return their capital. Another way of looking

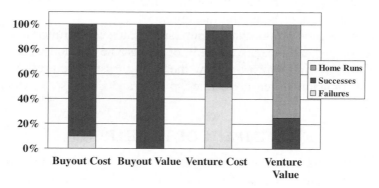

Figure 7.2   Impact of home runs on venture fund returns

at this is to say that it is left to the remaining 90% to contribute all the fund's value or return. I must emphasise that this breakdown is not based upon any hard data (which, so far as I am aware, is not available anyway) but on my own many years of experience of buyout funds.

The right-hand side of the graphic tells a very different story. Note that there is an extra category here: the home runs, defined for these purposes as any investment that makes at least 25×.

The first thing to note is that roughly 50% of all venture companies will fail. One of the hardest things with which venture GPs and LPs alike struggle to come to terms is that this is no reflection on anyone's abilities as a venture capitalist; it is just the way the venture model works. Even if you are the best venture capital firm in the world there is a chance that 50% of your companies by cost will fail to return their capital. However, this doesn't matter, and if you take a look at the home runs category you will see instantly why it doesn't matter.

The home runs represent about 5% of companies by cost. Yet this 5% by cost creates nearly 80% of the value. The stark reality is that it is almost completely irrelevant what happens to the other 95% of the portfolio by cost. Yes, the remaining 95% or so make some contribution, but only about 20% of the total. It is the home runs, and the home runs almost alone, which drive venture returns.

For example, Kleiner Perkins, perhaps the best known of the leading US venture firms, is rumoured to have bought 25% of Netscape at a post-money valuation of about $20M, to see the company later acquired (having first gone public) by AOL for $4 billion. There are many other examples, and Kleiner Perkins are far from the only firm to have achieved these sorts of multiples on individual deals, but it will give you some idea of the scale of what can be achieved.

This is why home run mentality is so important, and this is why the only thing you really need to look for in a venture firm (if you are an LP) is the ability to score home runs. Almost nothing else matters. Every successful venture fund in history has included at least one home run. One will frequently hear during industry discussions comments such as "oh yes, that was their Ciena fund"; in other words, the fund will often be associated in people's minds with, and thus identified by, the particular home run company which it featured.

We talked in the last chapter, for example, about the way in which many US venture firms have withdrawn from Life Science activity. One of the main reasons for this was that it was perceived as much more difficult (certainly this is what experience suggested, anyway) to score a home run in that area compared with IT or Telecoms. The European experience, as we noted, has been rather different.

We also need to be aware that there is in some parts of the world considerable scepticism as to whether the home run model constitutes a sustainable model of venture investment. In the more traditional corridors of European venture investing, for example, there is deep unease with such a fundamentally binary approach, and a contrary view that returns can and should be earned more evenly across the whole portfolio.

In part, this stems from a different cultural background in some countries, particularly amongst, say, the over-50s. In these more enlightened times it may come as a shock to some younger Europeans to know that only a few years ago the general rule in many European countries, including the UK, was that if you had been a director of a company which had gone into liquidation or receivership then it could be extremely difficult to become a director of another company; there was very considerable stigma attached to insolvency and corporate failure. Fortunately, a much healthier viewpoint has spread from the USA, which sees a failed business venture as worthwhile experience, a campaign medal to be worn with some pride. I remember, for example, a study in about 1999 which showed that the CEOs of most NASDAQ flotations had previously been the CEO of two failed companies.

However, old habits die hard and the traditional European mindset led to an undoubted reluctance to kill struggling companies and this, combined with a lack of value add skills compared with the USA, contributed to a widespread failure by the European industry to generate the number (and scale) of home runs which it needed to establish a record of healthy historic returns. We will look at this area in much more detail in the next chapter.

One small personal recollection may perhaps serve to illustrate this point. I used to be in a position where I was monitoring the performance of venture funds both in the USA and in Europe. I found that the quarter of the year in which companies were written off was fairly random in the USA, whereas in Europe there was a heavy concentration in the fourth quarter. This suggests very strongly that in Europe the imperative to kill a company was largely being driven by accounting considerations (i.e., the need to agree the necessary figures for the audited accounts) rather than strategic issues of portfolio management.

At the end of the day, though, the historic figures are all we have to go on, and they seem to show very clearly that the Europeans simply got it wrong, and that trying to draw intellectual distinctions about the basic concepts is largely irrelevant. The US experience shows overwhelmingly that the home run model is valid, and indeed, will ultimately impose itself upon any venture market given the right GP skills and enough capital. I have no doubt personally that it can and, indeed, does work in Europe, and that we will witness something of a revolution in European venture in coming years as some firms (generally the smaller and the newer) embrace it enthusiastically while others (generally the larger and the longer-established) attempt to soldier on much as before. The reason, incidentally, that I draw these distinctions is that it seems to me on the basis of my personal observations that it tends to be the smaller and newer European firms that are attracting people with genuine entrepreneurial experience as former company founders, and that it is these operating skills (previously largely absent from European venture firms) which are required to provide the sort of value add which will allow the home run model to work.

SUMMARY

- Venture deals, unlike buyout transactions, typically do not involve debt and so the analysis process is at first sight much simpler, at least at the most basic level.
- However, the mechanics of venture returns are in fact very complex, since several funding rounds will usually be involved, and each on different terms. The ability to model this, though, is usually restricted by the level of available information.
- The basic drivers are the post-money valuation of the round concerned (with the first round in which the fund participates obviously having the most impact) and the percentage of the company's equity which a fund holds.
- By far the most important measure of venture performance is the money multiple, i.e., the ratio of the total amount of cash generated by an investment to the total amount of cash invested. IRR is also important, not least for charting the progress of the J-curve, but is largely meaningless in the early to mid-stages of a fund – even more so than for buyout, given the longer average holding periods of venture funds.
- Valuation of current investments is much more of an issue for venture funds than for buyout and there have been some extreme

variations of approach and procedure, particularly in the USA, which have given rise for concern.

- Historically, European venture was subject to strict peremptory valuation guidelines while US venture was not. With the publication of new guidelines in Europe, the situation appears less clear-cut going forward.
- Home runs drive venture returns. Within the best US portfolios, companies delivering a multiple of at least 25× account for less than 5% of companies by cost but generate nearly 80% of final fund value. What happens to the other 95% is largely irrelevant. About 50% of all venture companies will fail to return their capital. Thus analysis of venture funds should concentrate on illuminating the ability (or otherwise) of the relevant venture capital team to score home runs.
- As well as examining what percentage of a company's equity is held by a fund, one needs also to look at what percentage of the fund itself is represented by any one investment. There is little point in having a company which returns 25× if it is only 1% of the fund.

8

Venture Returns

Just as we examined the historic returns that have actually been earned by buyout funds, so we will now do the same for venture. Some of the issues which we will be examining will be similar, but some will be rather different. How can we explain the different returns that have been earned in different geographic areas, specifically Europe and the USA? Are the European figures really as bad as they appear to be? Is there any correlation between returns and fund size? Can we dig a little more deeply into how returns are influenced by the stage at which one invests? Are the historic figures a good guide to future performance?

US OUT-PERFORMANCE VERSUS EUROPE

The really big issue here, though, is the radical difference between the historic returns of venture funds in Europe and the USA, respectively. Take a look at Figure 8.1, which shows the historic returns of the 1990s measured by Capital Weighted IRR.

Look at the huge extent to which US venture out-performed European venture during the decade. It looks as though the "European buyout and US venture" mantra really was justified throughout the 1990s. Remember, too, that we are here looking at the Capital Weighted Average rather than the Upper Quartile fund, which most people in the industry would consider a more realistic measure. Figure 8.2 shows that this difference is even more dramatic.

The conclusion is inescapable. Not only has US venture as a whole out-performed European venture significantly throughout the decade, but the best US funds out-performed their European counterparts quite dramatically. We need to consider not only these figures but also the implications and issues which lie behind them to see if they can help us understand just how and why this should have happened.

I am afraid that in this one area we are going to have to dig into the VentureXpert figures rather more deeply than we have hitherto, because one of the issues here is the extent to which the data population is representative and statistically significant. We will see, when we do, that

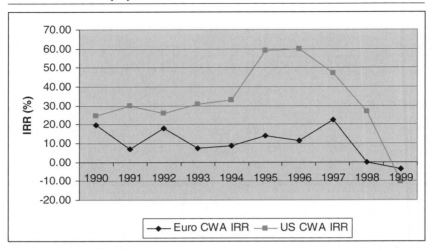

Figure 8.1 US and European venture – relative performance (1); Capital Weighted Average IRR, by vintage year 1990–1999

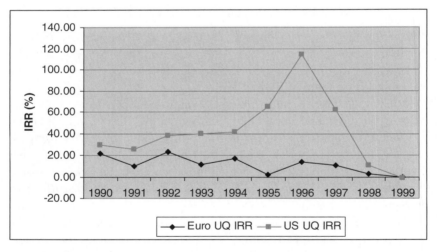

Figure 8.2 US and European venture – relative performance (1); Upper Quartile IRR, by vintage year 1990–1999

the contrast between European and US venture returns is not actually as stark as it might at first appear. However, let us leave this to one side for the moment. Nobody can deny that there has been a dramatic outperformance by US venture, and we need to analyse this so we can better understand it.

Money Multiples Drive IRRs

It is usually money multiples which drive IRRs. Let us see if this is so in this case.

Figure 8.3 clearly suggests a direct connection between higher money multiples and higher IRRs. In fact, we measure the correlation for this period between the Capital Weighted Average TVPI and the Capital Weighted Average IRR; it is 81% for both Europe and the USA. In other words, the ability to score high money multiples appears to drive high IRRs, just as we suspected, and this seems to be (exactly!) equally so in both regions.

As we have observed many times in this book already, it is multiples which drive IRRs, and not the other way round, at least not directly. The desire to chase a high IRR can result in GPs baling out of an investment before they should, which may of course result in a lower multiple than might otherwise be the case. (Remember my earlier example of asking you to consider which you would prefer: 60% IRR for 6 months or 25% IRR for 6 years. The sophisticated LP will of course choose the latter, but a GP who is about to go out fundraising might be tempted to opt for the former. This is an extreme example, but deliberately chosen so that the difference is obvious. More usually in practice it will be a more subtle question of degree.)

This example is strictly irrelevant, though, since it requires some form of conscious human intervention. The principle which I am

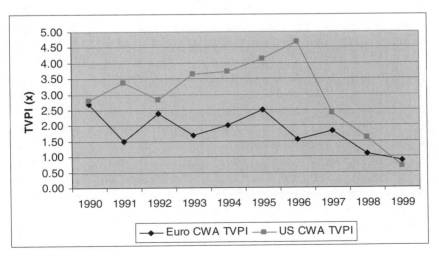

Figure 8.3   European versus US CWA money multiple; TVPI by vintage year

expounding is that in the absence of any intentional alteration of events then it is the multiple which will drive the IRR, rather than vice versa. Figure 8.3 supports this view. I think we can accordingly safely advance the hypothesis that the out-performance achieved by US venture during the 1990s was actually a manifestation of an ability to achieve high money multiples. Further, if we remember what we said about home runs, it must specifically have been a manifestation of the ability to score home runs. Sadly, that degree of data is not publicly available at the company level, but we may be able to find echoes of it in the data which we *do* have available at the fund level.

Home Runs and the Golden Circle

First, though, a little background: US venture returns have not only been driven by a relatively very small number of big winners at the company level, but also by a relatively small number of big winners at the fund level (which have been essentially those funds in which the big winners at the company level have been present). These funds have in turn been managed by a relatively small number of venture firms, to which some years ago I gave the name of the "golden circle". While no two venture industry professionals will agree on precisely the same list of names to include, there is general consensus on who is or is not likely to figure on the list, and it may be as few as a dozen names, and certainly no more than a couple of dozen. I am not suggesting that the funds managed by these firms consistently out-perform time after time; on the contrary, what research has been done suggests that it is extremely difficult for any two consecutive funds managed by the same venture firm both to out-perform. It is more a general pattern of out-performance, probably about two funds out of every five.

I base these observations on my personal experience of the industry rather than on any hard, publicly available data but they are broadly correct and I ask the reader to trust me on this point. In other words, if you had been able consistently to select (and access, which is another point entirely) funds managed by the golden circle then you would have scored very dramatic returns from your venture fund portfolio, whereas if you had not been able to select or access these funds then your returns would have been significantly lower, even if most of your fund picks had been in the upper quartile. As Phil Horsley, the founder of Horsley Bridge, memorably remarked: "venture is an upper decile game". Indeed, it is my contention that it is the absence of this annual cluster of golden circle type returns that has been the major factor in the differential between historic US and European returns.

What we need to try to do, therefore, is somehow to isolate and consider the track record of the (few) very best US venture funds in each vintage year, since it is here that the home runs are most likely to have been scored. Unfortunately, lack of transparency again arises to thwart our efforts, since the publicly available data in the Venture Xpert system does not allow one to identify the performance of individual named funds. However, we do know which individual funds make up the sample population in each vintage year, which allows a few educated guesses to be made, and we do know the performance of both the best and the upper quartile funds: in others words, we know the spread of the upper quartile since we know both its top and its bottom.

Table 8.1 shows the top and bottom of the upper quartile by TVPI for each of the vintage years we have been considering, and a "short list" of golden circle candidates from within that year, any one of which may well be represented by the "maximum" figure. Figures are for US venture funds, with the data being drawn as usual from Thomson Financial's Venture Xpert system.

You will see that in seven out of the nine vintage years under review there was at least one US venture fund that returned a very substantial double-digit multiple. In fact, given the very large gap between the top and the bottom of the upper quartile, it is reasonable to assume that in each of those vintage years there were in fact three or four that outperformed in this way. It is these funds that one needed to capture to achieve the sort of returns that were in fact achieved by a small number of private equity fund investors in the USA during the 1990s. You will see also that although for the sake of completeness I have included golden circle candidates for 1991 and 1999, the scale of their success at the fund level is not in the same league as for the vintage years comprising the rest of the decade.

I think there are different reasons for this. 1999 was of course the last vintage year under review completely to encapsulate the technology and internet bubble. One would therefore expect performance to be disappointing, given that many investments would have been made at high valuations and then either written off or sold a considerable time later at written-down values. Take a look at the Upper Quartile TVPI and you will see the stark reality: any GP who returns committed capital on a 1999 vintage year venture fund will be doing well. To make any significant return would be heroic indeed.

Table 8.1 Upper Quartile US venture analysis by TVPI (×)

Vintage year	Maximum (top of UQ)	(Bottom of) UQ	Golden circle shortlist
1991	5.7	3.6	Austin Ventures III, IVP V, Sierra IV, Sutter Hill Ventures
1992	14.1	3.6	Highland II, Kleiner Perkins VI, Matrix, Mayfield VII, Mohr Davidow III, Oak V, Sevin Rosen IV
1993	28.0	2.9	Accel IV, Hummer Winblad II, NEA VI, Sequoia VI
1994	13.7	4.3	ARCH II, Battery III, IVP VI, Kleiner Perkins VII, Mohr Davidow IV
1995	21.9	4.5	Benchmark I, Charles River VII, Doll I, Foundation I, Matrix IV, Mayfield VIII, Mohr Davidow V, Sevin Rosen V
1996	19.6	6.0	Accel V, Geocapital IV, Highland III, IVP VII, Kleiner Perkins VIII, Mayfield III (?), Sequoia VII, USVP V, Worldview I
1997	15.8	2.7	Benchmark II, Charles River VIII, Greylock IX, Mayfield IX, Menlo VII
1998	17.7	1.5	Accel VI, Benchmark III, Foundation II, Highland IV, IVP VIII, Matrix V, Mayfield IV (?), Sequoia VIII, Sevin Rosen VI
1999	5.6	1.0	Accel VII, Battery V, Benchmark IV, Charles River IX and X, Doll II, Kleiner Perkins IX, Mayfield X, Mohr Davidow VI, Sequoia IX, Sevin Rosen VII, WPG V

1991 is a different matter. I suspect that the truth here is partly that 1991 vintage year funds were too early to capitalise on the huge ramp in company values which occurred during the 1990s. It is also partly that at this time a lot of venture firms in the USA were still transacting a mix of Life Science and Technology deals, and we have already heard that the former performed disappointingly in general. Indeed, it was the fear that these were dragging down overall fund returns that led many American GPs to withdraw from the field and/or to hive off their Life Science teams as separate firms. The final reason is a purely statistical one. VentureXpert's sample population for the 1991 vintage year is only 41 funds, compared with an admittedly extreme 525 for fund year 2000. In part this reflects the explosion in venture activity which took place during the late 1990s, but I think it may also be a symptom of the fact that collecting fund data was still in its comparative infancy in 1991 and there was considerable resistance to the idea of making performance data public, even on a blinded basis as Thomson Financial do.

At the end of the day, though, 1991 is probably a very good example of the principle I have been expounding. The fact is that not a single fund was closed in 1991 by a clear-cut golden circle candidate, save for a very small ($5.4 M) expansion fund by Sevin Rosen. It may well be, therefore, that this provides yet more evidence to suggest that without the presence of the golden circle, venture returns will indeed struggle to find break-out performance. Perhaps significantly, the maximum TVPI for both the previous vintage years (when there *were* golden circle firms closing funds) is higher, though the Upper Quartile TVPI is lower, suggesting significant out-performance by one or two funds within the upper quartile.

Market Conditions

It is tempting to seek to explain US out-performance during the 1990s solely by reference to the amazing market conditions which flourished during the second half of the decade. We have already seen what happened to PE ratios during this period: the S&P PE ratio peaked at nearly 35 in 1999. While it is not strictly relevant to talk about PE ratios in the context of venture companies, since few have any earnings, this is nonetheless indicative of what happened to equity markets generally. At the end of 1990 the NASDAQ index stood at a lowly 374, while by the end of 1999 it had risen to 4069. That is why it is tempting to seek to dismiss such out-performance on the grounds that "a rising tide lifts all ships". If the equity market which provides your main exit route and your main exit valuation benchmark rises more then tenfold in a decade then, the argument runs, you would have to have been pretty stupid not to score good returns even if only by accident. Kleiner Perkins, for example, were reputed to have earned a transaction IRR in excess of 50000% on their investment in Amazon.com based on 1999 stock prices.

However, this argument is simplistic and pays little regard (or respect) to the very real skill-base which exists among the best US venture capitalists. Yes, by the end of the decade valuations had risen to ridiculous levels for companies which had absorbed in some cases hundreds of millions of funding and had yet to turn a profit (and in many cases, were based on a business plan that was unlikely *ever* to produce any significant profits). Yes, this was a genuine bubble and, yes, experienced and skilful venture capitalists who should have known better fell for its siren call in much the same way as others did, but much was achieved that was genuine and cannot be explained by this simplistic analysis.

Genuine companies were created which are today acknowledged global leaders, many of which are solid technology businesses, such as Cisco, Sun, Intuit and Lotus, in addition to internet success stories such as Google, AOL, eBay and Amazon. These are high quality companies which would have succeeded in any equity market environment because they were based on sound business principles and run by highly talented individuals. Yet the "value add" which their venture capital backers provided also played an essential role in their success.

Thus, while it is undeniable that market conditions boosted US venture returns during this period, high quality companies, and the high quality venture capitalists who backed them, would have thrived in any conditions, and still produced good (though not so exaggerated) returns. It is worth stating for the sake of balance, though, that the argument does have some relevance in two specific areas.

First, the spectre of almost unbelievable venture returns drew a large number of new investors into the marketplace. In 1991 $1.9 billion was raised by US venture funds. By 1999 this had risen to $60 billion, and in fact peaked at nearly double that amount in 2000 – a 60-fold increase in just 10 years. There were only two ways in which this much money could be accommodated. Existing firms increased their fund sizes (in some cases to $1.5 billion – more or less the whole amount that had been raised by 40 funds in 1991) and many new entrants came into the market (contrast those 42 funds in 1992 with 525 in 2000). This massive influx of new capital, much of it in unskilled hands, acted like air being sucked into the bottom of a furnace and fuelled the massive bubble which grossly inflated venture valuations. It is fair to say that while this happened in Europe to some extent, it was not on anything like the same scale. Valuations never reached the peaks they had scaled in the USA, and more importantly, everything was a year or two later, which meant that the scope for making high returns by getting into bubble-type companies and out of them again in time before the market collapsed was more limited.

Second, there is no doubt that the absence of anything like NASDAQ was a severe drawback for European venture capital firms, and had a definite negative impact on their returns. In retrospect, Europeans should have invited (even implored) NASDAQ to come to Europe with a view to creating a global exit market for venture-backed companies. A welcome corollary to this would have been that on their coat-tails would probably have come most of the leading US venture firms, setting up offices in Europe (as it is, only a very few have done so – see below). Instead, the Europeans decided to try to create their own version of NASDAQ. Named EASDAQ, it was a sad failure which only ever attracted a handful of companies and, like all such pan-European projects, became a highly political affair, with nobody being prepared to admit defeat. Ironically, NASDAQ were invited to take a controlling interest in it in 2001, by which time the damage had been done and European venture firms had been denied (in practice – in theory they could have relocated their companies to the USA as Israeli venture firms did in order to take advantage of NASDAQ) access to NASDAQ exactly when they could most have profited from it.

Nor does the London Stock Exchange emerge particularly well from the story. Two attempts at providing junior markets, the Third Market and the Unlisted Securities Market, both took hold but were then abruptly closed down by the LSE for no good apparent reason, leading to great scepticism about the LSE's commitment to this area. Ironically, AIM, the LSE's latest offering, has now become what EASDAQ was intended to be and is attracting IPO candidates from all over the world, including the USA. It is a sad indication of just what an opportunity might have been missed as a result of the LSE's arbitrary actions in the past.

EUROPEAN VENTURE – IS IT AS BAD AS IT SEEMS?

The answer to this is "no", but understanding why it is "no" requires me to explain a few things.

We have already discussed a couple of factors (NASDAQ and the bubble) which artificially boosted US venture returns, thus making European returns look worse in relative terms. We have also discussed the very different skill-sets which would have ensured that in any event US venture would have out-performed European venture during the 1990s. None of this is an issue. US venture capital firms (particularly the golden circle) achieved some amazing things during the 1990s and deserve every congratulation for having done so. We will probably never see the like of those returns again.

However, when we come to look at how European venture performed in absolute terms we hit an immediate problem and I am afraid that it is a problem with the available data. Since this is likely to prove a controversial topic, let me choose my words extremely carefully. The VentureXpert figures for European venture include a lot of funds that simply should not be there, and they do this to such an extent that the resulting figures cannot be taken as any valid measurement of European venture returns.

Let me say at once that a lot of this is not their fault, and has indeed resulted from excess zeal rather than lack of it. Many very small seed and development funds, usually operating on a very localised basis, and frequently either governmental (local or national) or attached to an academic institution, have been rightly anxious that they should be listed in the VentureXpert database. Arguably these are not even practising "venture capital" in the true sense anyway, but whatever the case virtually none of them would be eligible for investment by institutional LPs in any event because of their size or their nature. In a market the size of the USA, for example, this would not matter very much, though it would introduce some statistical "noise" into the system, but within a much smaller sample population it matters very much. The average number of European venture funds tracked in the five vintage years from 1992 to 1996, for example, is only 18; within such a small sample, any sampling error can potentially have a very significant effect.

In addition to these very small quasi-developmental type funds, there are funds run by entities such as banks, media companies and industrial groups which even if they are technically open to outside investors would not generally be considered (sophisticated LPs invest only with independent professional firms, to the extent that the merest possibility of any outsider being able to exert influence, either in investment decisions or otherwise, will usually bestow the kiss of death). There are also funds which would be ineligible because of their legal nature; VCTs, for example, are tax-friendly vehicles aimed at British retail investors.

Finally, there are some funds which either do not fit comfortably within the geographic range (there are many Russian and East European funds which should really be separately classified) and many funds which have just been wrongly classified in the first place. There are Asian and African funds, for example, and buyout, mezzanine,

Table 8.2 Analysis of VentureXpert data for European venture funds, vintage years 1990–1999

Year	Stated total	Real total*	% by number
1990	15	4	27
1991	20	1	5
1992	8	2	25
1993	17	4	24
1994	21	2	10
1995	22	5	23
1996	22	6	27
1997	43	15	35
1998	45	17	38
1999	68	22	32

Source: Thomson Financial's VentureXpert.
* (1) Independent firms, (2) conducting genuine venture transactions, (3) with a fund structure open to institutional LPs and (4) fund size >$20 M.

Funds of Funds, etc. So, let us see what happens if we notionally strip all these inappropriate funds out of the universe to leave only those which are institutional grade European venture funds (Table 8.2).

The difference really is very dramatic. You will see that even in the best year (1997) only 15 out of the stated 43 funds were eligible, while the average number of eligible funds for any one of the vintage years under consideration is only 27%. Put this the other way round, and we can state that in the average vintage year the figures are 73% inaccurate by number of funds. Needless to say, this is a pretty staggering result and underlines the fact that in this one area the normally excellent VentureXpert system breaks down, and that its numbers can in no way be seen as representative of real-life European venture performance.

So, where does this leave us? If we cannot rely on the VentureXpert figures, what can we do instead? Well, there are a few pointers. First, look at the figures achieved by the "maximum" fund in each vintage year (Table 8.3).

Clearly, there must have been at least one European venture fund in each vintage year that achieved stand-out performance. The figures shown in Table 8.3 would be completely acceptable as the performance measures of any quality US venture fund, and in some years (e.g., 1996 and 1997) are the sort of figures that could be achieved by one of the golden circle firms in the USA. Thus, it is facile to suggest, as many do, that it is simply not possible to earn decent venture returns in Europe. Not only is it possible, but people have actually done it.

Table 8.3   Performance of the best recorded European venture fund, vintage years 1990–1999

Year	TVPI (×)	IRR (%)
1990	11.2	55.1
1991	3.3	36.2
1992	3.0	26.2
1993	6.6	55.5
1994	6.2	27.4
1995	6.4	200.8
1996	14.7	103.9
1997	10.0	262.0
1998	8.2	180.5
1999	2.8	125.3

Source: Thomson Financial's VentureXpert.

The question, of course, is "who?" Unfortunately the figures do not help us very much here as they are of course blinded. It could be suggested that as we are for the most part concerned only with about a quarter of the data then we should take the upper quartile figure as essentially the bottom of the range, but this suggestion is not strictly logical as there can be no guarantee that the quarter with which we are concerned is indeed all clustered within the upper quartile. Just as there is undoubtedly at least one fund in each vintage year which has out-performed, there must surely be others which have under-performed.

However, experience suggests very strongly that if one is comparing institutional quality funds against non-institutional quality funds then the former are more likely to have over-performed than under-performed. Thus it is very probable indeed that most of them will be in the upper quartile, at least half of them anyway. So, if you were approaching the problem with a very broad brush, it is almost certain that the stated upper quartile is in fact more of a median, and probably even below that. Let us see what happens, for example, if we compare the stated European Upper Quartile TVPI with the stated US median (Figure 8.4).

Rough and ready though such an approach may be, it may well be that the position it suggests is not unrealistic. Yes, US venture still out-performed during the middle of the decade but perhaps the scale of it was not quite so dramatic as may appear at first blush. For the rest of the decade, European venture seems to have been very competitive in terms of the money multiples which it has generated.

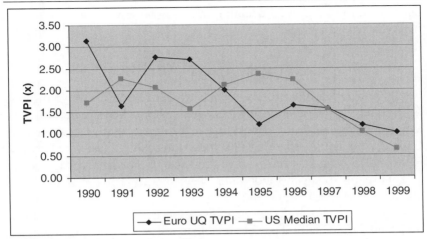

Source: Thomson Financial's VentureXpert.

Figure 8.4 Stated European Upper Quartile TVPI versus stated US median TVPI, by vintage year 1990–1999

We are straying into dangerous territory here, since we are now largely in the realm of supposition, yet when the official figures fail us we have little alternative and it seems preferable to me at least to make some attempt at independent thought rather than, as many in the industry do, simply to accept the figures at face value and never even wonder about what may lie behind them. I freely accept that my approach may flatter actual European venture returns. However, if they do, then they probably do not do so by very much, and certainly not by as much as the official figures seem to under-estimate them.

One other point to bear in mind before we leave this issue and move on is that there is undoubtedly much greater variation in European venture returns than in American, and in Europe this is concentrated within a much smaller sample. In other words, I am sure it must be true that in Europe there is a much greater proportion of funds which make truly awful returns than in the USA. In the VentureXpert figures for US venture, for example, there is only one vintage year in which a fund has made −100% since records began, whereas the European figures show five, and this within a much smaller sample. What does this mean? Simply that in Europe manager selection is even more important than in the USA. This has understandably led to European venture gaining a reputation as by far the most difficult of the various private equity classes, and to many LPs deciding that they simply do not want to be involved with it.

RETURNS AND FUND SIZE

Let us now repeat the exercise which we carried out for buyout funds by looking at the relationship between historic venture returns and average fund size. Let us look first at Europe. Figure 8.5 shows the Capital Weighted Average TVPI achieved in each vintage year between 1990 and 1999 against the average fund size of the same vintage year.

This seems to suggest a definite sweet spot in terms of fund size at about $150 M, both below and above which returns will suffer. So far as very small funds are concerned, experience does indeed suggest that they tend to fare badly. They are unable to follow on when other, bigger, sources of funding get involved at later stages and tend to get excessively diluted. Also, they are less likely to be trying to grow really large companies, in part because that is often not their raison d'être (they may, for example, be a university seed fund) and in part because they rightly identify in such efforts a high chance of (as they see it) unnecessary dilution. I can therefore happily accept that there is an efficient fund size in Europe below which returns will suffer; indeed, this is

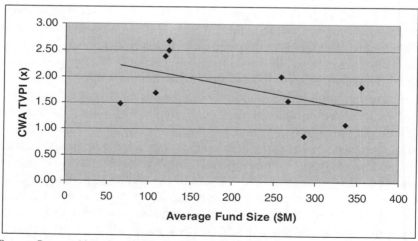

Source: Own workings from Thomson Financial's VentureXpert.

Figure 8.5 Analysis of European venture returns versus average fund size; TVPI by average fund size, vintage years 1990–1999

currently a very real issue, with even high quality European venture firms struggling to raise money.

At the other end of the scale, though, I think one needs to be a little more careful about accepting the figures at face value. We have to remember that these figures are highly questionable, particularly when we start talking about average fund size. There are, for example, a number of funds within the database where the fund size is stated as zero, which must inevitably skew the resulting averages. My own personal instinct is that the ideal venture fund size, certainly for those operating at the seed and early stages, is probably about $250 M, so that these figures probably all need shifting notionally to the right as you look at the graph. We will talk a little more about large fund sizes in a moment when we examine the US figures, since the issue is much more relevant there, but certainly there is a point beyond which returns will suffer, if only because a large fund size will inevitably push one's investment focus towards the later stages.

Because these figures seem to be somewhat skewed by false "zero" fund sizes I think it may be more useful to look at returns versus total capital raised in any one vintage year. Again, I am conscious that such an approach is far from perfect. It ignores, obviously, the number of funds that were raised and the sectors and stages for which the capital was intended. However, if we do not have the data which we need then we have to make the best of what we do have, and it strikes me that this will at least give us some indication of possible over-capacity in the system (Figure 8.6).

We have to be careful about what conclusions we draw here, since we cannot ignore the timeline of the 1990s. Yes, commitments to European venture funds rose quickly towards the end of the decade, but this was on the back of the bubble and we cannot just ignore the fact that the bubble happened. However, very cautiously I would suggest that these figures do seem to support the common-sense hypothesis that the less money there is available in the system then the better returns are likely to be. Even here, though, we must be careful. It may well be that once the amount of available capital dips below a certain point then this trend will reverse itself as it becomes difficult or even impossible to raise further financing rounds for companies, or to get funded in the first place. It could also drive firms to invest in fewer companies in each fund, thus lessening their chances of catching that one all-important home run. The years 2002–2005, for example, saw very low levels of fundraising in Europe. Figure 8.6 would suggest that they should be

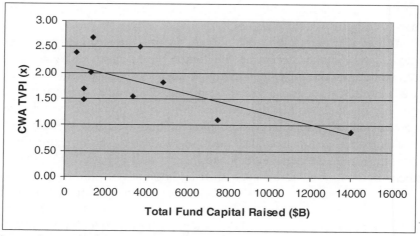

Source: Own workings from Thomson Financial VentureXpert.

Figure 8.6 European venture performance versus total fund capital raised; TVPI (×) by vintage year 1990–1999

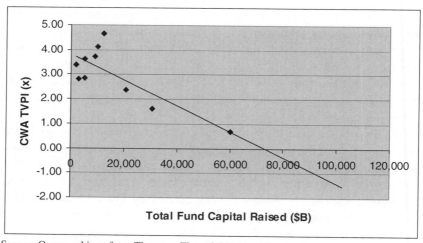

Source: Own workings from Thomson Financial VentureXpert.

Figure 8.7 US venture returns versus total fund capital raised; TVPI (×) by vintage year 1990–1999

very successful vintage years in terms of returns, but there is the very real danger that levels may have been so low that some of the phenomena I mention above may apply.

Let us now look at the same measure applied to US venture funds (Figure 8.7).

Wow! This seems to be sending a very clear picture of a direct inverse correlation between capital raised and vintage year performance. I must say right at the outset that I believe this picture to be broadly true, but there are a number of important caveats to state. First, there is the timeline effect just as with European funds. Second, this is probably exacerbated by the fact that the funds from the last couple of years (which were the really big ones) may not yet have had a chance to develop any realistic indication of their actual lifetime return.

However, these figures again seem to square with the common-sense hypothesis that an excess of money in the system will lead to a diminution of returns. This arises in a number of ways. First, American GPs have always drawn a distinction between what they call "smart money" and "dumb money". What made the funding bubble particularly harmful in the USA (and, by the way, it was even worse than these figures suggest – the original total raised for 2000 was over $120 billion before fund size reductions started to kick in) was that most of the new influx was "dumb money" from LPs who were determined to commit to US venture funds come what may, and did not particularly mind that it might fall into inexperienced or inexpert hands; 525 funds were raised in 2000, of which a very large proportion must have been first time funds. In other words, LPs were prepared to commit to funds which were likely to end up in the third or fourth quartiles of US venture performance rather than to funds which had every chance of ending up in the upper quartile of, say, European buyout. Given that even in the glory days of 1995 and 1996 the top of the lower quartile only returned 3.5% and 1.7%, whereas the upper quartile European buyout fund returned 20.3% and 22.9%, respectively, then it can readily be appreciated just how tragically mistaken this approach was.

So, quality was undoubtedly a new problem which was forced upon the US venture industry by LP behaviour, but so was quantity. As more and more money came into the system, company valuations rose dramatically, and fund sizes spiralled upwards to try to keep up with them. By 2000, firms which just a few years previously had been raising funds of $300M were suddenly raising $1.5 billion funds. While officially denied at the time, there can be little doubt in retrospect that these larger fund sizes in turn played their part in a continued increase in company valuations, even though these were already in many cases already at sustainable levels. I would argue that once the level of available funding reaches a certain level within any venture environment then this sort of outcome is inevitable, which is why I am comfortable with the general trend which Figure 8.7 identifies, even though I acknowledge that there were specific factors throughout the bubble period and the build-up to it which all made their individual contributions.

In fact, what we are seeing here is probably a natural cycle in which perceived out-performance in an asset class sucks more money into it until the excess availability of money pushes down returns sufficiently to make the asset class unattractive in relative terms, at which point allocation levels drop off, returns rise and the whole cycle starts all over again. We see this clearly in the USA, where 3 or 4 years of bumper fundraising followed 2 or 3 years of bumper performance. I think what made this possible was that whereas normally it would take several years for fund performance to become apparent, the prevailing climate of rapidly rising equity markets and fairly quick venture company exits into a booming IPO environment made clear very quickly the sort of returns that LPs in the top US venture funds of that era could reasonably expect. In more normal circumstances I would expect the cycle to develop more slowly.

Initial hopes that this cycle may have reversed itself very quickly were initially raised by the figures for, say, 2002 and 2003. In both those years roughly $11 billion was raised by roughly 100 funds even at a time when fund size reductions were taking place and so LPs should logically have had surplus capital to allocate; compare and contrast this with 2000, when 525 funds raised initially over ten times that amount. It is too early to say whether this reduction will have had any long-term beneficial effect of squeezing excess capital out of the system, but probably not, since many LPs seem to be returning quickly to their former ways. 2005 saw US venture fundraising return to very nearly 1998 levels,[1] while preliminary figures suggest that over $18 billion has been raised in the first 6 months of 2006 alone.

Recent evidence emerged that concern at fundraising levels was shared even within the Golden Circle when venture firm Sevin Rosen announced that they were abandoning fundraising for their Fund X on the grounds that "the traditional US venture model was broken" (their words, not mine). "While good returns from any given firm's portfolio are certainly a possibility," the firm wrote to its LPs, "the statistics have clearly shifted in an unfavourable direction. The venture environment has changed so

---

[1] $27 billion is reported to have been raised in 2005. Not only was this nearly as much as was raised in 1998, but it is more than was raised for the three years 1994, 1995 and 1996 combined.

that overall returns for the entire industry are way too low and even the upper quartile returns have dropped to insufficient levels."

VENTURE RETURNS BY STAGE

Accepted wisdom has it that the earlier the investment stage at which a venture fund focuses then the higher the returns they can realistically expect, and vice versa. We have already touched on this briefly, and I have to say that it accords with my own experience gained largely from US venture funds. Let us see how it works out in practice.

I think Table 8.4 shows broadly what one might expect. Observe that for both IRR and TVPI there is a slow but steady falling off as one progresses from early to later stages of investment. By the way, these figures show the fund's main investment focus, and will therefore be blunted somewhat since there is nothing to stop a later stage fund making a few early stage investments as well, or vice versa. The seed figures, though, are a bit strange and we need to dig a little deeper to see what has happened here.

We spoke earlier about the difficulty which very small venture funds have in avoiding dilution, and this is what I think we are seeing at work here. This problem is more acute in the USA than it is in Europe. In Europe, there is a feeling that a continuing good relationship with the other venture firm in question is more important than pressing what might be seen as a cruelly hard bargain on any one funding round. In the USA, the opposite is the case, and the prevailing maxim is "if you can't pay, you can't play", or in other words if you cannot participate meaningfully in a funding round then you must expect to be seriously diluted. Incidentally, this caused quite a few ruffled feathers when US firms first started doing deals in Europe in the heady days of 1998 and 1999.

Table 8.4 Analysis of US venture fund performance by stage; all funds from inception to end 2005

Stage	UQ TVPI (×)	CWA TVPI (×)	UQ IRR (%)	CWA IRR (%)
Seed	2.12	1.30	13.3	0.2
Early	2.25	1.58	16.3	13.2
Balanced	2.22	1.52	15.4	6.9
Late	2.09	1.44	14.8	5.8

Source: Thomson Financial VentureXpert.

Across business as a whole, and venture is no exception, US participants tend to be transaction-oriented whereas their European counterparts tend to be relationship-oriented, and I feel that each side needs to try to understand the other much more in this regard or further bad feeling is inevitable. As the bubble started to burst I lost count of the number of European GPs who complained bitterly to me that they had been badly treated by a US GP "who I thought we had a relationship with", usually followed by an expressed determination never to have anything to do with that firm again. Naïve, perhaps, but one could argue that the American attitude was just as mistaken, in its short-sightedness. What will happen when that US firm tries to re-enter Europe? People have long memories when they think they have been ill-used.

I suspect that the figures for US seed funds are a clear example of this inability to avoid dilution. The vast majority of the US seed stage funds listed by VentureXpert are less than $25 M in fund size, certainly way too small to "play with the big boys" as I have heard it expressed by US GPs. The absolute minimum effective size for a seed fund, bearing in mind the need to be able to follow in later rounds all the way through to exit, is probably about $100 M, and some would probably argue for an even higher figure. In fact, only 34 out of 525 seed funds in the database, or about 6% by number, are bigger than $100 M. This also helps to explain why the Capital Weighted Average IRR is so low. Just about all the larger funds were raised at the height of the bubble and their predictably low IRRs will be unduly depressing the result – hence the very large difference between the CWA and the Upper Quartile.

In general, though, I think Table 8.4 does indeed support the general view that later stage funds are likely to see lower returns than early ones. A sceptic might object that the differences are so small that they might safely be ignored, however they are drawn from a large sample and the trend which they display, though small, is statistically significant. More importantly, there is one key fact that they do not show. Remember that venture returns are driven by the stand-out funds largely managed by the golden circle firms? Well, you are no less than 15 times more likely to achieve at least a 10× return by investing in an early stage US venture fund than you are by investing in a late stage one.[2] For anyone who really understands venture returns, this is a killer point.

---

[2] Figures from Thomson Financial's VentureXpert system.

You cannot achieve the sort of returns we have heard talked about by the likes of Horsley Bridge, the Yale Endowment and others without capturing a good number of these stand-out funds within your portfolio; you have only a limited number of bullets to fire at that particular target, so why waste any of them on such a very long shot (no pun intended)? It is no coincidence that Horsley Bridge specialise almost exclusively in early stage US venture – they worked this out a long time ago.

WHAT OF THE FUTURE?

It is always a difficult business making predictions about what will happen to private equity in the future. I felt reasonably confident in doing so when talking about buyout returns since the prevailing trends seem to be suggested so strongly by the available data. Here, we are obviously in different territory.

First there is the effect of the bubble to consider. This had infinitely more direct impact on venture returns than it did on buyout. Buyout suffered indirectly through the associated ramp in equity valuations followed by what was almost a nuclear winter for some years as far as exits were concerned, but venture caught the full blast of it. This was hopefully a "once in a generation" event and so it seems hard to take the possibility of another such cataclysmic period into account, but human nature being what it is one trembles to think what might happen to investor sentiment should things such as stem cell therapy, fuel cell technology or cold fusion ever really take off; there is the even more likely prospect that something as yet completely uncontemplated could suddenly be hailed as "the next big thing". So faddism, or irrational exuberance, or cyclicality or whatever you might like to call it is probably something that must be factored into our expectations of venture returns in the future.

My concerns in this direction are heightened by the fact that venture fundraising does not appear to have fallen back, as one might have hoped when looking at the figures a few years ago, to the more rational levels of, say, 1994 or 1995. On the contrary, fundraising already seems to have regained the levels it enjoyed at the beginning of the bubble period and my instinct is that it will go higher yet. There are likely to be a good number of investors wishing to enter the private equity space over the next few years, and the advice they will probably receive is that they should be looking to put their money to work in US venture funds. Since access to the golden circle will be effectively impossible, this means that we will see the irrational intention of investing with potential third or fourth quartile funds perpetuated. This in turn will enable some firms who should probably not be able to raise a new fund in normal circumstances to remain in business.

As we saw a few pages earlier, my concerns are shared even within the Golden Circle itself; Sevin Rosen were raising their tenth fund when they withdrew from the Market. Interestingly, another factor which Sevin Rosen might have mentioned but didn't is that the US venture market is once again seeing large numbers of new entrants (just as in 2001 just before the bubble burst): 52 new US venture firms in the first three quarters of 2006 alone according to the NVCA.

Then there is the problem of coming to any sort of accurate view on what European venture has actually achieved in terms of historic performance, and in any event is historic European performance necessarily a good guide to future returns?

We have demonstrated that coming to any sort of accurate view of how European venture has really performed is virtually impossible. There is evidence that at least one fund in each vintage year has usually produced performance that would measure against the golden circle in the USA, although the golden circle effect as such is absent. However, there can be no doubt that European venture has badly under-performed, though it is impossible to say by exactly how much.

This is due partly to the absence of the golden circle, but this only tells part of the story. The absence of the US model of early stage investing, and skills, expertise and mind-set that this requires, have meant that with the exception of that odd one or two funds a year, European venture has under-performed across the board. The really interesting question, of course, is what will happen as the US model starts to be widely employed in Europe. Is there any good reason why it should not generate at least as good returns as it has done in America?

My instinct says "no". However, I am in a delicate position here. I am well known as an advocate of European venture and do not want to be accused of making fanciful claims with little hard data to back it up. It may, I freely admit, be seen as highly convenient that the historic data which seems to damn historic European venture returns turns out to be unreliable. Very well, here is some hard data. According to data provider VentureOne, there have only been eight venture exits in the world since the beginning of 2002 with an exit value in excess of $1 billion. It may surprise many that not only have four of these been European, but also that with the exception of Google, the European realised exit multiples have been higher than the others. Now, one swallow (or even four swallows) doth not a summer make, but surely this is at least circumstantial evidence that European venture capitalists are watching what has happened in the USA, learning from it, and applying it in Europe to good effect?

So, the future for venture may be unpredictable but certainly, for this most exciting of asset classes, is not going to be boring. Certainly the golden circle will continue consistently to out-perform. The question is what happens outside the golden circle. How will the returns of the run-of-the-mill US firms hold up in an environment which still looks over-funded and over-populated? Will the gap between the golden circle and the rest open up still further? Will the bulk of the golden circle come to rue their decision not to expand into Europe in the late 1990s?

My instinct says "yes", but I am unsure exactly how this might play out. I am aware of at least one European venture firm which has been approached with a view to becoming the European offshoot of an American firm, and this is certainly one way ahead, but I am not sure that it will prove widespread as an approach. Nor I am sure that US firms will actually come to Europe en masse in the near future. European expansion, or, at least, *successful* European expansion requires a mind-set which I think simply does not exist in US firms at present. It requires a willingness to adapt where necessary to slightly different ways of doing business, and to accept that companies planted beyond your own garden fence might prove just as successful as your own home-grown variety. It also requires a readiness to work with Europeans as equal partners. There are at least two honourable exceptions here,[3] but for the most part the best US venture firms seem to believe that none of this is possible without in some way fatally compromising the US model. I think they will come to see that they are mistaken, but it will take time and by then the real opportunity may well have been missed.

In the meantime they may well have decided to expand to Asia first. While illogical, since Europe represents an already established venture community, and a stable business infrastructure in marked contrast to, say, China, this would be consistent with what has happened in other areas of investment and also with everything I have heard from talking with American LPs. The roots of the American love affair with Asia,

---

[3] Accel and Benchmark, already mentioned.

and particularly with China, run deep and were planted a long time ago (at least 70 years ago and possibly longer). Asia is hugely seductive and it is a seduction that US investors feel unable to resist. One constant in human affairs is our apparent inability to learn from history. Those few of us with long enough experience of private equity will remember the ill-fated China funds which were set up almost exclusively with US money in the early 1990s, amid brave talk of expectations of 4× or 5× fund returns (since naturally something which was high risk must also produce high returns, mustn't it?). Yet sadly it seems that this is something that each successive generation of investors must learn for themselves all over again.

Please do not run away with the idea that I am somehow anti-Asian; I am not. Venture capital has become a global business and Asia has a vital role to play in global expansion of venture companies; Worldview, for example, has had business development offices in Asia for many years. Yet there is all the difference in the world between seeing Asia as a logical market for portfolio companies and investing in funds dedicated to conducting venture transactions within a particular Asian market. Here there is a significant perceived risk premium due to things like lack of transparency in business affairs and different attitudes to contractual commitments. It is important that investors go into markets like Asia and South America with their eyes open and with realistic expectations of extra return to compensate for this additional risk.

SUMMARY

- Historically, US venture has very significantly out-performed European venture. However, while taking nothing away from the superb achievements of US venture firms during the 1990s, the difference is not perhaps quite so dramatic as the official figures would have us believe.
- The official figures for European venture contain a large number of funds which either cannot be properly classified as venture, or are not of institutional investment grade, either because they are very small, or because they are not managed by independent venture firms. The level of accuracy in the average vintage years during the 1990s, measured by the number of such eligible funds, is only about 27%. Thus, while performance has been undeniably disappointing, it is difficult to be sure just how disappointing.

Individual European funds have proved successful, even achieving 10×, but it seems that such successes have been isolated and not reproduced across any significant portion of the industry.

- In statistical terms, much of the difference is due to the consistent success of the "golden circle" firms in the USA in producing funds which can return more than 10×. It is significant that in the only pre-bubble vintage year in the 1990s to produce less than exciting returns (1991), there was not a single such fund formed. Thus the ability to produce excellent returns from a portfolio of US venture funds is dependent upon the ability to successfully identify and access these funds.
- Early stage funds seem 15 times more likely to produce at least 10× than late stage funds.
- There seems to be a direct inverse relationship between the amount of capital raised in any vintage year and the returns of that vintage year, particularly in the USA.
- In practical terms the main reason for the differing returns was the absence in Europe of the US model, with everything that this implies (mind-set, skills, etc.).
- However, it should be remembered that no equivalent of NASDAQ existed in Europe to provide exits and drive valuations. Also, the bubble had much more opportunity (because of the relative time-lines) to create high returns for a brief time in the USA than it did in Europe.
- Levels of venture fundraising remain a concern in the USA. There are indications that these are returning to early bubble era pro-portions, despite a significant overhang of capital already in the system. This could well result in valuations remaining at relatively high historic levels, but will also see LPs being pushed inexorably down the quality chain in their fund selection.
- It seems highly likely that the golden circle will continue signifi-cantly to out-perform the rest of their US competitors. Indeed, it is possible that with high levels of available capital enabling third and fourth quartile firms to stay in business, this difference will become even more pronounced.
- The huge unknown is what will happen as the US model becomes increasingly widely practised in Europe. Recent billion dollar exits, though small in number, suggest that Europe may well be able to at least match US returns in future. Given that very small

amounts of capital are currently being allocated to this area, European venture could be seen as representing a classic contrarian opportunity.

- It is possible that the vast majority of US venture firms may live to regret having missed a strategic window for expansion into Europe in the late 1990s. It is unlikely that this situation will change any time soon; indeed, it is quite possible that most US firms have Asia ahead of Europe on the agenda.
- Whatever the case, venture is rapidly becoming a global business, and the key test for any venture firm in the future may well prove to be how they rise to this challenge. With one or two honourable exceptions, international expansion by venture firms has proved highly problematic in practice.

9

Due Diligence

The making of any private equity investment is a twofold process. First comes the decision in principle as to whether this looks like an attractive prospect. If this ends with a "yes" vote then you will have decided to make the investment "subject to due diligence" and this second part of the process will now follow. In practice, the distinction between the two is becoming increasingly blurred, since you will have needed to investigate a lot of the facts very thoroughly in order to make your decision in principle in the first place, particularly if these have been identified as specific issues. However, for ease of discussion we will assume that these two parts of the process are separate and discrete.

Due diligence is a huge subject, particularly so in this case since we need to cover all the different types of private equity investment. However, there is much that is common in the approach to each one, and so I will begin by describing the process in general and then focus on what you should look for in each particular case.

I would recommend that during the initial decision process you keep a list (putting it on a flipchart works very well) divided into three columns headed "pros", "cons" and "issues", respectively. The objective of due diligence is to focus on each of the issues until it is possible to resolve it, hopefully transferring it to one of the other columns in the process. Of course, this is not always possible and there will be some issues that remain issues right up to the time the final decision is taken. Generally speaking with private equity you make any decision to invest despite the existence of various issues. This is just the way it is (chiefly because in many cases your decision is largely a decision to back certain individuals, and human beings are notoriously difficult to understand and classify) and if you seek a perfect situation where there can never be any possible doubt what the right decision may be then I am afraid you will never make a single investment. You must do your best, exhausting every reasonable avenue of enquiry in the process, but you cannot achieve certainty. Indeed, it is in this final layer of uncertainty that the skill and judgement which distinguishes a truly good private equity investor from an also-ran resides.

The fact that due diligence carries on from the initial stages of the investment process is in fact a great help, since you should already have identified those issues which you need to explore. Incidentally, there is an important lesson here which is ignored by the vast majority of private equity investors, both at the fund and at the company level. Due diligence does not take place in a vacuum. If you have a standard due diligence checklist which you dutifully and meticulously follow in each case (or, even worse, a standard questionnaire which you expect the investee to complete) then you are completely missing the point. Yes, of course there are certain things which you will always need to check, but the main purpose of due diligence is to satisfy yourself on those specific issues which you have identified during your initial investigations and analysis. Sadly most investors seem to fail to recognise that the aim of due diligence is to help them make better decisions, and prefer to see it as a means of covering their backs in advance should anything go wrong with the investment in the future.

In many cases, particularly where the LP relies on the investee supposedly to do their work for them by filling in interminable questionnaires asking for their grandmother's date of birth, due diligence at the fund level may consist largely of recalculating the relevant historic cashflows to check that the stated IRRs are indeed correct. In passing, I would query whether this is really necessary when, for example, the figures have already been specifically audited by a major accounting firm, or verified by a reputable placing agent, but let that go. Such investigation may be a very good way of papering the due diligence file, but fails to address the key questions, which are not "what is the IRR?" but "how does it compare to the IRRs of similar funds from the same vintage year?", "if it is different, why is it different?", "how have the returns been influenced by the relevant drivers?", "what evidence do the figures show of this firm doing things differently to other firms, or differently to how the same firm used to do things in the past?", etc. In other words, even financial due diligence needs to be intelligent and geared towards answering specific questions, not just verifying the data which has been proffered.

At the company level, of course, particularly in the case of buyouts, verification *is* vitally important and will usually be addressed by way of an investigating accountant's report. Yet even here, financial due diligence will go way beyond verification and the exploration of contingent liabilities, etc. The buyout firm will be flexing the forecasts and management accounts to see how much extra cashflow can be squeezed out to service debt, or investigating the effects of possible asset or business unit sales.

However, it is on the "soft" issues that due diligence become the most difficult, partly because people are always reluctant to speak frankly about their associates, and in particular reluctant to say anything negative about them. For some reason this problem is particularly acute in France, where effective "people" due diligence is all but impossible; even if you make the effort to have the conversation in French all anyone will usually say is that the object of your enquiries is "well connected". A good way of getting around his problem, if you can, is to track down anyone who has left the firm recently; even the insights of quite junior staff on things like team dynamics can be very helpful. This raises a further important point, by the way. By all means make a few calls to the names you have been given, but this should be largely a matter of form since they are most unlikely to tell you anything really valuable. Most of your calls should be "off the list". In addition to recent leavers, try to find the CEOs of portfolio companies which may have got into difficulties, any other private equity firms who co-invested in such deals, and any LPs who committed to previous funds but have now stopped doing so.

As a matter of form you should verify the personal details you have been given by contacting previous employers and educational institutions. It is amazing how many people lie about their class of degree, for example. It is a pity that this is not done more often as a matter of routine when checking offering documents and the like. I have so far come across someone who claimed to have a degree from a prestigious British university when in fact he had been expelled in his first year, and someone who put the letters "LLD" after his name – something which went unnoticed for some time despite the fact that this can only be awarded as an honorary degree to a major public figure, whereas this particular gentleman turned out to be a struck-off solicitor's clerk. My cast of characters over the years has also included a phoney barrister and someone who changed the spelling of his name in an attempt to conceal a string of bankruptcy orders (and who also turned out to have spent time at Her Majesty's pleasure, described rather inventively as "voluntary work overseas").

All this should be routine, but often is not. The scope of due diligence is bounded only by your imagination and the amount of time which you have available, but you should never lose sight of the real objective, which is to resolve any outstanding issues which you have with the fund or company. In the case of a fund, all your enquiries should be leading you towards one thing: exactly how does this group do its deals, and how does this differ from other people in the same space? This will include things such as dealflow (Ian Simpson of Helix Associates once memorably drew attention to a computer virus which had invaded the computers of private equity practitioners inserting the phrases "proprietary dealflow" and "upper quartile performance" at random into people's presentations), but also how they develop their portfolio companies during the post-investment phase.

BUYOUT FUNDS

We have seen in an earlier chapter how to model and analyse buyout returns. You need to be able to examine exactly what contribution each of the buyout drivers has made, since this will give you a good idea of how the firm creates value for its investors. Top of your list of preferences should be any firm that is able consistently to increase company earnings in real terms (i.e., after adjusting for inflation) since this is a group that will be able to make money in any market conditions.

However, you should also use your driver analysis to compare what the firm has been doing against other buyout firms over time; obviously this will only become possible as you add more buyout firms to your portfolio over the years, but once comparative data *is* available then this can become a very revealing exercise. Is one firm using more or less debt than the others, for example, or paying higher multiples for its companies? There is often a surprising variation in the former measure, while the latter can be an indicator of a group that is struggling for dealflow.

Incidentally, this is one reason why doing due diligence on a firm is never wasted. Even if you decide at the end of the day not to invest, then your due diligence material can be saved and used for comparative purposes when analysing other funds. However, I am not suggesting that you should embark upon due diligence routinely just to acquire data for these purposes. There are quite a few LPs who do seem to do this, and they rapidly acquire a poor reputation amongst GPs and placing agents. Due diligence should only follow a decision in principle to invest, and if you are not committing to at least two-thirds of the funds on which you perform due diligence then something is wrong; specifically, you are starting a full due diligence process when a little limited information gathering could probably have killed the project at a much earlier stage. Due diligence time is precious, particularly if you are going to do things properly by speaking to lots of people. Use it wisely to do really meaningful work on those few funds you believe to be key prospects.

Dealflow is key for buyout firms and one of the things you should be analysing is exactly where each deal comes from. For the larger players, just about every deal will nowadays go through some sort of auction process, so be very wary of deals which are described as "pro-active" or "exclusive" in origin. Similarly, most will today involve a consortium of investors, possibly with equity syndication outside the consortium as well. A word of warning here: every buyout firm involved in a consortium will claim to have led it, and that their involvement was the reason why the deal was offered to the consortium in the first place (e.g., "we had been chasing this deal for five years", "we knew the company very well", "we have recognised expertise in the sector", etc.). Take such claims with a pinch of salt and see if you can find independent verification (perhaps from the investment bank which handled the deal, from a lending bank, or from someone who has recently left one of the buyout firms involved) of exactly what really happened.

Equally important is to try to find out which deals they were chasing but did not manage to close. Were they on the short list of potential purchasers? If not, which of their competitors were preferred, and why? If they were on the list but did not close the deal, why was this? Is it possible to check, for example, that the price they offered was lower than that of the winning consortium, and, if so, by how much, and why?

With smaller buyout firms due diligence can take on a more traditional flavour since here it is perfectly possible that they may be sourcing deals on an exclusive and/or proactive basis, but again do maintain a healthy scepticism. The tentacles of the auction process now reach a very long way down the size scale. Times have changed since a management team used to hire an accountancy firm and go to see two or three buyout firms. These days most company vendors will use some sort of intermediary who will solicit offers from a wide variety of purchasers.

Team dynamics are key and require careful teasing out. How many of the executives share in the carry and the management fee profits, and in what percentages? There can be some very large sums of money involved, particularly in the case of mega funds, and having the equity ownership contained within too tight a group of people is generally an unwelcome sign, as it can be an omen of executive departures or an unhappy ship.

Similarly, exactly who takes the investment decisions, and how are these made? Is it majority voting? Does any one person have a veto? Does it have to be unanimous? Incidentally, do look out for situations where an outsider, i.e., someone who is not a member of the executive team, plays any part in the investment decision process. This will not normally be an issue since it will typically only occur where a group is not independent but is part of a larger organisation (usually a bank or an insurance company) and you would not normally consider a fund managed by such a team in the first place. However, it is still quite common in continental Europe for one or two prominent outsiders to play a role. Another way in which the issue can occur is if an outsider has previously played a role but the team has got the message that this is bad news for investors and has removed the person from that role. The problem here is that sometimes all that happens is that the name disappears from the Offering Memorandum but the individual carries on playing the role de facto; you need to be very careful (but discreet) in checking what is going on here. The general rule is that if you have any doubt at all that decisions are not being made exclusively by the executives themselves, then do not proceed.

VENTURE FUNDS

Many of the points which I have already made in relation to buyout funds are relevant here too, particularly in so far as they relate to team dynamics. Indeed, within a venture firm this is even more important, as they tend to be more of a collegiate, equal partnership type of organisation rather than the more hierarchical structure of the typical buyout firm. Some venture firms, for example, have an "only partners" policy, and thus they do all the work themselves rather than delegating it to principals, associates, analysts, senior vice presidents, junior vice presidents, middling vice presidents, etc. In such a situation the relationship of each partner to the others is all-important and should form a large part of your initial discussions and due diligence work. Again, the best people to ask are almost certainly not the partners themselves but people who have dealings with the firm and who, ideally, have been involved in one or more of their transactions (including ones that have not worked out).

We have already seen that what distinguishes a good venture firm from its competitors is home run mentality, and all your due diligence should be focused on identifying the presence or otherwise of this.

Unfortunately, just as every buyout firm will claim to have proprietary dealflow, so every venture firm will claim to have a home run mentality, so this is very much an area where you will have to rely on what you see and hear for yourself, rather than on what you are told.

With an established firm which has been in business for 10 years or more there is a very simple litmus test which can tell you straight away if this is an offering on which you wish to spend any time or not. If they are now on, say, Fund IV and none of their earlier funds seem likely to return at least three times their money or to produce a home run (and to do one without the other is difficult) then I think you are entitled to assume that this is a good indicator that the firm is unlikely ever to achieve this. Remember, we are defining a home run as something which has the potential to return the whole capital of the fund at least once, so even if there has been a big winner (25× or better) it does not count as a home run if it only made up, say, 1% of the fund.

This raises an important point, and something which is not appreciated (and certainly not carried out) by most LPs who do due diligence on venture firms. It is crucial that you analyse the money multiple made by each deal relative to what percentage of the fund it made up. Ideally, of course, what you want to see is a good correlation between big bets and big winners. This is a very good indicator of home run mentality; a firm that is identifying and killing off its losers quickly and devoting its resources to those few companies which emerge as having home run potential. While a perfect result (a trend line from bottom left to top right) will rarely be possible, a cluster of companies in the top left-hand corner would almost certainly be a clear reason not to invest with that firm.

The percentage of a company's equity which is held by the fund is also often a good indicator of how they are doing business. The ideal is a fund which can get into a company early, secure a good equity percentage (anything up to about 40%) and protect that against subsequent dilution as much as possible, ending up with 15% to 20%. If a fund shows consistently low percentage holdings then either (1) they are not doing a good job of protecting their position or (2) they are predominantly coming into other people's deals at a later stage.[1] Neither of these approaches is likely to result in the scoring of home runs.

---

[1] I was once making a reference call to the CEO of a company in which a venture fund had taken a very small stake late in the day, and when I explained that I was calling about XYZ Partners he asked "who?".

Obviously there are exceptions when a company's valuation really explodes, as happened recently with Skype, but I think the general principle will be clear. It is much easier to score a home run if you have a large percentage of a company's equity, since you will capture proportionately more of the gain, and if it represents a good percentage (at least 4%) of your fund, since it will have a much greater effect on the fund's money multiple. We want to invest with venture firms which have the maximum chance of scoring home runs, so we will tend to avoid those which exhibit either of the above tendencies.

The other aspect of a home run mentality which needs to be thoroughly tested is the ability to contribute value add. This is best done by speaking to other venture capitalists who have invested alongside them and CEOs whose companies have been backed by the firm in the past, and quizzing them about what the individual GPs actually did for the company. Here there may well be a dramatic difference in the responses depending on whether you are in Europe or America.

In the USA you will hear about GPs helping with product development, drawing up sales presentations, making introductions to key customers, hiring executives, etc. The CEO is likely to be very clued-up about venture best practice, particularly if he is an experienced entrepreneur, and may well be able to draw direct comparisons with other venture firms. When conducting due diligence on a traditional European venture firm, CEOs are likely to say "well, he comes to the board meeting once a month – after all, that's what venture capitalists do, you know". Happily, things are changing in Europe but clearly a response like this is not likely to inspire confidence in a firm's ability to score home runs.

There are lots of other things that you can do when looking at a venture fund. You can check to see how their pre-money valuations compare with other deals, how their performance may differ by sector, and whether their investment focus is moving earlier or later by stage (this may well be a function of fund size – larger venture funds typically push a firm later in stage focus). At the end of the day, however, home runs are all that matter in venture capital and all your due diligence, no matter what form it takes, should be geared towards answering the fundamental question: how likely is it that this fund will end up with at least one home run in it?

With venture becoming an increasingly global business, you also need to look very carefully at how a firm might be able to grow a company across national boundaries if they are operating in sectors where this might prove necessary. For example, if a Californian firm is doing deals in the mobile space, how is it going to access European markets? Similarly, how is a European firm going to relocate a software company to the USA? This is currently seen, rightly I think, as much more of an issue for European firms, who commonly complain that it is impossible for them to get the attention of the leading US venture firms when they try to interest them in becoming a US co-investor in their deals. However, I have written elsewhere that I think the failure of the best US venture firms successfully to colonise Europe (with two honourable exceptions) may well prove to be a source of major strategic weakness in the future.

CO-INVESTORS

As an essential part of the due diligence on a venture fund you should look carefully at the venture firms which co-invested in portfolio companies. Quality venture firms want to invest in quality companies alongside other quality venture firms, and the identity of co-investors is a very good indicator of levels of peer recognition and respect, both for the firm generally and for its portfolio companies. Indeed, if you want a "quick and dirty" indicator of firm quality you could simply look at the identity of their co-investors and the number of home runs they have scored. However, please be aware that this measure, though still valid, is less just in Europe, where capital is typically in short supply and venture firms frequently have to take it where they can find it.

Incidentally, this is an issue too in buyout funds, but for different reasons. We have already noted the practice of buyout funds gathering together in consortia to bid for various companies. We are now also starting to see evidence of equity being syndicated immediately after completion to other buyout funds, who may have been members of unsuccessful consortia bidding for the same deal. This needs to be carefully monitored, as it threatens to commoditise buyout returns. In particular, if you see evidence of two or three buyout firms habitually acting together then you need to think very carefully about whether you can validly invest with any more than one of them. Conversely, if you see evidence of a buyout firm that can act alone and still win deals, or perhaps involve other firms infrequently and on a random basis, then this offers genuine potential for a unique pattern of returns.[2]

---

[2] But beware – this could be uniquely bad as well as uniquely good!

CROSS-FUND INVESTING

With both buyout and venture funds you need to keep a very careful eye on instances of cross-fund investing. I mention this here because traditionally it has been more of an issue with venture funds, although there have been a couple of high profile cases involving buyout funds in recent years. The reason it is more of an issue with venture funds is that venture companies will have serial funding rounds, whereas typically buyout companies will have only one. Thus, in buyout situations it normally arises either where a company is making an acquisition, or where it has got into severe difficulty and an injection of new equity is proposed, or (and this may surprise you) where it is being sold and the buyout firm involved decides to make a new investment into the deal from its current fund alongside the purchaser. Space forbids a detailed examination of these situations, but suffice it to say that each of these buyout situations involves at least the potential for massive conflict of interest (since the LP membership of each fund will be different) and the need for a strong and disinterested advisory board of independent views is paramount (but unfortunately rarely realised). The best advice I can give is that if you come across such a situation that seems a particularly unfair use of current fund capital, then this is probably a firm best avoided.

Within a venture fund, other issues arise in addition to the obvious one of valuation. Principally you will need to ask what went wrong with the reserves for future funding rounds within the firm's prior fund, and question to what extent the effect of such follow-on investing may shift the investment stage focus of the new fund away from early stage towards late stage. The general principle should be that an early stage venture fund should not be investing in a company for the first time at a later stage, full stop. To do so is to diminish its chances of scoring a home run, to which end every penny of fund capital should be utilised.

BUYOUT COMPANIES

Buyout firms perform due diligence on prospective portfolio companies in much the same way that any prospective corporate acquirer would in any M&A transaction and this is one reason why buyout professionals are often drawn from the ranks either of investment bankers or accountants; the disciplines of M&A and buyout are very similar in the investment and exit modes, though a buyout firm will be looking at a company with different objectives in mind.

So, full financial due diligence is the order of the day and, as we have already seen, this will usually include commissioning a report from an investigating accountant. This is partly in the nature of an audit process but more importantly (since the most recent audited accounts will usually form the subject of reps and warranties anyway) looks at things like the company's currency exposure, leasing and borrowing arrangements and working capital generally. The objective is to make quite sure that the cashflow assumptions which the buyout firm is making can in fact be relied upon. This is hugely important since, as we saw in an earlier chapter, the ability to service and repay the acquisition debt is an essential requirement for the success of any buyout.

The buyout firm will also want to make sure that key personnel will stay in place during the post-deal stage. Typically, they will try to do this by persuading the individuals concerned to take either some part of the sweet equity personally or some share options, and at the same time sign agreements which tie them to the company for a certain length of time as a condition subsequent to their equity entitlement. However, in some cases the buyout firm is not allowed access to the management team, or only under strictly regulated conditions, so this is very much a delicate area and one where some of the black arts of the buyout world come into play.

You will also need to examine the various supply and distribution channel agreements to which the company is party. This should be not only in the nature of a legal audit (there may for example be a change of control provision) but also to investigate what is likely to happen in practical terms. If, for example, the relationship with a key customer has been handled by one individual for a number of years and that individual is leaving the company, you might consider inserting some sort of earn-out provision to protect you should turnover and earnings fall sharply. If they are staying as part of the management team, then you might also be thinking about what you put in that individual's contract as well as introducing further people into the relationship as a practical measure.

Where a very large business is concerned, which is increasingly the case given the much bigger fund sizes that we are seeing, you will also need to due diligence the competitive situation for fear of falling foul of anti-trust (USA) or monopolies (Europe) legislation. This can lead to a lengthy and costly investigation at the end of which the deal may be vetoed or only allowed under certain conditions (usually of business units or rights being relinquished artificially to create greater competition). Personally I have never seen the point of such legislation in a capitalist system. It seems rather like saying to a tiger "it's all right to have teeth as long as you don't actually bite anyone", but the fact remains that it is an increasingly important factor in the buyout world and you would be well advised to seek advice in advance from the law firms and strategic consultancies who specialise in such matters.

Another area which has become of vital importance in these days of pension deficits (at least in the UK) is the question of the company's pension scheme. This can be a particular problem where the company being bought is part of a larger group and the group scheme is in deficit. Here, the acquiring entity (buyout fund) may have to not only make good the deficit (measured artificially for accounting and regulatory purposes) but also bring it up to what is called "buy-out" level. Confusingly, this has nothing to do with the private equity meaning of the term but refers to the cost of buying annuities for all the scheme members, which can be up to 40% higher.[3] At the time of writing this is a very topical issue. According to a survey carried out by Mercers, over 20% of buyout firms polled said they had pulled out of a deal solely for this reason.[4] However, it now seems that in the UK new Inland Revenue rules will allow an alternative solution whereby the business unit and its workers simply carry on paying into the pension scheme of the former parent group, but it has yet to be seen how this will work out in practice. Whatever the case, detailed actuarial analysis of the company's pension position will continue to be an essential part of buyout due diligence.

VENTURE COMPANIES

The issues surrounding venture companies will be different, and thus due diligence needs to be aimed in different directions.

The main concern which any venture firm will have about a new investment will be whether the product or service will be successful commercially, and successful on a large enough scale to provide the potential for growing a very large company. This can be addressed in different ways, but much will come down to the particular sector knowl-

---

[3] See an article by Phil Davis in the *Financial Times*, 11 September 2006.
[4] "Pension liabilities bad for private equity", www.globalpension.com, 14 September 2006.

edge of an individual GP, and this is why personal entrepreneurial experience is so important. A venture capitalist who can look at a prospect from the perspective of his own recent start-up, and who is acquainted with the company's potential key customers clearly has a huge advantage. This is a vital part of the US venture model which has until very recently been largely absent in Europe.[5]

This process will inevitably be largely subjective and collegiate – the GP will discuss the prospect on an ongoing basis with the other partners in the firm, and venture partners and EIRs will also often be able to add their personal perspective. The process can be more formalised, however. I know of one European venture firm, for example, who will not make a new investment until after they have taken the entrepreneurial team on tour around a number of prospective customers worldwide and have watched and discussed their reaction to the team's "pitch". Should the firm continue with the investment then this process of course has a multiple purpose since it represents not only valuable advance marketing to possible alpha and beta customers, but also provides input on product design and specification.

At a scientific level, the venture firm will need to assure themselves of the soundness of the design, i.e., that the product will actually work. Many of the best GPs have these technical skills themselves, but most venture firms also maintain a panel of consultant technical experts, many of whom will be senior academics or research scientists.

The firm will also need to satisfy itself on ownership of the intellectual property of the technology involved. Here again use will be made of outside specialists, this time patent agents and lawyers.

Venture investing is a question of investing in people, perhaps even more so at the company level than at the fund level. After all, the typical venture company proposition is, at least at seed and early stage, "two guys with an idea". Thus much time will be spent getting to know the individuals involved on a personal basis (frequently by one or more GP, VP and/or EIR from the firm going and working with the team for a period of time). Another important point will arise here. The team members need to understand that they will almost certainly not be the right people to lead the company long term, and unless the venture firm is absolutely sure that this recognition is both clear and genuine, then

---

[5] An informal survey conducted by the writer a couple of years ago across 10 leading European venture firms suggested that only about 4% of their IT and Telecoms partners had themselves founded a start-up company.

they should not proceed. The prospects of many a promising venture company have been destroyed by the refusal of an intransigent founder to stand down in favour of a professional CEO, and this has been a particular problem in Europe, where venture firms have typically striven heroically to avoid any undue confrontation in such situations.

If all this sounds a little unstructured that is probably because if buyout investing is a science, then venture investing is an art, in which soft issues such as people qualities and market instinct are more important than financial engineering. However, while this is undoubtedly true, I would not wish to over-play it. The venture firm which neglected hardcore due diligence on things like background checks and intellectual property would soon find itself in trouble, no matter how sound its instincts.

FUND OF FUNDS

The issues before an investor when considering investment in a Fund of Funds will vary according to the structure, time horizon and investment focus which the investor desires. Sadly, the subtlety of realising that different Fund of Funds managers can offer different things is frequently lost on LPs, particularly those who resort to the tender process,[6] but this is nonetheless the ideal at which one should aim. Yes, of course there are large multinational Fund of Funds players whose funds are both generalist and global in scope,[7] but there are also niche players who might specialise, for example, in US venture or European buyout and a sophisticated LP, even if embarking on a Fund of Funds programme (which is not only a perfectly valid approach but probably very sensible in many cases) will be seeking to understand exactly what coverage is offered, not only so that they may fine-tune this as necessary but also to know in what directions their due diligence should be aimed.

Due diligence on a Fund of Funds is almost a vicarious experience as much of it will consist of examining how the Fund of Funds manager carries out due diligence on its own potential investee funds. Having a good idea now of the sort of things to look for when examining both buyout and venture finds, you will in turn have an idea of what they should be doing and (importantly) why.

---

[6] For an article on the tendering process, particularly as it affects European pension funds, see "Got time to kill?", *Pensions World*, Vol. 35, No. 1, January 2006.

[7] Officially, at least. In fact, European venture is usually conspicuous by its absence.

The most important area of due diligence, though, particularly as regards any firm which promises a large coverage of US venture, is the question of access. Test the level of exposure which they have actually achieved for their investors in golden circle US firms (beware, here, that they may well try to stretch this definition very considerably). In many cases it will be 5% or less of their total fund capital (sometimes considerably less). If so, this should raise questions as to why they are raising so much money. If their target for US venture is, say, 30% overall, then even if they wanted to match their golden circle exposure dollar for dollar with other hopefully first quartile funds, they should still only be raising about one-third as much total fund capital. It should also raise questions about their asset allocation. If they can only get 5% into the golden circle then is it really sensible to be putting five times as much into other US venture funds? They may have perfectly good answers to these questions, but it is here that the bulk of your due diligence should be focused, not filing away voluminous questionnaires full of largely irrelevant information.

In fact, this is so important that let us make this point just once more. The most important factor in analysing any private equity fund (and Funds of Funds are no exception) is the investment model. Is it valid? Can the firm keep to it? Does it make sense in the context of current and possibly changing market conditions? Is it consistent with the amount of money which they are raising? As you will have seen from earlier chapters, it is this last question in particular which many firms may struggle to answer convincingly. Similarly, let me repeat one final time: the way to do this is by full and frank face-to-face meetings, the content of which is targeted at specific issues and discussed internally afterwards, not by papering the file with questionnaires. If you want to make the transition from a simple functionary to an intelligent investor, for goodness sake tear up your questionnaire and throw it away.

The final point with a Fund of Funds is of course people and performance. The latter should be fully set out in whatever OM is available. If not, it is a good idea to prepare a one-page summary of fund history, showing the age, vintage year, TVPI and IRR to date of each individual fund. Indeed, a good OM should already contain this as a matter of course. So far as people are concerned, all my earlier remarks apply.

Incidentally, while conducting due diligence, it is worth remembering the following principle, sometimes known as "the 3 Ps":

People + Process = Performance

I have seen this used by many firms in different disciplines (most recently by hedge funds) and authorship is claimed by many people. However, for what it's worth my instinct is that, as with so many things in private equity, it probably originated many years ago with Phil Horsley.

MONITORING PRIVATE EQUITY FUNDS

Many people feel that once they have done all the hard work of the investment decision process and due diligence they can relax and sit back. In fact, this is what many actually do, simply attending the fund's annual meeting and, one suspects, gathering up all the quarterly reports for their auditors once a year.

This is not, however, how a sophisticated investor will approach things. Once made, the investment must be monitored. You want to know that the firm is sticking to its agreed investment model, that it is investing efficiently, and that the team dynamics are still as they were when you carried out your due diligence. In particular, you want to know at once if any key player within the team is thinking of leaving.

In short, unless the firm is actually hiding things (which would obviously carry very serious implications), you should never discover anything new at the annual meeting, and if you do then I would suggest that you have probably not been doing your job properly. Of course, if a firm does choose to hide things there is little you can do save determine not to invest with that firm again or, in an extreme case, seek to sell your LP interest in the secondary market so as to bring your relationship with that firm to an end.

I have to say that the vast majority of GPs are honest, professional and highly reputable, and will not only practice full disclosure but will seek to bring any particular issues to your attention specifically, and in many cases canvass your views before taking any action. I have only personally experienced downright concealment on three occasions, in each case concerning the departure of a partner or partners, but when it does occur then loss of trust tends to be both rapid and total.

Formal monitoring will take two forms. First, you will be entering the deal data contained in the quarterly reports into your buyout or venture model as appropriate and analysing it on an ongoing basis. You will find that most funds do not provide the level of detail you need to be able to do this, but most are happy to provide supplemental information, particularly if you promise to show them, on a blind basis, how they rank against some of their competitors on the key drivers.

Armed with this information, the second part of your monitoring process will be regular update visits with the group, ideally at least twice a year. It may be an idea to show them your analysis material in advance and to stipulate those issues upon which you wish to focus. Otherwise, there is a real danger that the firm will simply "run the clock" and the meeting will degenerate into a general chat about the market. By the way, an hour is rarely adequate for these meetings and you should insist on two hours being set aside, particularly if there is a potentially significant issue which you wish to discuss (such as why an early stage fund is suddenly making lots of late stage investments, or why a buyout fund seems to be paying higher earnings multiples than its competitors).

Informal monitoring consists of keeping one's ear to the ground generally. In addition to everyday conversations with other people there are now a number of good online news sources. It is necessary to distinguish between the useful and the dangerous, however. Into the former category would fall hearing from a banker friend that a buyout transaction's debt is being offered at a discount in the marketplace. Into the latter would fall comments of the "I spoke to (insert name as desired) at an annual meeting and he doesn't like them" variety.

There are other things that can give you a clue that all is not well. Chief among these is timely reporting and it is puzzling that so many GPs should over the years have failed to realise this. Not only are consistently late reports and accounts indicative of sloppy processes within the firm, but they can give certain classes of investor, most notably Funds of Funds, very real problems regarding the provisions in their own legal agreements governing their reporting to their own clients. It can be easy, and even appealing, to write this off as a minor administrative irritant, but I do urge you not to neglect this key indicator. It may be a coincidence, but I have only encountered two cases of really bad and consistent late reporting, and one of them was also one of the three "concealment" firms alluded to above.

Remember too that what you learn through your monitoring of the current fund will form part of your due diligence for the next fund, so the better your monitoring, the easier and quicker your next round of due diligence is likely to be. In particular, the report pages from your venture or buyout model will form the starting point for your quantitative due diligence.

Finally, do remember what I said in the Introduction about the relationship between the GP and the LP. The power is all with the GP, provided you are committing to quality funds. There is accordingly no point at all in trying to throw your weight around during the monitoring process; indeed, this is likely to prove counter-productive. Ignoring for a moment no-fault divorce provisions [since (1) a detailed discussion of fund terms falls outside the scope of this book and (2) this is not something that you can use by yourself, but only in association with a majority of the other LPs] then your options as a disgruntled private equity fund investor are two, and two only. You may choose not to invest in the firm's next fund, and you may choose to sell your existing interest in the secondary market.

The monitoring process is designed to help you primarily with the first of these decisions. Your monitoring activities may already have disclosed by the time the next fundraising cycle comes around that this is not a firm you wish to back again. I would stress, though, that such situations are comparatively rare and will usually only occur where a firm has had key GP departures, failed to keep to the agreed investment model, acted in perceived conflict of interest, or whose investment metrics have deteriorated unacceptably. Fortunately, such situations are unusual, and the norm will be that when you sign up for a fund you are in reality signing up for at least the next one, and possibly two, as well (since the performance of the first one may not have become apparent even by the time the third one is raised).

Since you are thus committed to a long-term relationship with the firm no matter what happens, conducting your monitoring in a friendly and considerate manner is not only a matter of practical common sense, it is also your best chance of getting something you don't like changed. Incidentally, this can be a good reason for not sitting on advisory boards (though I readily acknowledge that there are different schools of thought on this).[8] Advisory boards generally do not make a good job of what

---

[8] I think my argument holds broadly true with quality US and European venture firms, who typically do a very good job of keeping their investors informed. I freely admit that the situation with buyout firms, particularly in Europe, may be different as there is a regrettable tendency to cultivate an inner circle of those few LPs who sit on the advisory board while keeping the rest in relative ignorance. However, provided that you are having update meetings on a regular basis and conducting them properly, then unless a firm is actively concealing something, not being on the advisory board should not be a problem.

they are supposed to do (protect LPs against conflicts of interest), and open discussion in a formal setting is not the best way to approach sensitive issues. As an independent voice who has cultivated a good personal relationship with at least some of the GPs, you often have a far better chance of getting something done through friendly chat than by attempting to use a bargaining position that it is effectively non-existent.

SUMMARY

- The decision to invest in a particular fund or company is usually a twofold process, although in practice the boundaries between these two neatly defined areas tend to become somewhat blurred. In theory, a decision to invest in principle will be taken first, and this decision will be subject to satisfactory due diligence which will then follow.
- It may be found helpful to maintain a running record of "pros", "cons" and "issues". Due diligence is aimed at resolving all outstanding issues, and should be specifically targeted in this way. It should not be regarded as an unfocused information-gathering process. Still less should it take the form of a standard form questionnaire. It is a way of facilitating decision-making, not a process of papering the file to protect individuals from the internal consequences of making bad decisions.
- It is generally far more helpful to seek out your own "referees" than to rely on those given to you by the fund or company. In particular, try to find individuals who have left the organisation recently, and find out why. Co-investors and portfolio company CEOs can also be sources of very useful information, particularly where the investment concerned has not performed well.
- Buyout fund due diligence should be based on the buyout transaction analysis discussed earlier, and on how well placed the firm may be in terms of dealflow channels, and how expert it is in its financial engineering.
- Venture fund due diligence should be based on the venture transaction analysis discussed earlier and should focus on the firm's ability to score home runs.
- Buyout company due diligence will be very similar to the standard M&A due diligence performed by a prospective corporate

acquirer. However, particular attention should be paid to key members of the executive team and their level of commitment to the proposed transaction.

- Venture company due diligence will focus on the qualities of the individuals concerned, and the level of market risk which their product or service will need to overcome. Also key is the potential for the company, if successful, to be sufficiently successful to become a home run.
- Fund of Fund due diligence will focus on historic performance (track record) and the firm's ability to access the very best private equity funds.
- Due diligence flows naturally into monitoring. However here, at the fund level, your focus will be on facilitating your decision whether to invest in successor funds, while at the company level it will be on checking the financial performance of the company and, in the case of venture companies, the healthy and timely development of the company's product or service.

10
Planning your
Investment Programme

Hopefully having read this far you will have a good idea of what buyout and venture capital are, what drives their returns, and what to look for when selecting funds in which to invest. You have also had a chance to consider the historic returns of each asset class, arranged by geography, and to take a look at how these might be influenced not just by transitory outside factors such as bubbles and market conditions but also to discern the workings of more lasting trends.

I would like to turn now to the nuts and bolts of how actually to put money to work in the private equity field. It is all very well having a working understanding of buyout and venture, but if you are suddenly presented with an allocation of, say, $100 M for private equity, how should you go about drawing up an action plan and implementing it?

CASHFLOW PLANNING

Let's just remind ourselves of the way in which any individual private equity fund works by looking again at something we saw earlier.

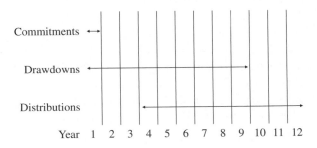

Remember, this is the profile of one individual fund, whereas we will be looking to commit to quite a number (ideally at least six in each vintage year). In planning our programme, therefore, we will have to overlay the profiles of a large number of funds onto an overall cashflow model. Thus, at any one time within our planned programme, we will have some funds that are in investment mode, some that may not yet have drawn down any significant amount of capital at all, and some that will already be harvesting their investments and returning money to investors.

You will of course need to assume some money multiples, since once a fund programme is mature the cash that is flowing back to the investor will always be greater than the money which is flowing out by way of drawdowns. I would suggest that you start with some very conservative default multiples – say 1.7× for a buyout fund and 2.3× for a venture fund – and adjust these to match actual performance as you go along.

Remember too that just as the J-curve will be the same basic shape for each fund but may be either squashed or elongated according to the fund type and market conditions (and may move within different ranges according to the amount and timing of cashflows), so too the pattern which you see set out in the figure above will occur either more quickly or over a more extended interval depending on whether the investment focus of the fund is on early stage venture (longest/slowest), buyout or later stage venture (roughly as depicted) or secondary transactions (shortest/quickest).

We are looking here specifically at private equity funds, but it is of course quite possible that, in deciding your overall investment policy, you might decide also to participate directly in individual private equity transactions, particularly in the secondary market where various LPs commonly operate alongside specialist secondary funds. We will be looking specifically at this area later in this chapter.

The purpose of this sort of outline cashflow modelling is not to provide a forecast of income and expenditure for accounting purposes. We are dealing here with cashflows which are essentially unpredictable both as to their timing and their amount, over a period which stretches a long way out into the future. Such an exercise cannot possibly produce anything other than a guesstimate, at best. The chances of your cashflows in any one year conforming exactly to what has been predicted at the outset are virtually nil. If you are an accountant, you might find it hard to understand why in these circumstances we would wish to embark upon the exercise at all. Yet to criticise it in this way, or label it as pointless, is fundamentally to misunderstand the reason for embarking upon it. It is not to have something available as a yardstick against which to judge just how closely actual cashflows in future years may conform to what we predicted at the outset (indeed, the very word "predicted" is inappropriate – it would be much more correct to say "projected"). It is so that we plan our exposure from the outset in a methodical manner; it is always open to us to fine-tune this as we go along, but it is essential to have an overall plan within which to operate (and not to allow ourselves to be unduly distracted from it as we go along by short-term issues).

ALLOCATED, COMMITTED AND INVESTED CAPITAL

In Chapter 1 we looked at the difference between allocated, committed and invested capital. It might be an idea just to glance at these definitions in the Glossary to remind yourself of the distinction, since an understanding is crucial to what we are now going to be discussing.

Almost as soon as you embark on the cashflow modelling exercise I have been describing, this distinction will be brought home to you very strongly. In the early years of a private equity programme you will find, for example, that, left to their own devices, invested capital may represent only a tiny fraction of allocated capital and it may seem that almost as much is getting drawn down in fees as is getting put to work in investee companies. You will notice that I say "left to their own devices" since there are actually some very straightforward things that can be done to alleviate this situation and which, bafflingly, many investors and their advisers simply ignore. We will look at these in detail later.

Successful management of a private equity programme requires these three different but directly related entities to be managed intelligently and proactively. This in turn requires active and knowledgeable monitoring of your portfolio funds. If many European buyout funds suddenly start exiting companies at the same time, for example (which is entirely possible given that such things are usually driven by exit market conditions), their LPs will fall into two broad categories: those who saw this coming and have planned in advance as far as possible how to deploy these cashflows back into some sort of private equity or quasi-private equity bucket, and those who did not and end up being forced to give it to their treasury department to invest on the money markets.

Similarly, if GPs invest their money either more quickly or more slowly than their usual fund cycle would suggest, then the time to do something about it, in terms of considering what this means for your future commitment programme, is straight away, not when you find yourself performing due diligence on five funds but realising that you need to commit to at least ten, or no more than one.

Please bear this distinction between allocated, invested and committed capital in mind, as it will be crucial as we now turn to look at two of the main mistakes which are made by investors when entering the private equity arena: failure to diversify by time, and failure to set proper commitment levels in the first place.

DIVERSIFICATION BY TIME

When studying the historic returns of both venture and buyout we came to the conclusion that they were subject to two broad categories of influence: those which are relatively constant and long-lasting, such as fundamental return drivers and long-term trends, and those which are transitory such as bubbles, exit windows, equity market conditions, fundraising levels, etc.

It is the job of a private equity investor, whether at the fund or the company level, to study and understand the former and shape investment policy accordingly. It is not part of the job to react to the latter, or, even worse, try to predict them and "market time" one's investments. How, then, do we treat these? The answer is that we simply ignore them. Private equity investors deal with cashflows which are unpredictable both as to their timing and as to their amount which stretch a long way into the future, becoming even more unpredictable with every extra year which is added to our projections. This unpredictability is such that any attempt to market time involves the prediction of market conditions and investor sentiment a long way in the future, and also involves assuming not only that this prediction will be correct, but that it will continue to be correct for a long enough period for all the planned and necessary inflows or outflows to take place. This is effectively impossible.

Instead, the sophisticated investor aims to commit capital evenly every vintage year so that there will be a roughly equal exposure to every vintage year within the portfolio. Consider what would have happened, for example, if one had taken the view that 2000 was going to be a bumper year for US venture and had decided to commit one's entire allocation to 2000 vintage year US venture funds. Or had decided to stop investing in US venture between 1994 and 1996 because the likely returns of your 1991 vintage year funds were not looking good? It is impossible to assess in advance how a particular vintage year is going to perform; one does not even usually have a final figure for total fund-raising until at least 3 months (in the USA) or about 6 months (in Europe) into the following calendar year.

You may think that the first example I quote in the preceding paragraph is fanciful. It is not. Not only is it drawn from life, but there were a number of new entrants to the market who did exactly that. I will not mention names, but a well-known company came to me for advice in or about late 1999 on how to plan their new private equity programme and I gave them roughly the counsel which is contained in this chapter. Imagine my surprise when I subsequently learnt that not only had their private equity team blown their entire allocation in the space of about 6 months almost entirely on US venture funds with a dot.com focus, but they had gone back to their board for a greatly increased allocation, much of which they proceeded to treat in similar fashion. Without giving too much away, the same company closed down their private equity operations a couple of years later, and while of course I was sorry to hear it, I did not allow my regret to get in the way of picking up a couple of very attractive secondary opportunities.

This is obviously a counsel of perfection, and like all counsels of perfection there are times when it is just not possible to do exactly what you would like to. European buyout, for example, can be a particular problem because there tends to be "bunching", with several funds coming to market at the same time and intervening fallow periods. There is no particular reason for this; it just happens, rather in the same way that you wait for a bus for an hour and then four arrive all at once (although I now understand that there *is* apparently some arcane mathematical explanation for this after all). Do you pass up the opportunity of investing with a quality fund in one year simply to keep your commitment levels in trim, or do you try to steal a bit of capital from another vintage year?

The answer is threefold. First, it is inconceivable that any LP is going to be investing solely in European buyout, so there may be scope for under-committing slightly that vintage year to other private equity classes in order to over-commit slightly to European buyout. Second, if you want to borrow a little money from any particular year then probably little harm is done. Third, many fund closings stretch in practice across year ends – this is done deliberately for precisely this reason. However, the key words here are "slightly" and "a little"; some fine-tuning is perfectly acceptable, and indeed probably even desirable, but significant tweaks are not.

Diversification by time is probably the single most important concept that should drive any private equity fund investor. Write it on the wall of your office. Chant it to yourself as you take your morning shower. Practising diversification by time will not of itself make you a successful fund investor (you still need to be able to identify and access the right funds), but it will very significantly boost your chances, and is definitely preferable to a future in long-term unemployment.

PROPER COMMITMENT LEVELS

The second common mistake made by LPs who are new to the asset class is not to set proper commitment levels. Basically, this comes down to a failure to understand the difference between allocated, invested and committed capital.

If you run the sort of broad brush cashflow exercise that we were talking about at the beginning of the chapter you will quickly see that you will have money coming back from your earliest funds well before you finish paying in to those to which you commit in later years. This will of course be exacerbated by the fact that in normal circumstances the money coming back will be some multiple of the money paid in. To those who cherish the principle of the payback period, this is good news as it means that a fund programme can become self-financing after the first 7 years or so. To those who understand investment returns it is a disaster, as it means that money coming back having earned a private equity return is going to end up invested on the money markets, and you are never going to get anywhere near your overall target allocation figure. So, how do we get around this problem?

The answer is quite simple, but many investors seem to have a conceptual problem with it nonetheless. You must over-commit. As a rough rule of thumb you multiply your allocation by anything between about 1.5× (conservative) and 2× (aggressive), then divide it by eight and look to commit that amount every year for the first eight vintage years. You will obviously have to keep these amounts under review as your programme progresses; most probably you will need steadily to increase the amount you are committing every year.

So, to take our earlier example, if you have an allocation to private equity of $100 M and you decide to take a conservative approach, you need first to multiply this by 1.6 and then divide it by eight with the result that you now know you need to target fund commitments of $20 M a year for the next 8 years.

Simple, yes, but surprisingly often completely overlooked or ignored. It just isn't possible to invest in private equity funds any other way. Unless you over-commit in this way you will be very lucky ever to end up with much more than about 50% of your capital actually invested at any one time. The problem is often that those setting out asset allocation policy at senior levels within institutions do not themselves understand the difference between allocated and committed capital, in which case there needs to be some sort of ongoing education exercise. They need to be reassured that there is no danger of the allocation level being breached in the real world, given proper cashflow planning; certainly I have never once known it to be a problem for anyone in my personal experience.[1] Even if some sort of unimaginable financial cataclysm gripped the investment world for a prolonged period, then in extremis existing interests could be sold as secondaries, and/or future commitment levels reduced.

DIVERSIFICATION BY
SECTOR AND GEOGRAPHY

This is a more controversial subject on which there are a number of different views. Let me put to you the two arguments at different ends of the spectrum.

On the one hand there will be the traditional investment view that diversification is always attractive in its own right and that an ideal private equity portfolio should therefore aim in any one vintage year for a roughly equal split between venture and buyout, and between Europe and the USA, perhaps with a dash of Asia thrown into the mix for the sake of completeness.

---

[1] I have known the problem to occur in a different way through mistaken internal accounting. During the bubble period in the USA, shares in public companies which had either been retained in venture funds or distributed in specie subject to lock-up continued to be classified as "private equity" by some LPs when it was demonstrably now no longer private equity. This caused a problem as these were at very high valuations, and unbalanced the private equity percentage allocation compared with less well performing asset classes. Not only was this approach mistaken from a reporting viewpoint, it was also irrational. Logically within the next 6 to 12 months all the value represented by those shares would either have been realised in cash or, in the event of a market crash, would have disappeared. Either way, it would no longer be an issue. Yet some LPs were forced to decline involvement in leading venture funds, damaging not only their level of diversification by time but also their prospects of ever being able to get back into future funds managed by the firms in question.

Properly constructed, any such portfolio should tend to give a composite return that is the private equity equivalent of a passively managed global equities programme. It will effectively return the global private equity index, so the argument goes, if such a thing existed. It is what I attempted to capture in my last book[2] in considering how private equity as an asset class fitted into an overall asset allocation approach, when I calculated a global Capital Weighted Average IRR for private equity funds. I acknowledged at the time that this was an essentially artificial measure, but hoped it would prove acceptable to those raised on a diet of global indices and benchmarks.

The reader will by now know more than enough about private equity to be able to spot various flaws in the above approach.

First, not all private equity classes have returned equal returns; indeed, the returns of some classes vary widely even within themselves, most notably US venture and European buyout. It is clear, then, that not only must manager selection play a great role in selecting a private equity fund portfolio but also that the stage and sector (in venture) or the size and geography (in buyout) of a fund's investment focus will also be legitimate considerations. I am not aware of any portfolio anywhere in the world, for example, which currently gives anything like an equal weighting to European venture.

Yet we have seen that the returns of any one private equity class fluctuate from one vintage year to another, and that it is impossible to predict such returns in advance. So are we not, an advocate of the balanced approach might argue, simply adopting a sort of market timing by stealth if we start tweaking our mix in this way? Should we not simply try to choose the best managers within each class in each vintage year and leave the relative performance of each class to fall where it may?

Second, we have seen that in each class there are a small number of managers who may consistently out-perform, most notably in US venture but also to a less extreme extent in other areas. Suppose that in order to make up our quota of, say, the US buyout funds which are raising money that year we would be obliged to choose a respectable but potentially unexciting candidate when we could use that money instead to commit to a leading US venture fund. Is it not more likely that whatever happens to the respective returns of US buyout and venture as a whole, the leading venture manager is likely to give us a higher return than the unexciting buyout manager? Ah, says the

---

[2] *Multi Asset Class Investment Strategy*, already referenced.

balanced investor, but suppose the vintage year in question turns out to be 2000? In that case you might end up thanking your lucky stars that you stuck to your principles and did not throw extra capital into US venture, no matter how attractive it might have seemed at the time.

This leads us rather neatly into the opposite view, which we might term the Silicon Valley theory, for want of anything better. This runs as follows. There is one asset class within private equity, US venture, that has consistently out-performed all others. Further, there is a small group of firms within it, the golden circle, that has consistently out-performed the rest of the class. So why not simply seek to identify and access these potential golden circle funds and simply ignore everything else within private equity? Yes, there will be the occasionally poor vintage year but you are protected against this by diversification by time and, in the case of golden circle US venture, the dramatic returns which you make in the good years will more than compensate you for the occasional bad one.

These are interesting arguments and each has its attractions, though in fairness I should point out that the Silicon Valley theory has been totally vindicated by those who have chosen to apply it and been able so to do. However, in the words "and been able so to do" lies the Achilles heel of this approach. I am sure you will have spotted it already.

In order to be able to adopt it, you must be able both to identify *and* *access* potential golden circle funds. Yet access is a huge issue in US venture capital; even Horsley Bridge, the supreme exponent of this approach, is not able to access every single US venture fund. To be fair, in their case this hardly matters since they have so many of the others, but just consider what your position might be if you are not fortunate enough to be Horsley Bridge, or to have invested with them over the years.

I have in the past attempted to analyse how much money might be raised in any one vintage year by the US golden circle firms, but this has become a thankless task with the fundraising figures going up and down like a yo-yo and, given that they are published in arrears, my efforts have often been superseded almost as soon as they have been published. Suffice it to say that in any one year the amount of demand for golden circle fund capital hugely exceeds available supply.

Much of the capital is taken up by the GPs themselves and their strategic investors (which will include the likes of successful entrepreneurs whom they have previously backed and with whom they may wish to work again, and technology companies who may be potential key customers and development partners for portfolio companies). Depending on the firm, this can be anywhere up to two-thirds of the fund size. Then there are the Horsley Bridge type players who have backed the firm for many years and are guaranteed a sizeable chunk of what is left. Then there are a number of endowments and foundations who will again typically have been long-term supporters of the firm. Finally there are a large number of institutions fighting on the fringes of the pack for whatever scraps may remain.

It is in trying to estimate the amounts involved in any one particular year that one can come to grief, but it is probably safe to assume that in any one year the amount available for fringe players (into which category would fall any new entrants to the asset class) would be certainly no more than $1 billion and probably a lot, lot less, perhaps as little as $100M. Given that every investor in the world would logically want as much of this as they could have, then you can probably say that whatever amount it is will be at least a hundred times and maybe a thousand times over-subscribed.

In other words, access to the golden circle for the average investor is as near impossible as makes no difference. Unfortunately this is yet another very basic truth which appears to be little understood, prompted in part by the less scrupulous Fund of Funds managers who fudge the true figures (and the classification of what may or may not genuinely be a golden circle fund) and claim to be able to achieve significant coverage for their clients when in fact this simply is not (and indeed cannot) be the case. Yes, there are Fund of Funds managers who can genuinely put some reasonable part of their capital into these funds, but they are few and far between and in many cases neither investors nor those who advise them seem to have a very clear idea of which they may be.

So the Silicon Valley approach simply is not available to the average investor, and that really changes the picture quite dramatically. If you cannot gain access to the golden circle, and the same problems as to access apply with gradually diminishing severity as you descend the quality scale, then you will be struggling to achieve US venture results which even match the upper quartile; in fact, it is quite likely that some significant number of your fund picks will end up in the second or third quartiles.

If you are struggling to achieve upper quartile US venture returns, is it still a valid approach to say that you will target that private equity class, and that class only? Clearly not. Can one, then, fall back on the balanced theory in the hope that you will be able to achieve some sort of blended global return? Well, in theory yes, but I do think that the objections which we raised to such an approach merit careful consideration, and probably argue against a strict application of such a pure and uncompromising policy. In particular, I would be really troubled by the possibility of having to pass up a very high quality opportunity in one category just because one would not otherwise fulfil one's quota in a different area. In fact, all my experience suggests very strongly that any sort of rigid pre-allocation at all is the enemy of optimal returns.

We have seen several times during the book so far that private equity differs from other classes in various ways and this is another important one. The differential in return which can be earned through successful manager selection is almost infinite. Choosing one quoted equity manager over another might make a difference of 1 or 2% a year; choosing the right private equity manager can make a difference of 100% a year in venture or maybe 10 or 15% a year in buyout. Viewed in this light, the risk of missing out on an outstanding manager is just too great to allow pre-allocations of this sort to get in the way.

So, I think that the answer lies somewhere between the two extremes. By all means discuss some broad outlines as to how you would like your portfolio to look in terms of venture (sector, stage and geography) and buyout (size and geography), but be flexible, and concentrate on selecting the best managers in any one category as you go along rather than strictly fulfilling a quota policy in any one vintage year.

TOTAL RETURN

With an understanding of the differences between allocated, committed and invested capital comes a realisation that the return which you earn across your whole private equity allocation will be very different from the wonderful IRRs that are peddled to you during presentations on private equity funds and Funds of Funds. This is in one sense a necessary consequence of the way in which private equity returns are measured, but can also betray a lack of understanding of the asset class generally.

As we saw in an earlier chapter, a private equity fund is a sequence of cashflows and the proper measure of its performance is an IRR. I do not seek to criticise this in any way; far from it. Save only for money multiples, the IRR is the only valid way in which private equity fund performance can be measured. Certainly I hope that we have well and truly dispelled any notion that annual returns can ever be appropriate.

However, what an IRR or a money multiple measures when used in this way is the performance of a *fund*, whereas what you will be (or should be) concerned about is the performance of your *programme*.

Now, as we have seen, even if you do everything humanly possible to reduce its impact, you are going necessarily to suffer from under-investment (or, perhaps more accurately, sub-optimal utilisation) of capital. I would hope this is obvious. You will not be committing some of your money for several years, and, even when you do, it will take the GP of each individual fund a few years to draw all that money down and put it to work in investee companies. Hence the sub-optimal utilisation. The optimal use of that money is to be invested in the portfolio companies of buyout and venture funds. Thus, any time that any money is not so invested, it is being used in a less than optimal fashion.

Yet, if this is so obvious why is it that so few LPs take any serious steps to plan what they are going to do with their cash while it is not actually invested in underlying companies? "I'm only 10% invested after three years" is the sort of thing which you hear on a regular basis, to which I'm afraid I usually respond "well, what did you expect?". The way in which a private equity fund programme operates is hardly rocket science. You can model the cashflows in outline, as we have seen above, and it will become instantly apparent that even if you do all the right things in terms of over-commitment there is still going to be a very slow and protracted take-up of capital.

This in turn means that when many investors refer to "our private equity return" what they really mean is "our return on that small portion of our allocation which we have actually managed to invest in private equity assets". Even for someone with a mature programme this is only ever likely to be some part of the whole, and in the case of a new entrant it may be practically nothing. That is why I feel it would be helpful for people to think in terms of their Total Return across the whole allocation rather than just that amount which is actually sitting in underlying companies.

Which prompts the question: what should we do with our allocation in the meantime?

HOW TO DEAL WITH UNINVESTED CAPITAL

The need to think in terms of Total Return means that we can rethink our philosophy of private equity returns. Accepted wisdom teaches that you should chase the very best possible returns and this of course is true when thinking about committing money to primary funds; if you have $20 M to commit in any one vintage year then you want to try to ensure that you choose from amongst funds which you can access and which are likely to produce the very best returns. However, where capital which is allocated but as yet uninvested is concerned, different considerations apply.

In this situation we should be content to accept slightly lower rates of return. Logically, we should accept any rate of return which is likely to be higher than that which we could earn through any alternative use of that capital. In order to assess this it would of course be necessary to know what that alternative use might be, and this would almost certainly vary from one investor to another. Some leave the money with their treasury department, while others might leave it within their allocation to quoted equities and still others might invest it in quoted private equity vehicles.

It would be cheering to report that they adopted this latter course in order to earn some sort of private equity proxy return, but in fact this is not the case. I suspect that they do so merely as a way of ticking the "private equity" box on their checklist, and in any case the overall allocation to private equity is frequently so small that in truth it is not going to make any significant difference anyway. I rehearsed in my last book[3] the reasons why this is not a good idea. Such vehicles are frequently cash-rich themselves and thus the problem is shifted rather than resolved. Largely because of this, it is effectively impossible to earn anything like a proper private equity return from them (why do you think that sophisticated investors the world over prefer to invest in institutional partnerships, even though these come at a much higher cost?). Also, since such vehicles are quoted they must be subject at least in some part to the vagaries of public equity markets and thus lack of correlation with your quoted equity holdings (which is one of the two main reasons for having a diversified portfolio in the first place[4]) will inevitably be compromised.

For the sake of argument, let us assume that the alternative use of funds would be quoted equities. This is probably not a bad assumption to make, since quoted equities are still generally regarded as the most "high risk" (whatever that might mean) asset within many institutional

---

[3] *Multi Asset Class Investment Strategy*, already referenced.
[4] The other being the ability to access high return asset classes such as private equity.

portfolios. Thus, to use classic corporate finance theory, we should accept all projects for the use of our capital that offer a potential rate of return which exceeds the likely return on quoted equities. Given our concerns about correlation and diversification, as well as the internal requirements of staying within our investment mandate, we should however qualify "projects" by saying something like "projects of a private equity nature, or offering a private equity-like return which exhibits low correlation with the rest of our portfolio".

This clearly opens up other possibilities which should be considered but, alas, rarely are by investors in this position.

SECONDARIES

Secondary transactions offer a private equity return (hardly surprising since they are actually private equity investments!) in terms of IRR, but this is created by accepting lower money multiples for shorter periods. Bearing in mind our motivation for making such investments, namely putting temporarily surplus capital to work, we have no problem with this. On the contrary, a private equity investment that returns its capital within a short time period is ideal for our purposes.

In practice, most LPs will make such investments through the medium of specialist secondary funds and while these do an excellent job I would urge investors not to be afraid of venturing into the market themselves on occasions in addition to their secondary fund investments, particularly if they have a good relationship with the buyout or venture GP managing the fund in which the secondary interest is held. However, for many (those without an established private equity programme, for example) this will simply not be possible as it will prove very difficult for them to originate deals, or to execute them with the speed that is usually required, so that the best they are likely to be able to do is to co-invest alongside secondary funds in which they have invested.

The fact that there is a thriving secondary market in private equity fund interests is conveniently overlooked by those who give a fear of being locked into a fund for 10 years or more as a reason (excuse?) for not having an allocation to private equity. In fact there is a large and thriving market which provides ample liquidity for anyone who wants it.

There is as yet no publicly available data on the total value of secondary transactions in any particular period (this is one of the last areas of private equity gloom to be penetrated by the light of transparency), but we can make some intelligent deductions. A Dow Jones publication[5] states that over $5 billion was raised by secondary funds in each of 2004 and 2005 and suggests $8 billion as a possible target figure for 2006, though in my view this latter estimate is likely to prove conservative. Given that the average secondary fund these days tends to invest its capital over about a 3-year period (but in individual cases this can be much shorter), and given also that they are not the only players in the market (Funds of Funds[6] and institutional LPs also buy and sell secondary interests) then it seems reasonable to assume that somewhere between $5 billion and $7 billion of secondary interests are being bought and sold every year, and practitioners believe that the market has probably been at this sort of level for the last few years.

Two things are clear: the secondary market is already big, and getting rapidly bigger with every year that passes – certainly it is growing at more than 10% a year and sometimes substantially more than that. In my view this is one area that could see quite dramatic growth in the future as more LPs wake up to the need to use secondaries to help manage their cashflows and capital levels, and as awareness grows of the need to use Total Return investing.

One important point needs to be made before we leave the subject of secondaries. You often hear investors saying "we don't do secondaries", or perhaps "we will only look at secondaries where we are already invested with that GP". Such statements betray a confusion over secondaries policy borne of a lack of understanding of the different ways in which they can (and should) be used. There are two different types of secondaries, and it is important properly to distinguish between them: portfolio secondaries and treasury secondaries.

Portfolio secondaries are purchased because an investor wants exposure (or additional exposure) to a particular private equity fund, and seizes the opportunity when the secondary interest becomes available. It may be that access to the fund was restricted when it was raised and the LP was not able to get into it, or not able to invest as much as she would have wished. It may even be that the LP is buying the interest defensively, to stop any third party from being in a better pro rata bargaining position when the next fund is raised. A common situation is where an LP has invested with a successful GP and is offered a

---

[5] *Guide to the Secondary Market*, Private Equity Analyst 2006.
[6] Harborvest can apparently put up to $2 billion of their current Fund of Funds into secondaries.

piece of one of the GP's early funds, perhaps dating from a vintage year even before the LP entered the private equity space. Such opportunities offer a twofold advantage: the potential to strengthen the relationship with the GP and the chance to gain further diversification by time with exposure to a vintage year not already contained within the programme.

A treasury secondary, by contrast, is purchased solely for reasons of cashflow and capital management. Here the precise nature of the secondary interest is irrelevant. All that matters (and needs to be analysed) is the likely amounts and timing of its remaining cashflows. Indeed, my inclination would be not even to record the names of these investments separately within a private equity programme but simply to lump them all together simply as "treasury secondaries" to make this distinction explicit.

This is an important point since there is a very real danger that GPs (usually) and LPs (often) will assume that some level of lasting relationship is created by the purchase of a secondary interest. Thus, respective expectations need to be carefully and sensitively managed, or embarrassment and bad feeling can result the next time the GP goes fundraising. The distinction is equally important internally. Those making the investment decisions within an LP need to understand that the decision to purchase an interest in a particular fund as a treasury secondary does not carry any overtones of endorsing the qualities of the GP involved, and this can if necessary be made clear externally.

So, secondary investments represent the clearest way of managing surplus private equity capacity, and any intelligent LP should be looking to make heavy use of them. Remember that with secondary funds the vintage year of the fund is largely irrelevant, since the vintage years of the fund interests which they purchase will all be different. Indeed, one further level of future sophistication might be for secondary fund managers to begin offering different products categorised by vintage years; they might, say, offer a "2001–2003" fund and undertake that at least 75% of the interests which it purchases will fall within those three vintage years.

The reason this is important is that it means there is no logical objection to an LP putting a large amount of their private equity allocation in secondary funds in their very first year of private equity activity, and then reducing the amount on secondary fund commitments as they go along and the amount of their primary commitments increases. Indeed, I can see no particular reason why they should not commit all of their allocation in this way across year 1, hoping to be something in excess of 50% invested by the end of year 2.

MEZZANINE

Mezzanine, that is to say convertible debt, would also be a candidate for the use of non-invested capital. As we saw earlier when we analysed how buyouts work, this is the financing strip that sits between the equity and the senior debt of a buyout transaction and thus, unsurprisingly, is designed to give less than a buyout equity return but more than a buyout debt return. Its attractions to us in our present position are twofold. First, it is part of a private equity transaction and thus is undeniably private equity in nature (this may be important for the more officious of internal processes). Second, the debt servicing element of its cash-flows are entirely predictable both as to timing and as to amount, since these will be laid out in legally binding documentation, and this makes it possible to plan exactly where such investments might fit into our overall cashflow planning model.

For those who do not wish to venture into the convertible debt market directly there are specialist funds, just as there are for secondaries, but these usually function on a primary basis, i.e., providing the mezzanine element of buyout deals over a period of 3 years or so in just the same way as a buyout fund does with equity. This obviously makes mezza-nine much less attractive for our present purposes, since we are giving up one of the key advantages (predictability). However, it is becoming increasingly possible to invest in existing (secondary) mezzanine inter-ests and this is another area where I feel we will see increased sophis-tication in the future as Total Return investing becomes more widely accepted, possibly with funds offering a selection of interests with specific maturity profiles.

PRIVATE EQUITY PROXIES

Here we stray into the more controversial area of using the returns of completely different asset classes which have no direct connection with private equity to produce a return which might in some way approxi-mate to or be correlated with a private equity fund return. Indeed, I have spoken with pension funds and other institutional investors who believe that they can use such an approach as a substitute for making any private equity investments at all. Some, for example, use a selection of small cap quoted equities and try introducing some leverage through debt, or some hedging through derivatives.

I showed in my earlier book[7] that this approach does not work any better than the alternative policy of investing in quoted private equity vehicles. Whenever I have discussed this approach with one who is an advocate of it I find that the private equity return which they are using as a benchmark is commonly much too low, because an inappropriate measure (such as a median or average return) has been selected either through ignorance, or sometimes, I suspect, on a self-serving basis to justify the solution that has already been chosen.

There are those who claim to have detected a strong correlation between private equity returns and the NASDAQ index. In my earlier book I tried very hard to reproduce these results since it would have actually suited my purposes so to do, but was unable to. Using annual returns, an approach which is clearly artificial for private equity purposes, it is possible to establish correlation with US venture (logically the closest private equity asset class to the NASDAQ, which functions at least in part as an exit market for US venture companies) of about 70%. Using vintage year returns it is possible to get this up to about 76% for private equity as a whole. Whether this is acceptable is a matter of subjective choice; to place it in context, the correlation between the NASDAQ and S&P 100 is about 88%.

Of course there are those LPs whose internal thought police simply would not allow them to make this sort of decision in any case, since in no way can either the NASDAQ or small cap quoted stocks be properly classified as "private equity". However, where the option is a possibility I think I would be relatively relaxed about using the NASDAQ index as long as this is a final fall-back option for use only after secondaries and mezzanine opportunities have been exhausted, and is thus only ever likely to form a very small part of our portfolio. It would definitely be preferable to allowing the capital to be invested on the money markets and also to adding it to our existing quoted equity holdings.

TOWARDS A NEW WORLD OF PRIVATE EQUITY PROGRAMMES

This is a new and controversial concept which I believe is here being set out for the first time ever, and so I do not wish to go overboard about

---

[7] *Multi Asset Class Investment Strategy*, already referenced.

its merits, or to become unduly dogmatic as to what needs to be done. However, it does seem to me that it is both unrealistic and unreasonable to judge a private equity programme on the basis only of that very small part of it which is actually invested at any one time, given that the elimination, or at least amelioration, of the results of slow capital take-up is something that can and should fairly easily be addressed. Once we view this as a key skill of a private equity LP, just as much as choosing the right funds, then surely it is appropriate to judge LP performance across the whole allocated amount? It is for this reason that I advocate Total Return investing for institutional investors everywhere.

This clearly impacts not just upon the LP but also upon those who offer products and services to them. Why should a Fund of Funds manager, for example, be paid a fee on the whole committed capital of their fund when only a small part of it will actually be invested at any one time? To take one obvious example, if a Fund of Funds has a 1% management fee and after 1 year is only, say, 5% drawn down (not impossible), then the effective management fee for that year is not 1% but 20% – quite a difference!

Would it not be more logical to expect the Fund of Funds manager to draw down the money up front and be judged on a total return basis over the life of the fund? After all, the only thing that has really changed is that the money is now in the hands of the manager rather than the investor; yes, ownership of the problem has been transferred but the manager is likely to be better placed to address it than the investor, and is being paid to do so. Granted the increased (and different types of) work would merit an increased management fee overall, but (1) when measured as a percentage of invested capital this would be a fraction of what the present fee arrangement really represents, and (2) the manager will be disinclined to charge too much as his performance (upon which depends his ability to raise future funds) will still be measured on a net cashflow basis, i.e., net of fees and carried interest.

Like all new ideas, I think this one will catch on slowly, but catch on it will, and totally change the face of private equity fund investing in the process. It should prove very attractive to LPs, since it will transfer from them to their manager(s) the burden of what they see as a particularly difficult problem. I anticipate that it will be resisted by Fund of Funds managers, since it will involve them in extra work, and the acquisition of different skills and dealflow channels, while having the effect of depressing the high levels of return which they have been accustomed to quoting. However, with change comes opportunity and there will surely be some who choose to embrace the new way of doing business and turn it into a specific selling point.

SUMMARY

- When planning a private equity fund programme it is essential to draw up an outline cashflow model showing the various funds to which it is intended to commit, even though it must be recognised that given the essential unpredictable nature of private equity fund cashflows this will serve as only a rough guide.
- When creating your model it is probably advisable to use default multiples of 1.7× for a buyout fund and 2.3× for a venture fund. These should be kept constantly under review in each individual case and changed if necessary as specific data on that individual fund becomes available.
- A failure to understand and remember the difference between allocated, committed and invested capital lies at the heart of many of the problems experienced by private equity LPs. The two main issues are:

  1. Unless you over-commit (minimum 160%) you will never be much more than about 50% invested.
  2. Returns are calculated traditionally only on invested capital less fees and carry. This is both unrealistic and unreasonable. Investors should seek instead to calculate their Total Return on allocated capital.

- Having multiplied your allocated capital by a minimum of 160%, now divide it by eight to give you the amount of money you need to commit each vintage year. This is essential not only to address the problem of under-investment, but also to ensure proper diversification by time.
- To achieve acceptable levels of Total Return, endeavour to find alternative private equity or private equity-type uses for uninvested capital rather than allowing it to be drawn into bonds or quoted equities. Secondary and mezzanine interests are the prime candidates. The NASDAQ index might be considered as a final fall-back solution for a small part of the overall allocation.
- Aim to commit the bulk of your allocation to secondaries initially, and then use the secondary cashflows which result to fund primary drawdowns.

- Total Return investing may be a totally new concept but it will catch on, and will involve some fundamental changes to how LPs approach private equity investing. Some Fund of Funds managers may prove resistant to the idea, but some will see it as an opportunity to develop a differentiating advantage over the competition.

Glossary

3G
Abbreviation or acronym for so-called "third generation" mobile telephone technology. Strictly speaking this should only apply to UMTS, but partly due to delays in rolling this out it has come to be applied by some to GPRS, which is much less powerful but much more widely and cheaply available.

A Round
Successive rounds of funding for a venture company are given successive letters, i.e., the A Round will come first, followed by the B Round, etc.

An A Round is usually defined as the first round in which a professional venture investor participates, but this is misleading as it could equally refer to a seed round, depending on the stage in a company's development at which it takes place.

An A Round may be preceded by one or more angel rounds as well as by a seed round.

A shares
Different classes of share are customarily created for different funding rounds in a venture company. Traditionally, A shares are issued for the A Round, B shares for the B Round, and so on.

Advisory Board
A committee of LPs within an individual fund delegated by the GP to give clearance and guidance on any situations involving a possible conflict of interest.

ADSL
Asynchronous Digital Subscriber Line. A means of using traditional copper telephone lines to carry broadband.

AFIC
The French venture capital association.

Allocated capital
The amount (usually calculated as a percentage) of its overall capital that an investor chooses to devote to private equity. Can be thought of as representing the rough amount of capital which an investor would ideally like to have invested in private equity at any one time.

Allocation
Another expression for allocated capital, usually when expressed as a percentage of the whole, e.g., "a 15% allocation to private equity".

Alpha and beta (customers and product)
"Alpha" and "beta" are used differently in different situations by different people. I would offer the following classification.

Alpha customers are those who are trialling product which is still very much at a pilot stage, i.e., it is likely that based on the customer's feedback significant changes and development may yet be made to the product.

Beta customers are those who are trialling something that is supposed to be essentially the finished article. The intention is that only minor changes will need to be made, principally to correct technical glitches that arise during the trial.

Angel
Someone who invests in venture companies, typically at a very early stage, but is not a professional venture capitalist. In the USA these are quite likely themselves to have been successful entrepreneurs, and to be well adapted to dealing with the venture industry.

In Europe, angels tend to be successful business executives, to have less money available for investment than their American counterparts, and frequently to view venture firms with suspicion rather than seeing them as useful co-investors.

Angel round

A round of venture funding in which only angels participate, i.e., in which no professional venture firm is present.

Annexe fund

A separate fund formed by the LPs of a fund to provide a pool of top-up capital when the reserves of the fund have proved inadequate, with the aim of avoiding the issues raised by cross-fund investing.

Anti-dilution

Provisions commonly found in the funding agreements governing rounds of investment in venture companies under which the shareholdings of certain shareholders (typically early stage investors and entrepreneurs) cannot fall below a specified percentage of the whole.

Average (when applied to returns)

The arithmetic mean of any sample population of fund returns. This measure suffers from a grave drawback in that it gives equal weighting to all funds within the sample, even the very small ones which will probably not be of institutional investment grade. The Capital Weighted Average (see below) is greatly to be preferred.

Average holding period

Σ Holding period$/n$

where n is the number of companies.

Average leverage (or gearing or debt)

$$\frac{\Sigma \text{Debt}/n}{\Sigma \text{Enterprise value}/n}$$

where n is the number of companies.
    See gearing ratio, below.

B2B

Online business which deals with business customers, e.g., wholesale, business services, business exchanges, etc.

B2C

Online business which deals with retail customers. Amazon would be one of the best known examples.

Baggage

American expression used to describe the amount of time which GPs are going to have to spend looking after the portfolio companies of prior funds.

Basis point

One hundredth of 1%. Thus 50 basis points is 0.5%, and so on.

Bid premium

That part of a public company's value which may be ascribed to the possibility of it being taken over (bid for). Where there is a controlling or blocking shareholding there can by definition be no bid premium.

BIMBO

Acronym for Buy-In/Management Buyout. A type of buyout transaction which combines the features of both an MBO and MBI (see below). In most cases a senior executive who has worked within the same sector (and may even have worked for the target company in the past) forms a management consortium with existing managers from within the target company.

Blind or blinded (of data)

Fund data is blinded when it is impossible to identify exactly which individual fund matches which individual data entry. Thomson Financial's VentureXpert system operates in this way.

The disadvantage is that you cannot assess the performance of any one fund. The advantage is that GPs who may otherwise be reluctant to submit their data are reassured sufficiently to do so.

Book

"The Book" is the selling document (often called a Sale Memorandum) which is prepared by the investment bank retained on behalf of a business seller (vendor). It describes the business to be sold and will be circulated to a (usually restricted) group of potential purchasers, who will typically include at least two or three buyout houses.

Note: this term may also be used in other ways, i.e., by brokers during share issues as meaning a list of underwriters or subscribers.

Bottom up
The way in which analysis of private equity funds must be carried out, by modelling the individual transactions within a fund in order to build up a picture of the whole.

Buyout
Generic name for a group of transactions in which debt is used to assist the acquisition of a control position in a company. One of the two main categories of private equity, the other being venture capital.

Buyout drivers
There are usually said to be three main drivers of buyout returns: earnings, (earnings) multiple and leverage. In fact there is also a fourth: time.

BVCA
British Venture Capital Association. Despite its name, it represents overwhelmingly by fund value the interests of pan-European buyout firms based in London, not the British Venture Capital community.

EVCA (see below) is subject to similar terminological inexactitude.

Capital call
A demand by a private equity fund for some part of the money which has been committed (i.e., promised) to it by investors. Each such demand, and the payment made pursuant to it, is called a drawdown.

Capital Weighted Average (CWA)
An average return calculated for any given sample population by reference to the capital size of each individual constituent fund. Save only for Upper Quartile returns, it is submitted that this is the most realistic measure of private equity returns.

Carried interest
That share of the profits made by a private equity fund which is reserved for the management team ("GPs"). This is typically 20%, but can be as high as 30% for some top US venture funds and usually drops to 10% for a Fund of Funds.

Carry
Another term for carried interest (see above).

Cash sweep
As part of the banking arrangements for a buyout transaction, a cash sweep refers to the process of checking all the company's bank accounts on specified dates and automatically gathering up any spare cash balances to offset some or all of the outstanding loan balances.

Change of control provision
A clause in a business contract which stipulates that if ownership of a majority of the equity of a company changes hands, then the other party to the contract has a right to cancel, usually without liability for paying any compensation.

Class rights
Rights (such as a liquidation preference) attaching to a particular class of shares in a company which cannot be varied except with the consent of the holders of that class of share.

Closed-end or closed-ended
A vehicle such as a Limited Partnership, which has a stated lifetime at the end of which it will be wound up. Contrast with open-ended or evergreen vehicles (see below).

Closing or close
The signing of an LPA (see below). Every fund will have a first close, after which it has legal status and may begin operations, usually followed by a series of other closings. Typically the final close will be required to take place not later than one year after the first close.

Commitment
A legally binding promise by an investor to make a certain amount of money available to a private equity fund on demand.

Committed capital
When used by an investor, the total of all current commitments to all funds by that investor.

When used by a fund, the total amount of capital currently committed to that fund by all investors.

Condition subsequent
Used where a certain legal entitlement (for example to some share options in a buyout company) is granted subject to a certain thing remaining true, e.g., the individual remaining employed by the company for a specified time.

Constituent fund
A fund which forms part of a specified group for return purposes. For example, a European buyout fund formed in 1997 which turns out to have a return equal to or greater than the upper quartile, will be a constituent fund of the "1997 vintage year upper quartile" group.

Controlled auction
A process whereby the potential seller of a business will appoint an intermediary (today usually an investment bank) to prepare a sale memorandum ("the book") and send it to an agreed list of potential buyers, who will then enter an auction process. Practice varies, but classically there will be at least two stages, with only some of the candidates being selected to move on to the next stage. The ability to figure on this list of potential buyers represents a huge barrier to entry for first time large buyout funds.

Convertible
A share (usually a preference share) or loan note which carries the right in specified circumstances (i.e., on a particular date, or on the happening of a specified event) to be exchanged in whole or in part for equity in the company. The conversion ratio may be fixed or on a sliding scale contingent, for example, on the performance of the company.

Cross-fund investing
Where a firm invests in the same company at different times from different funds, i.e., uses their current fund towards a financing round in a company which forms part of the portfolio of one of their earlier funds.

Development capital
A quasi-buyout transaction which can typically be distinguished from buyout by the lack of (1) shareholder control and (2) any significant amount of acquisition debt.

Distributed to Committed Capital (DCC)

The multiple (ratio) of total money distributed to date to the total committed capital of the fund. Like DPI (below) this is only really meaningful right at the end of a fund's life.

Distributed to Paid in (DPI)

A multiple commonly used in analysing private equity funds. It represents the ratio of money distributed (i.e., paid out) by the fund to money paid in (i.e., drawndown). This ratio is referred to as the realisation ratio, but is only really meaningful in the very late stages of a fund's lifetime.

Distribution

The process of a fund paying money to an investor after exiting an investment. This can sometimes take the form of an in specie distribution of shares, particularly in the case of US venture funds.

Diversification by time

The need to invest private equity money, whether at the company or fund level, steadily over several vintage years in roughly equal amounts. Lack of diversification by time is one of the most common mistakes committed by new LPs entering the asset class.

Dollar-weighted (returns)

A misleading term when compared with time-weighted returns (see below).

Simply the calculation of the IRR of a series of fund cashflows, i.e., the compound return over time. This is the classic measure of private equity returns, and is to be commended.

Great care should be taken not to confuse this measure with time-weighted returns which, contrary to first impressions, actually means something completely different (and should be avoided at all costs).

Dot.com

There are both narrow and wide senses in which this phrase is used.

Narrowly, it refers to e-commerce businesses, ranging from the spectacularly successful such as Google.com and Amazon.com to the spectacularly unsuccessful such as Pets.com, eToys.com and Boo.com. In most people's minds it is probably most closely associated with online retailers (B2C).

Widely, it became applied to all participants in the technology and internet bubble of the late 1990s, to the extent that this is often referred to as "the dot.com bubble".

Downside
Negative returns within a fund or a fund programme. May be used in particular when looking at which companies within a fund lost money compared with those that made money. When used by an investor, may refer to the risk of any one fund failing to return its capital.

Drawdown
See capital call.

Please be aware that this term is used in a completely different sense in other areas, e.g., hedge funds, where it can mean periods of downside.

Drawdown notice
Another term for a capital call. Properly speaking, the mechanism by which a capital call is effected.

Drawndown capital
When used by an investor, the total amount of committed capital which has actually been requested by its private equity funds.

When used by a fund, the total amount of committed capital which it has actually drawndown from its investors.

Due diligence
The process of performing background checks and rigorous financial analysis on a private equity fund (for an LP) or on a potential investee company (for a GP).

Since due diligence is a lengthy and costly exercise it will normally only be entered into once a decision to invest in principle (i.e., "subject to due diligence") has been taken.

Earn out
A provision which used to be commonplace but is now increasingly rare whereby the buyer of a company agrees to pay the seller a fixed multiple of the actual profits of each of the next two or three years.

The alternative is often to try to get certain minimum levels of future profits made the subject of a warranty, but this is now very difficult to achieve except in the case of a forced sale or a classic traditional-style MBO.

Earnings

Usually thought of as a company's earnings after deduction of all accounting items, e.g., interest and tax. Can be thought of as the earnings which would normally be available for distribution to shareholders. Forms the basis for the PE ratio (see below).

EBIT

Earnings Before (deduction of) Interest and Tax.

Probably a more appropriate buyout measure than earnings, but still not a true cashflow proxy since it includes non-cash items such as depreciation.

EBITDA

Earnings Before Interest, Taxes, Depreciation and Amortisation.

Probably the best of all buyout earnings measures and certainly the one used by buyout firms themselves. Of limited use for comparative purposes, however, since it is a non-GAAP measure and the manner of its calculation can fluctuate from year to year.

EIR

Entrepreneur in Residence. Many American venture firms will have three or four of these at any one time, encouraging them to incubate their next business start-up idea in their offices.

End game

The management of quoted distributions. This is a much underestimated requirement of any investor in US venture funds, calling for specialist skills and processes.

Enterprise value

The total value of a business, the price at which it may be sold. Can be thought of as earnings × PE ratio (or any of the other earnings measures × the appropriate multiple) or as equity value + debt.

EPS

Earnings Per Share.

Equity value

The value of the equity in a company. Can be thought of as enterprise value – debt.

ERISA

Employee Retirement Income Security Act, which governs the way in which US pension plans can invest in private equity. Private equity funds must be "ERISA compliant" in order to qualify for capital from these sources.

EVCA

European Venture Capital Association.

Evergreen

Refers to an investment vehicle which is open-ended, unlike an institutional limited partnership, which will always have a stated lifetime and will thus be closed-ended. These used to be very prevalent in continental Europe where there were both legal and cultural obstacles to investing in limited partnerships, but a number are quoted on the London Stock Exchange, 3i being the best known example.

These vehicles can give rise to particular problems when it comes to analysing returns, since they typically do not return capital to investors, and thus think in terms of Net Asset Value and dividends rather than compound returns based on cashflows.

Exclusivity

An agreement that the potential seller of a company will deal only with one specific potential vendor for a specified period, on pain of financial penalties (usually refunding the buyer's costs) for any breach.

Expansion capital

Another term for development capital, usually applied in the case of "money in" transactions (see below).

FDA

The (American) Food and Drug Administration. Responsible for licensing all medical products for use in the USA. Chiefly relevant to drug discovery and related areas, e.g., genomics.

Firm

Yet another area of transatlantic ambiguity. I use the word in its European sense of a private equity management entity, whereas in North America it is frequently taken to mean a venture company, i.e., an entity in which a fund will invest.

In North America the words "group" or "GP" are typically used for a European "firm" or "manager".

Flotation

Known as an IPO in America (see below), the process by which a company's shares become quoted on a stock market and thus publicly tradeable.

French auction

Named after some infamous goings-on in France during the early and mid-1990s. An auction in which there is no guarantee that the highest bidder will win, and that may be reopened to allow the preferred bidder to re-bid.

French solution

A euphemism employed by French politicians, investment banks and business sellers. Translated, it means "we are going to offer this company on the open market, and anyone can buy it as long as they are French".

Fund I, etc.

Private equity funds are traditionally given roman numerals. Thus, Doughty Hanson II would be the second fund to have been raised by Doughty Hanson, Apax V would be the fifth fund to have been raised by Apax, and so on.

Fund cycle

The natural rhythm of a fund's operations. Very broadly, this will usually take the form of an investment period (typically about 3 years, though venture funds will continue to invest money into companies for some years), followed by a development period and a harvesting period, when exits are effected.

Fund of Funds

A private equity firm which invests in buyout and venture funds, rather than directly into buyout and venture companies. Fund of Funds managers are frequently also active participants in the secondary market.

Fundraising
The process of finding investors (LPs) to commit to a new fund.

Fundraising cycle
The period between raising one fund and its successor fund. Typically about 3 years for primary funds and about 2 years for secondary funds.

GAAP
Generally Accepted Accounting Principles.

Gearing
Another word for leverage (below), describing the effect of debt on a transaction or company.

Gearing ratio

Usually expressed as $\dfrac{\text{Total debt}}{\text{Enterprise value}}$

Golden circle
A phrase invented by the writer and now in common use to refer to that very small number of US venture firms who have managed more than one fund which has significantly out-performed. While it defies precise definition, it is probably no more than about 20 names.

GP
In the USA, and increasingly in Europe, a manager of a private equity fund is known as a GP (General Partner) since most private equity funds take the form of Limited Partnerships, and these are required by law to have a General Partner to manage their affairs.

GP can refer either to the management entity or to individual partners within such entities. (In Europe this ambiguity is avoided by using the word "firm" for the entity but this creates fresh confusion as the word "firm" is used in North America to denote a venture company – oh, dear!).

GPRS

General Packet Radio Service, sometimes called 2½G, as it was meant to be a stepping stone on the way to 3G (above). In the event, technical problems delayed the introduction of 3G and GPRS has in many cases come to be adopted (but wrongly described) as 3G.

Great Train Robbery

Colloquial epithet for the railway privatisation deals entered into in the UK in the mid-1990s, in conditions of considerable political risk.

Group

Frequent American usage for a "firm" or "GP".

Hard circle

Reference to an investor, or group of investors, who have made a firm decision to commit money to a private equity, subject only to agreement on the legal terms and any outstanding due diligence.

Hockey stick

Another name used for the pattern made by the J-curve (see below). This should be avoided if possible, since it can properly be applied to all sorts of situations including where annual returns are being considered, whereas the J-curve applies specifically to returns plotted on a cumulative compound basis.

Home run

A baseball term that has been imported into venture capital parlance. In baseball it is when the striker hits the ball out of the park into the crowd (equivalent to hitting a six in cricket, but more so in that its scoring is potentially open-ended and can have a dramatic effect on the overall team score, since all the players who are currently on base can run home).

Strictly speaking it means an investment (company) that returns the entire capital of the investing fund all by itself, but as a matter of practice, this has come to be generally accepted as being any investment which returns at least 25×.

Home run mentality

The attitude of mind which recognises the overwhelming importance of home runs, and sets out to achieve them. Includes the need to

reject an investment opportunity which does not have the potential
to be a big winner, and the focus on building a business quickly into
a large company.

Sometimes called "swinging for the fence" (another baseball
expression).

Hurdle

Used in its commonly accepted sense of a hurdle return, i.e., the lowest
possible return which a particular investor will accept.

However, also used specifically to describe a return which a GP has
to at least equal before any carry is calculated or payable. This mechanism is commonly found in buyout and development capital funds, but
rarely in venture funds.

In specie

A Latin phrase meaning literally "in its actual form". It is used to
describe a distribution of shares, rather than a distribution of the money
raised from selling those shares.

See "end game" and "quoted distributions".

Invested capital

The total amount of drawndown capital which has actually been invested
in companies. In practice, this will be equal to the amount of drawndown capital less amounts which have been used to pay fees, or which
are awaiting investment.

Investee company

A company within a private equity fund, i.e., an entity in which the
fund buys shares, and/or to which it provides finance in some form of
convertible instrument.

IPO

Initial Public Offering. American term for a flotation (see above), which
is steadily coming into common usage in Europe as well.

IRR

Internal Rate of Return (so called because it was originally used to calculate the return on different projects within a company). The compound
return of a series of cashflows over a specified period (usually several
years), used as one of the two main measures of private equity returns.

The strict business school definition is that compound return, found by iteration, which will reduce the NPV of any stream of cashflows to zero.

J-curve

The effect of all private equity funds, irrespective of final performance, exhibiting strongly negative returns in the early years as money is drawndown into the fund, reversing as distributions begin to be made. So-called from the shape made by the returns when plotted on a cumulative compound basis.

Kicker

A kicker or equity kicker is that part of the terms of a share or loan note which confers the convertible rights (see above).

LBO

Leveraged Buyout. In one sense all buyouts are LBOs, since they all involve the use of debt. However, this now has two main connotations: (1) a very large transaction, frequently with multiple business activities and (2) a transaction which is not initiated by a management team. It may be convenient to think of it as an industrial acquisition where the acquirer just happens to be a buyout firm (or consortium).

Leverage

Describes the effect of debt on a company or transactions. See also gearing (above).

Liquidation preference

Commonly found in venture funding agreements, particularly in the USA. A particular class of shareholder will reserve the right to have their investment paid back either once or some other multiple from any exit proceeds before the interests of any other investors are considered. Originally designed, as the name suggests, to provide protection in the event of a winding up, these have now come to be used almost routinely in all circumstances.

Historically less common in other parts of the world, such as Europe, where simpler capital structures and a more friendly, co-operative relationship between investors have been preferred.

LP

In the USA, and increasingly in Europe, an investor in private equity funds is known as an LP (Limited Partner), since most private equity funds take the form of Limited Partnerships.

LPA

Limited Partnership Agreement, the document which constitutes a Limited Partnership. These will be the subject of discussion and negotiation prior to first closing.

M&A

Merger and Acquisition. The process of buying and selling companies.

Manager

In Europe, a GP was traditionally referred to as a manager, and many still use this term.

Market timing

The practice of adjusting your investment approach in reaction to, or as a result of prediction of, conditions in financial markets.

In brief, because this approach requires a relatively short-term approach and, in particular, the ability to liquidate investments at short notice, it is an impossible approach to private equity investing, regardless of whether it may or may not work in relation to other asset classes. A failure to appreciate this is one of the most fundamental mistakes made by private equity investors (particularly LPs). See "diversification by time" (above).

MBI

Management Buy-In. A type of buyout transaction where a group of experienced executives buy not their own business but one which is operating in the same sector. Also includes a situation where an executive leads the buyout of a business where he has worked previously, but this will usually be a BIMBO (see above).

MBO

Management Buyout. A type of buyout transaction in which the team of executives managing a business buy it out from the parent company with the support of a buyout firm.

Median

The observation within a sample population that sits exactly in the middle of the observations ranked by value. Sometimes used as a measure of private equity returns (especially by those outside the industry) but its value as such is questionable, particularly where there is a small sample size or a heavily skewed range of values.

Mezzanine

Convertible unsecured debt which sits between the equity and senior debt layers of a buyout structure. In the USA, the term can also be found applied to pre-IPO funding rounds for venture companies.

Money in

Describes a development capital deal where the private equity fund acquires new shares in the target company, thus providing it with funds for growth. Such deals are frequently referred to as expansion capital.

Money out

Describes a development capital deal where the private equity fund acquires existing shares from the business owner. In other words, the money goes to him rather than into the company and is thus seen as analogous to him taking money out of the company.

Negative control

Where a buyout firm, though they may not control a majority of the target company's shares, impose a right of veto over certain decisions, most notably executive remuneration, share dividends, capital expenditure, borrowing, and changes in business activity.

Newco

A term used in structuring discussions and diagrams by lawyers, accountants, investment bankers and private equity professionals to describe a new company that will be formed specially to take some defined role in a corporate transaction or series of transactions, frequently as the acquisition vehicle (i.e., the new holding company) in a buyout transaction.

NVCA

National Venture Capital Association (of America).

Observation
Any single value within a sample population.

Offering Memorandum
An OM is a document issued by or on behalf of a private equity firm with the object of raising money from the investment community. Sometimes referred to as a Private Placing Memorandum (see below).

Open-ended
See evergreen.

Operating debt
Debt which is present naturally within a company as working capital for its business activities. This can be reduced through lowering stock levels, extending the time taken to pay creditors, or persuading debtors to pay their invoices more quickly.

Operating experience
Refers to what is used in contributing value add (see below). Chiefly used in a venture context, though some buyout firms also refer to it, and maintain a panel of key executives with different business backgrounds.

Overhang
Capital raised by private equity funds but as yet uninvested. This can become acute when levels of investment fail to keep pace with levels of fundraising.
Overhang will tend to put upward pressure on valuations, raise suspicions that deal quality may be sacrificed in order to put money to work, and may also stretch out the fund cycle.

Payback period
The length of time which it takes to recover your initial capital on any investment, i.e., for the investment to return 1×.
Once widely used as a means of evaluating rival projects or investments for capital allocation purposes but now largely superseded by IRR.

PE ratio

The Price/Earnings ratio is a way of stating the valuation of a company in a way which can be applied to and compared with those of other companies:

$$\text{either} \quad \frac{\text{share price}}{\text{EPS}} \quad \text{or} \quad \frac{\text{enterprise value}}{\text{earnings}}$$

PEIGG

Private Equity Industry Guidelines Group, a body which has produced a set of advisory valuation guidelines in the USA.

Pharma

A term used to refer to drug discovery activities, and also collectively for the very large multinational companies in this area.

PICC (Paid In to Committed Capital)

The ratio of total money drawndown by a fund to date measured against its committed capital. Can be a useful measure where there is a suspicion that a firm has raised too much money for their current fund and is struggling to put it all to work.

PIPE

Private Investment in Public Equity. Where a quoted company agrees to produce an instrument, which is typically not itself quoted, which can potentially offer a private equity-type return. These transactions have so far largely been confined to the USA.

Placing (or placement) agent

A business which acts as adviser and a source of introductions to LPs for GPs who are looking to raise a fund.

Pooled return

A method of calculating returns whereby all the constituent funds are consolidated together and treated as if they were one large fund.

Portfolio secondary

A phrase invented by the writer to mean a secondary investment which is made not for reasons of cashflow or capital management but specifically because the investor wants exposure (or additional exposure) to that particular private equity fund.

Cf. a treasury secondary (see below).

Post-money

Refers to a valuation of a venture company including the amount of money contributed by the venture round in question.

Pre-money

Refers to a valuation of a venture company before taking into account the amount of money contributed by the venture round in question.

Primary

Primary interests are commitments by investors to new funds, as distinct from secondary interests (see below). Once the fund is operating, i.e., making investments, then the interest would become a secondary interest.

A good way of remembering the difference is to consider the parties involved. In making a commitment to fund, the only relationship will be that between the LP and the GP. In disposing of an existing interest, the key relationship is between the LP and the other investor who is seeking to buy the interest and take the place of the LP.

Private Placing Memorandum

Or PPM. Another expression for an Offering Memorandum (see above).

Quoted distributions

Distributions in specie. That is to say, a distribution by a private equity fund to investors which takes the form of shares in an underlying company rather than cash produced by selling those shares. Such shares may frequently be restricted stock (see below).

See also end game (above).

Realisation ratio

The ratio of money paid out by a fund compared with money paid in. See D/PI (above).

Recapitalisation or "recap"

A very important but little understood contributor to buyout returns. Where a company has more earnings and/or cashflow than was originally envisaged, equity is returned to investors and replaced where necessary with new debt.

Reps and warranties

Representations and warranties by the vendor placed in the sale agreement when a company changes hands. They most usually cover things such as contingent liabilities, the company's tax position and the accuracy of the most recent audited accounts.

Reserves

Fund capital which is notionally set aside to provide subsequent funding rounds for portfolio companies. The level of reserves should be kept under constant review, particularly since when a company is written off it will be necessary to decide how to use the reserves set aside for that company which will now no longer be needed.

Except in the case of a roll-up, this is almost exclusively an issue for venture funds.

Residual Value to Paid In (RVPI)

The ratio of the current value of all remaining investments within a fund to the total amount of capital paid in to date.

Restricted stock

Shares which form part of a flotation (IPO) but which are not freely tradeable for a specified time – usually 6 months. In the USA this occurs automatically by operation of market regulation. In Europe it is a matter for contractual agreement, and thus can be varied if, for example, there is greater demand for stock than anticipated.

Roll-up

A buyout transaction where a fragmented industry is targeted, and a number of small businesses are bought before being consolidated together into one large entity.

Secondary

A secondary interest is an ownership position in an existing fund which may or may not be fully invested, but has not been fully exited and wound up. Such interests are usually more or less freely transferable and a thriving secondary market has grown up to cater for such transactions, a number of specialist firms having been set up for the purpose.

Cf. primary (see above).

Sector
Strictly speaking both buyout and venture deals can be subdivided by sector, but it is of less importance in buyout than it is in venture, where it is one of the two main ways of classifying venture deals (the other being by stage). Historically, venture companies have been divided into three broad categories: Life Science, Information Technology and Telecoms. The latter two are often referred to together as "Technology", and the distinction between them is becoming increasingly blurred.

Seed round
A round of venture funding which takes place during the seed stage. May be preceded by an angel round, but in this case it risks being defined as an A Round instead unless it occurs fairly soon after the seed round.

Seed stage
The start-up stage of a company's existence.

Senior debt
Strictly, debt which takes priority over other layers of debt in the buyout structure, both as to repayment and on liquidation. However, today it is used generally to refer to "straight" debt which will not normally have a convertible element and will usually enjoy some form of security.

Soft circle
Reference to an investor, or group of investors, who have indicated that they are likely to make a commitment to a fund, but who have not yet taken a firm decision.

Stage
The period in a venture company's life at which investment is made. Stage is one of the two main ways of classifying and distinguishing venture transactions (the other being by sector) and is divided into seed, early, mid and late.

Strip
Not as exciting as it sounds. A vertical slice of the buyout financing structure, usually taking a piece of each of the senior and mezzanine debt layers.

Sweet equity
Shares issued on preferential terms (most commonly for nominal value, i.e., at a much cheaper price) which are used to give management teams a much larger equity stake in a buyout than would be justified strictly by the amount of money which they are able to invest. Such cases are frequently structured as an option to acquire such shares based on pre-agreed performance targets and conditional upon staying with the company until an exit is achieved. More controversially, they have also been used occasionally by buyout firms as a substitute, or even additional form of carry.

Take private
A buyout transaction where a public company is acquired and then de-listed to become a private company.

Telco
Literally, any provider of telecommunications services, but taken usually to mean one of the incumbent players, i.e., one of the old monopolistic utilities such as BT (in the UK), Deutsche Telekom (in Germany) and the various Bell companies in the USA.

Thin equity
A capital structure in which there is a large amount of debt and very little equity. Various countries have adopted "thin equity" rules in an attempt to limit the tax effectiveness of financial engineering by buyout houses.

Time-weighted (returns)
A most misleading term as it actually means the exact opposite of what it suggests.

Instead of calculating the actual IRR of a series of cashflows over a given period (i.e., the compound return over time), time-weighted returns calculate the geometric mean, i.e., the average of the annual percentage return in any one year.

This measure of returns exists for historic reasons only. It is completely irrelevant (worse – misleading) for private equity purposes and should be ignored.

Total Return
A phrase invented by the writer which refers to the return which an LP earns on the whole private equity allocation, as opposed to just that part of it which is at any one time invested in underlying buyout or venture companies.

Treasury secondary
A phrase invented by the writer to mean a secondary investment which is made purely for reasons of capital and cashflow management, and the exact nature of which (save as to the likely amount and timing of the return) is thus irrelevant.

Cf. a portfolio secondary (see above).

Turn (an investment)
To turn an investment is to buy it and then sell it again quickly. In such situations, a high IRR can be generated from a low multiple.

Turnaround
A buyout of a company which is struggling and possibly even loss-making. Such deals are relatively rare and are an exception to the principle that a buyout target company will usually have earnings (or at least cashflow) which can be used to service debt.

Total Value to Paid In (TVPI)
The ratio of the current value of remaining investments within a fund plus the total value of all distributions to date to the total amount of capital paid into the fund to date.

Perhaps the best available measure of performance before the end of a fund's life.

UMTS
Universal Mobile Telecommunications System, popularly known as 3G. A technology that allows digital communications to be carried at broadband-type speeds to mobile telephones. A great idea, the successful introduction of which was plagued by technical problems, including the development of a sufficiently powerful battery.

Upper decile

The individual fund which sits 10% of the way down the statistical sample, or colloquially all funds which sit above this point. It is used conceptually when talking about the golden circle (see above) as in "venture is an upper decile game", but data including it as a statistical measure is not publicly available.

Upper quartile

Commonly used as a measure of vintage year returns. It is the return of that individual fund which sits at the bottom of the upper quartile, i.e., one quarter of the way down a ranked list of observations. It is *not* the pooled returns of all the funds which sit within the upper quartile. However, it is used colloquially to refer to all the funds which sit within the upper quartile, hence the confusion.

While statistically useful, its limitations should be recognised. In particular, it gives no indication of the spread within the upper quartile, which can be enormous, especially where venture funds are concerned. It can also be very misleading if the sample from which it is drawn is not properly representative (as is often the case where European venture is concerned).

US model

This refers to the traditional approach of US venture firms, particularly those active at early stage. Its main components are (1) a focus on the seed stage, (2) home run mentality and (3) value add.

Interestingly and excitingly, there are a number of European firms now adopting the US model.

Value add

An American expression referring to the ability to contribute company building skills gained at first hand to the development of a venture company, usually on a hands-on basis.

VCOC

Venture Capital Operating Company, a term used in the ERISA regulations (see above).

Venture capitalist

An individual professional within a venture firm.

Venture company

An investee company within a venture fund. Often referred to as a "firm" in North America.

Venture partner

Might be thought of as something between an EIR and a GP within a venture firm. A venture partner will usually be someone who has been a successful entrepreneur and will be used by the firm to look at prospective investment opportunities within their own area of specialist expertise.

Venture partner is frequently a temporary status. Typically a venture partner will be expected either to join the management team of an opportunity which he finds exciting, or to progress into being a GP. The status is also sometimes used for someone who has retired as a GP, but wishes to retain a part-time role within the firm.

Vintage year

The year in which a fund, or group of funds, was formed.

Vintage year returns

Vintage year returns show (in respect of any one vintage year) the compound return of all constituent funds formed during the vintage year, from the vintage year to the date specified.

Write down

To reduce the stated valuation of a portfolio company. Under both the EVCA and BVCA guidelines, there are some situations where a 25% write down is mandatory.

Write off

To reduce the stated valuation of a portfolio company to zero.

Write up

To increase the stated value of a portfolio company.

Index

Index compiled by Annette Musker